IT in Business

IT in Business
A manager's casebook

Edited by
David Targett
David J. Grimshaw
Philip Powell

OXFORD AUCKLAND BOSTON JOHANNESBURG MELBOURNE NEW DELHI

Butterworth-Heinemann
Linacre House, Jordan Hill, Oxford OX2 8DP
225 Wildwood Avenue, Woburn, MA 01801-2041

A division of Reed Educational and Professional Publishing Ltd

A member of the Reed Elsevier plc group

First published 1999

British Library Cataloguing in Publication Data
A catalogue record for this book is available from the British Library

ISBN 0 7506 3951 2

Typeset by Avocet Typeset, Brill, Aylesbury, Bucks
Printed and bound in Great Britain by Biddles Ltd,
Guildford and King's Lynn

Contents

Preface

At any moment, and throughout the world, hundreds of thousands of business school students are working on projects as part of their degree programmes. These projects usually have a practical orientation and many are company based. They result in reports for both the business school and, if there is one, the sponsoring company. The reports are taken very seriously by the students since they are a significant part of the degree and normally carry a heavy weight in the assessment procedures. Business school teachers can testify to the substantial effort students put into their projects. The projects are not doctoral (PhD) research, taking three or more years to deliver their findings. They are the projects carried out by undergraduate students on business administration courses and postgraduate students (MSc or MBA) on full- or part-time programmes. They deliver results in weeks or months. Some of the work is of the very highest quality, by academic or pragmatic standards.

Some sponsoring organizations make substantial use of the reports but not all do so and the reports rarely reach the public domain. Generally they sit on shelves 'in case the external examiner wishes to see them' only to be discarded two years later as shelf space becomes a scarce resource.

This book is an attempt to bring the best of these projects into the public domain, concentrating on one specific area of study – information technology (IT) and information systems (IS). What is the difference between IT and IS? IT is the equipment, the computers and telecommunications devices; IS are the channels of communication along which information flows. Broadly IT is what capital is spent on; IS are the structures produced by the IT. If the analogy is railways then IT is the locomotives, stations and track; IS are the network of routes along which passengers and freight travel. The area has increased in importance in recent years as IT has moved from the periphery of organizations, automating functions of marginal business importance, to a place at the core of the business as a major determinant of competitive success (or failure) and business profitability. The role of IT used to be a means of achieving incremental efficiency gains, for example computerizing inventory control and thereby reducing staff levels. While such activities still continue IT now has a more important and visible role at the centre of initiatives to improve competitiveness, transform businesses, re-structure organizations and streamline management processes. These current activities have the potential to produce radical, rather than incremental benefits.

IT's new role means that it is no longer an issue that can be left to the technical experts in the IT function. IT must be managed by general managers – at all levels including the most senior. This is particularly true given that IT's record is by no means one of total success. There are certainly many cases where IT has been part of major business successes, for example, virtual organizations (based on partnership, collaboration and networking rather than a formal structure of directly employed people) such as Benetton, telephone banking and insurance, and novel business structures such as Nike and Sun. But there are also many cases of IT disaster, for example the abandoned TAURUS system at the London Stock Exchange. At the time of writing there is concern about the UK's new air traffic control system, which has already been substantially delayed, and the so-called Millennium Bug which, some prophesise, will bring about the cessation of life as we know it in the early months of the year 2000.

The paradox runs deep. While IT expenditures are higher than ever (fifty per cent of capital expenditure in Western organizations is said to be IT-related and some organizations spend ten per cent or more of their turnover on IT), some research has suggested that, at the aggregate level, IT has produced no discernible productivity gains. According to Lester Thurow, 'IT is everywhere, except in the productivity statistics'. Other research disputes this view.

The debate on the value of IT continues but it is clear that it has become indispensable to the operation of organizations. Health services may be accused (in the UK at least) of wasted expenditure on IT but they would be unable to continue their present activities without IT. As a result managing IT has become a major concern for organizations. There is a rapidly increasing demand for people who have business *and* IT skills and knowledge, and this is reflected in the salaries offered to graduating students who can claim to have them. The critical shortage seems to be for people who can operate at the interface of business and IT.

It is for these reasons that three highly-rated UK business schools – The University of Bath's School of Management, Cranfield School of Management and Warwick Business School – have come together to find an outlet for the best of their students' work in the area of IT/IS. The projects are of two types, undergraduate projects carried out by groups of students and postgraduate projects carried out individually by MSc and MBA students. The projects were largely carried out in 1997 and 1998. The project reports have been selected (from a wide range of project reports at all three business schools), edited and converted into book chapters by the three editors of the book, David Targett (Bath), David Grimshaw (Cranfield) and Philip Powell (Warwick). Each postgraduate project was supervised within the relevant business school by an academic supervisor whose name has been added to that of the chapter's student author(s).

The undergraduate projects are assignments set as part of the assessment process in third year courses on the business impact of IS on organizations. The purpose of such assignments is to determine whether the students are aware of the ways IS can affect organizations, externally and internally, in radical or lesser ways. The students have to choose an organization or industry and investigate its use of IS. Typically students choose an organization they already know, perhaps because they have worked there on placement or have other contacts with it. They might choose an organization they find interesting and exciting, for example the travel industry. Alternatively, they might choose an organization they would like to work for in the future, seeing the project as a way of finding out more in preparation for the interviewing process and, they hope, the start of a subsequent career.

Having chosen an organization they are asked to pursue questions such as: Have IS made a difference to competitive positioning, to their relationships and alliances with other organizations, to the structure of the supply chain? Have IS played a part in business and process transformation? Have IS been part of changes to internal management? In short, the task is to choose an organization or industry and then examine whether IS have made a significant impact and, if so, how. In general the students choose to pick up on issues concerned with competitive impact and strategy, the high level issues. The work is based on secondary research – in the library searching for relevant articles in journals, newspapers, research reports and elsewhere – together with some primary research – interviews, surveys, personal observation. The reports produced tend to be of 3000 or so words and the chapters presented in this book have been edited but not scaled down.

The postgraduate chapters came about in a different way. The culmination of most MBA and MSc programmes is normally a large-scale project or dissertation which carries a high proportion of the overall marks for the course. Students choose an area to investigate, often with an organizational sponsor but not always. Since more time is available for the work the project reports are long, perhaps 30,000 words or more. This presents an opportunity to look at a wide range of issues in real depth – for example, organizational structures, human resource issues, IS planning methods. The work involves some secondary research – to find out what is already known about the area of study – but is substantially based on primary research, often with a survey together with interviews and other types of data collection. Frequently the research also makes it possible to write a case study. The editing task for these chapters is therefore different from that with the undergraduate projects. The task is to select portions of the report which can be presented as a coherent whole but which then need to be scaled down to produce a self-contained report of chapter size. Most of the chapters are case studies but some involve issues which required a broader investigation across more organizations.

However, the structure of the book is not based on a division between undergraduate and postgraduate chapters. The structure is based on topics, with four main parts. These topics were not pre-selected; they were emergent. The projects chosen for the book were selected on two broad criteria. First, they were selected because the underlying research was of high quality. The students had carried out some in-depth probing and produced a lot of data. There were also some innovative aspects, for example that there had been particularly good access or some counter-intuitive evidence had been unearthed. Second, the research findings were, on the one hand, practical and relevant to managers and students of business studies, and, on the other hand, publishable in the sense of containing findings and evidence that was of general interest and was newsworthy.

Once selected the projects were grouped according to the topics and issues with which they dealt. The resulting four parts are detailed below.

Part 1 Competition and Business Impact

Most of the chapters in this part are case studies which look at the way IS have influenced the competitive or, in the case of the public sector, strategic position of the organization. The organizations cover a wide range of industries – food retailing (Tesco), glass manufacturing (Demaglass), housing management (Pinnacle Housing), newspaper retailing (Johnsons News) and public health (UK Department of Health). There is one exception to the case study format. One chapter looks at a whole industry, the music industry.

Part 2 Information System Planning

Two of the four chapters in this section are case studies, looking at the planning processes which develop IS strategies and lead to decisions on IT investment and deployment. The companies are BP Acetyls and an anonymous computer vendor. Another chapter analyses the experiences of several UK companies in adopting BPR (business process re-engineering) initiatives and final chapter provides an overview, and examples from different business sectors are presented together with a critical assessment of the BPR concept.

Part 3 Managing the IS resource

The first two parts consider the early stages in the deployment of IT, the strategic impact and strategic planning. This part moves further down the IT deployment process and looks at aspects of the internal management of IS. All four chapters are case studies. The first (Bayford Thrust) focuses on IS implementation, paying special attention to the problems faced by smaller organizations.

The second (a UK utility) asks where the IT function should be positioned within the corporate structure. The third (an anonymous bank) is concerned with disaster recovery procedures. The final case (a power generator) is about the failure of an electronic requisitioning system.

Part 4 Communications and Information

The fourth part is concerned with the products of IT/IS configurations, communications and information. Two chapters are case studies. One looks at EIS (Executive Information Systems) in a hospital trust; the second examines how the UK Overseas Development Organization can derive business benefits from the information contained in a large database. The other two chapters deal with highly topical issues. One presents a major survey of the use of groupware (Lotus Notes), quantifying its use and drawing lessons on how to implement and manage the software. The second provides evidence from a number of organizations concerned with the ongoing issue of IS appraisal but with a concentration on the question of the appraisal of IT infrastructure.

In the book each of these four parts has its own introduction which describes the chapters and how they relate to one another in more detail.

The book has three main objectives:

1 To publish some important and original findings which are of practical value to both general and IT managers in all organizations. Because of the short time scales involved in student projects, the research is up to date; because of the business focus, the research is practical and relevant.
2 For similar reasons the second objective is to provide case and other material for teaching purposes – this project work can usefully feed back into business school courses.
3 The third objective is to exhibit some of the excellent work on the management of IT and IS which is continually taking place in business schools. It is hoped that this will result in a better dialogue between business schools and industry and eventually lead to improved education for current and aspiring managers who see information systems as the critical management area of the future.

The book would not have been possible without the cooperation of three groups. First, the organizations named in the cases have been generous in granting permission for access, allowing their names to be used and agreeing that the case study data could be made public. Authors and editors alike are extremely grateful to them. Second, the editors wish to record their thanks to the students for allowing their work to be published and, perhaps more importantly, for going a further mile and doing extra work on their projects so that they were suitable for publication. Third, the academic supervisors have played their parts in producing projects of a standard worthy of publication.

Special thanks must be given to Jill Hollis the administrator of this publication project. She has borne the brunt of the extensive liaison work between business schools, the publisher and, at Bath, many of the students. She has coordinated the multiple signing of the publishing contract and dealt with many of the legal problems which inevitably rose to the surface.

David Targett
David Grimshaw
Philip Powell

About the authors

David Targett

David Targett is the Professor of Information Management at Imperial College Management School, University of London. For eight years, 1990–98, he was the Professor of Information Systems and Director of the Centre for Research into Strategic Information Systems (CRSIS) at the University of Bath. Previously, he was at the London Business School and before becoming an academic he was an industrial engineer in the motor industry.

His work has been concerned with the impact of information systems on strategy and general management. As Director of CRSIS he is leading several major research projects but his main research interest is the evaluation of IT investments. A recent government funded project examined evaluation and decision-making by tracking the development and implementation of IT investments within twelve major organizations in both the public and private sectors. He teaches on all types of business school programmes – undergraduate, MSc, MBA and doctoral. He has written ten books, numerous articles, book chapters and conference papers.

David J. Grimshaw

David Grimshaw is Senior Lecturer in Information Systems at Cranfield School of Management. He was previously at the University of Leeds and Warwick Business School, University of Warwick. Current research interests include the use of geographical information by business and industry. He is the author of *Bringing GIS into Business*, second edition published by John Wiley Inc., and has published many papers in academic journals and the professional press. He is a Founding Member of the AGI Special Interest Group on GIS in Business and was recently elected to the Council of the AGI for 1999–2002.

David has wide teaching experience, with undergraduates, post-experience and executive programmes. He has also taught in Australia, Hong Kong, Malaysia, Portugal, Russia and Singapore. He has been Visiting Fellow at Curtin University, Australia and the National Center for Geographic Information and Analysis, State University of New York at Buffalo.

Previously he was a Visiting Professor at the International Management School, St Petersburg and at the Graduate School, University Utara Malaysia.

As an independent consultant David has advised many companies on strategic information systems planning and on geographical information systems.

Philip Powell

Philip Powell is Professor of Information Systems at Goldsmiths College, University of London. Formerly, he was Reader in Information Systems, ICAEW Academic Fellow and Director of the Information Systems Research Unit at Warwick Business School. Prior to becoming an academic he worked in insurance, accounting and computing. He is the author of four books on information systems and financial modelling, numerous book chapters and his work has appeared in over forty international journals. He is Managing Editor of the *Information Systems Journal*, Book Reviews Editor of the *Journal of Strategic Information Systems*, an Associate Editor of *OR Insight* and he is on a number of editorial boards. He is a Board Member of the UK Academy for Information Systems. His main interests are in the organizational impacts of IS and IT, especially decision support and expert systems, and the ways such systems might be evaluated.

Part One
Competition and Business Impact

David Targett

In broad terms the chapters in this part ask the following questions. Have IS affected the competitive and business situation of the organization? If so, what has been the nature of the impact – how has competitiveness changed? – how has business been changed? Four of the chapters in this part are case studies of private sector companies, covering a wide range of industries – food retailing, glass manufacturing, housing management and newspaper retailing. A fifth chapter is a case study on the operations of the UK government's Department of Health. Standard theoretical concepts, for example Porter's Five Forces framework, are used to analyse the impact of IS. The final chapter looks at the music industry. It is issue-based, examining the link between IS and time-based competition.

Perhaps the most striking case is that of Pinnacle Housing a company that has used IS in an innovative way to create a new national business in an area – the management of rented properties – which has previously been localized. The chapter describes the beginnings of an attempt to transform a business and gain competitive advantage.

Like Pinnacle Housing, Demaglass operates in an industry which is not known as a major user of IT. Like Pinnacle, Demaglass has an adventurous strategy to deploy IS in new ways which can improve its competitive situation and achieve its objective of becoming a world-class manufacturer. The chapter examines the development of a system which is intended to re-engineer processes and be a major catalyst of change.

Unlike housing management and glass manufacturing, the distribution of newspapers and magazines has long been an information intensive business and so it is not surprising that information management is a crucial activity. The case of Johnsons News, the fourth largest news wholesaler in the UK, is concerned with the use of EDI (Electronic Data Interchange), part of a continuing effort to develop systems which can give and sustain competitive advantage.

Second to financial services, food retailing may be the most information intensive industry. In recent years several major business thrusts, intended to deliver and maintain competitive advantage, have depended upon IS for their success. The list of initiatives is long – for example, just-in-time, supply chain re-engineering, loyalty cards, banking – and Tesco have been at the forefront in their deployment of IT, as well as being the industry's major IT spender. The case describes a number of Tesco's IT initiatives.

The use of IT by public sector organizations cannot be discussed in terms of competitive advantage. Nevertheless it can be discussed in terms of business impact and business benefits. Has IT delivered efficiency and effectiveness? Has it brought about major change? Has it transformed processes? The Department of Health case looks at the ways in which a particular, large-scale project (OIS – Office Information System) has effected the business and management activities of the Department.

The above cases deal with industries which range from ones which, up to now, have not been information intensive to ones which have long been so. Possibly the industry with the most potential for an exciting and radical move from one extreme to the other is the music industry. The information revolution is affecting both the product, as music is digitized and new media are being developed, and the retailing process, with possibilities for internet trading, product sampling, stock databases. The chapter describes these developments and goes on to speculate about the future.

1 Pinnacle Housing and Direct Let

Richard Shardlow, Charlotte Smitheman,
Edna Thrane-Steen, Daniel Webster
School of Management, University of Bath

This report describes and evaluates the strategic role of IT as part of the competitive strategy of Direct Let. Direct Let is a subsidiary of Pinnacle Housing. It was created in 1997 to take advantage of a business opportunity in which IT played an important part. Both the industry and firm are described and then evaluated using strategic IT frameworks. The objective is to evaluate whether Direct Let has gained business benefits from its use of IT and whether the use of IT is strategic in nature. The primary research is based on interviews and observation within Direct Let. The interview questionnaire is shown in Appendix A.

Introduction to Pinnacle and Direct Let

Pinnacle Housing entered the property management industry in 1988 after the introduction of a tax break for those wishing to invest in residential property for letting. Financial institutions were particularly interested in this tax break as they had large portfolios of repossessed property that they were loath to sell in the depressed housing market. Instead of liquidating the property at a discount they decided to move into the rental market.

The tax scheme required that certain regulations had to be met. The portfolio of properties had to be registered under the ownership of a BESCO (Business Expansion Scheme Company), which had to be capitalized at a maximum of £5 million. Investors had to hold onto their shares for a minimum of five years. In the event financial institutions incorporated as many BESCOs as their portfolios of property required.

No single property management firm was capable of managing such voluminous portfolios, due to a number of factors, which will be discussed later.

Pinnacle Housing, acting as a broker, bid for portfolios, split them up into areas and sub-contracted the management to regional property management firms.

Pinnacle saw that a demand was not being satisfied. This was that no single property management firm in the UK was capable of actually managing large or dispersed portfolios of properties. They considered that this was due to the inability of firms to maintain and process the vast amount of data that such a venture required. Pinnacle concluded that if they could develop an information system capable of tracking this data they would be able to enter an area of the market that had until now proved impenetrable to single property management firms. Thus, the direct management of large or dispersed portfolios without the need to use sub-contracted agents would be possible.

In December 1993 the Government ended the tax break and the BESCOs were expected to liquidate by December 1998. Pinnacle Housing's directors realized that the financial institutions would, given reasonable market conditions, sell the properties. This would be a huge loss to Pinnacle. The Financial Director estimated that BESCO business was fifty per cent of Pinnacle's total. Although Pinnacle's core business was the brokerage of BESCO portfolios there were plenty of other large portfolios in the market which were not BESCO owned. Pinnacle believed that with a suitable information system they could establish themselves as the market leaders in the management of large or dispersed portfolios.

Direct Let Ltd was therefore incorporated on 1 January 1997 as a subsidiary of Pinnacle Housing for the purpose of moving into this new area and to evolve into the core business of the group in future years. Other firms in the past had attempted to become an integrated national property manager but had failed because of the diseconomies of scale experienced through the management of the information and the cost of maintaining shop fronts in every area of operation. Pinnacle's strategy to overcome these diseconomies was based around these two aspects:

1 Centralize the administration by designing a suitable information system.
2 Replace high street branches with area managers.

IT/IS and the property management industry

The property management industry is highly regionalized. In any town across the country one can expect to find a mixture of local independently owned property managers and national firms such as Black Horse Agencies and Savills. Although firms like Savills have a national presence their offices are autonomously run and simply attempt to offer a similar service across the country. By visiting a cross section of property management firms in Bath (see Appendix B) it became clear that no one firm has invested in IT strategically to the extent that business practice had been transformed or competitive advantage gained. In recent years the property management industry had only used IT to gain administrative cost savings. Apart from Pinnacle Housing no single firm had developed an IT/IS strategy. These other firms had used IT in a very limited way. Few offices used network facilities; stand-alone PCs were used for administration and simple databases, which contained details such as lists of properties or contact addresses; most firms had a stand-alone PC that ran an accounts package, some of which were specifically designed for letting. However, these packages were little more than automated bookkeepers. All the firms interviewed used a manual paper system in their office, involving big filing draws containing a separate dossier for each property. Using the MIT90s five levels graph (Venkatraman, 1991) these firms would be situated at the localized exploitation stage.

As we can see from Figure 1.1, this implies that these firms have a very low degree of IT based transformation and there were few business benefits. Any benefits would tend to be cost savings relating to administration. The model illustrates the non-strategic use of IT in the property management industry.

The findings of the primary research were revealing. It was clear that all the interview firms felt that IT was not of any strategic importance within the industry and none of them admitted to having an IT strategy. The main reason given was that they believed no IT system was sufficiently flexible to operate in the property management environment. The firms seemed to be supplier

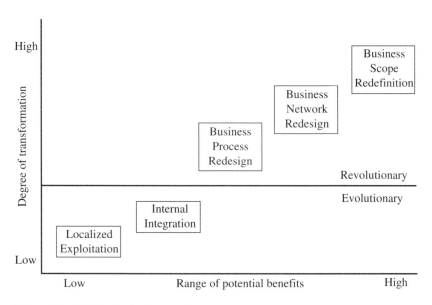

Figure 1.1 *MIT90s five levels graph*

led, preferring to keep the landlords happy even though it might result in incremental administration costs.

IT and Direct Let

Direct Let Ltd was incorporated in Bath as a national call centre from which customers could arrange a tenancy anywhere in the country. Using the database tool Microsoft FoxPro, Pinnacle's IT department designed and programmed, in-house, a property letting management system that they called PLMS (Property Letting Management System). PLMS was designed to be flexible enough to also serve Pinnacle's brokering operation.

Referring back to Figure 1.1 Direct Let is placed at the Business Network Redesign level. The new information system is at a revolutionary level in that it has transformed the whole process by which business is being done between organizations. This level of transformation implies a high level of risk, which is why it was important that PLMS had the full backing of the board. For example, a new IT department was formed. The directors believed that the benefits derived from their investment in IT would be well worth the level of risk they had to accept. Examples of the benefits PLMS provides will be covered once a more detailed explanation of the system has been given.

In an interview a director of Direct Let confirmed the vital importance of PLMS to the business. Without it the firm would collapse. She added that IT would also be of vital importance in the future, as it will define the nature of competition in the industry. At the time of writing the directors are not marketing the service that Direct Let offers because they realize that there are few barriers to prevent other firms from imitating their strategy. Presently Direct Let is acquiring regional property management firms and their client bases so that they will be the dominant firm when they launch the service in the market place.

This evidence suggests that Direct Let's use of IT is strategic in terms of McFarlan's definition of the word. Direct Let is placed in the top right hand corner of McFarlan's Strategic Grid (McFarlan, 1984). See Figure 1.2.

Our primary research suggested that most firms in the industry would be located in the support cell of this grid, which implies few benefits.

The investment in PLMS was part of a strategic move, which would allow Pinnacle to break into the property management industry and establish them as the only firm capable of managing whole portfolios from one centralized office. This expertise was expected to be a highly lucrative asset.

The primary research also suggested that Direct Let is a leader in the deployment of IT within an industry, which makes nominal use of IT. The situation is paradoxical. The property management industry is one in which lots of varying information needs to be managed. One would therefore expect a

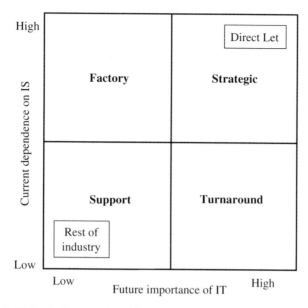

Figure 1.2 *McFarlan's strategic grid*

high level of IT deployment. But, given the differing nature of landlords, the information intensity and complexity is extremely high. So high that most firms regard it as impossible to design a system, which would be sufficiently flexible to cater for all their needs. In most cases these firms react by choosing to deal with clients who have small portfolios of property. This results in the companies having a high ratio of landlords to managed properties. They have a plethora of landlords all with differing opinions on how their property should be managed. It is a service that is tailored to the client and results in excessive amounts of paper and information. By keeping records manually it is no surprise that none of these firms are capable of managing more than a few hundred properties. In order to manage large volumes of property the service needs to be highly standardized and information needs to be much more readily available.

Making the data manageable

Standardizing the service is exactly what Direct Let did. Instead of the client defining the way in which properties are managed, Direct Let offers a prescribed service. Rationalizing the service in this way simplified the business process and allowed Direct Let to produce a fully integrated information system.

An example of this is the maintenance department. Tenants often call Direct Let with maintenance requests. The heating system may be malfunctioning, or the pipes are leaking, or furniture needs replacing. Some of the requests are a necessity but others are more ambiguous and there is often a dispute as to whether the landlord or the tenant should foot the bill. As property manager it is Direct Let's responsibility to see that maintenance is carried out on the property. With other firms this can tend to be a lengthy exercise, involving gaining permission from the landlord, quotes from suppliers and settling any disputes. As part of the service that Direct Let offers, the client agrees to a budgeted amount, usually a percentage of expected annual rental income, which is at the property managers discretion to spend on maintenance. Anything above this expenditure is then checked with the landlord.

Standardizing the service in this way means that Direct Let is free in most cases to go about its business without the client getting in the way. The same applies to the annual review of rent, which is also outlined in the contract with the client. The rental amounts are raised in line with the annual increase in the government calculated RPI. Again this nullifies the need for the client to get involved. Examples of slight standardizing to the service are prevalent throughout but we will not detail them any further. The point being made is that these minor adaptations to the service were necessary in order for the system to be successful. It also took the focus of the business away from the client and more towards the product. PLMS was designed to integrate fully with the processes that existed within the company. It is central to the firm's operations and, as will be explained later, conforms to modern management's idea of 'lean management'.

How PLMS operates and its business benefits

The whole office is networked to a server which processes all the information. Every member of staff has a PC with a Windows 95 operating system through which all the applications are run. One of these applications is PLMS.

PLMS was designed using the database tool Microsoft FoxPro. The interface is very user friendly and resembles other Microsoft applications such as Word and Excel. Users can reach their desired window through the GUI (graphical user interface) with its drill down menus. Clicking on one of the items on the drill down menu opens a window through which the relevant information can be viewed, updated and saved. When creating PLMS the designers attempted to cater for every process of information that the business required and then divided them up into relevant areas. Different departments in Direct Let tend to perform most of their work through the specific windows which apply to their tasks. Virtually every department in Direct Let uses PLMS, which is represented by Figure 1.3.

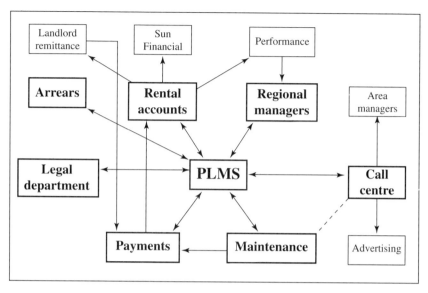

Figure 1.3 *Users of PLMS at Direct Let*

When users have selected the required window there are a number of ways the specific property can be identified. Each property has a unit reference number, an example of which is given below.

RP7/4543/003
Landlord ref./Property ref./Tenant ref.

This is a combination of a reference to the landlord, the property itself and the tenant. The user can enter this, or the address of the property, or the tenant's name to access the specific data. And even if the user does not know any of these exactly, part of them can be entered and a search performed.

This method makes the data extremely user friendly. Instead of opening the entire file on the property, the user can pinpoint the area of information required by selecting the relevant window. Because the landlord reference is an element of the unit reference number the user is also able to collate all the properties under the ownership of the same landlord and hence run a personalized report for each client.

Being run from a server all staff can access data at the same time. Even if data on the same property is required by more than one member of staff, the others can access the data in a read-only file while the first member of staff edits information.

Although these improvements were necessary for Direct Let to engage the larger clients they have also derived large cost benefits by rationalizing the administration of the information. These cost benefits are a considered by-product of the strategic nature of the project and they arise because of the following factors:

- The information is easier to maintain.
- Access to information is quicker and more precise.
- The data is more detailed and better presented.

The impact of PLMS on the organization

By far the greatest benefit that Direct Let's strategy imparted was the improvements it made to the business process and the resulting structure of the organization. As we will explain Direct Let provides a property management service that is fundamentally different from the rest of the industry. The MIT90s framework (Scott Morton, 1991) shown in Figure 1.4, aims to show that if there is a push or pull on any one area of the organization the other areas must change for the organization to remain in equilibrium.

The organization of the majority of property management firms is based around individual negotiators who deal with accounts at every stage from the

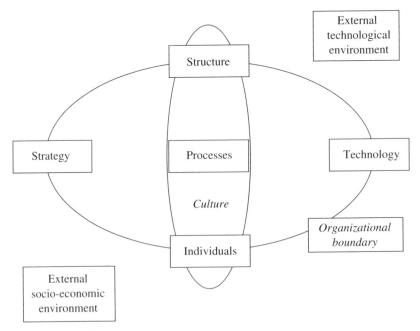

Figure 1.4 *MIT90s framework*

landlords to finding tenants to organizing maintenance. They spend a lot of their time acting as go-betweens.

As discussed earlier Direct Let is entering the market with an entirely different strategy and use of technology compared with the rest of the industry. The forces applied to the organization by the changes in strategy and technology have implied knock-on changes elsewhere which can be related to the MIT90s framework.

As explained earlier in Figure 1.3 the roles of the individuals have changed and hence the structure of the firm had also to change. Individuals work in departments with specific functions. The standardization of the product and the sophistication of the information system enables the staff to specialize in particular fields. There is no need for any one person to oversee every detail of a client's account as the relevant information is available to whomever requires it. This means that the culture of the organization is far removed from the 'negotiator' based culture of the rest of the industry. It is a culture that enables Direct Let's staff who are expert in an area carry out all relevant work, e.g. winning portfolios, chasing arrears or marketing vacant properties.

An example of how the business process has changed the structure of the firm and the role of the individual is evident when customers inquire about a property. Traditionally, a prospective customer would phone the property management firm in response to a vacancy advertised in the paper or on the off-chance that a property was available. The agent would search through files and arrange to meet the customer at a later date. In Direct Let the customer phones the call centre where staff can access a list of vacant properties in the desired area. A brief description of the property is also stored on file. Every call centre operator has access to a Microsoft Schedule for each area manager so that if a customer requires a viewing they can schedule the meeting into the diary of the area manager. Once the call is finished the operator simply calls the area manager and advises him of the arrangements. Area managers live locally and are issued with a company car and a mobile phone. Therefore, once they have been advised of a meeting they simply drive to the relevant property. This arrangement eliminates the need for local branches, which is a huge cost to firms in the industry.

These changes in organizational culture have a knock-on effect to how Direct Let is perceived in the marketplace. This will be particularly pronounced when Direct Let goes to market fully. This is part of the aim, to be seen to offer more of a *product* and to operate more efficiently, thus enabling the lower commissions that Direct Let charge.

Evaluation

The success of Direct Let's IT strategy as a competitive weapon can be evaluated by applying McFarlan's six questions (McFarlan,1984).

1 Can IT create defensible entry barriers?

When Direct Let goes fully to market there will be little to prevent other firms imitating Direct Let's IT/IS strategy, however they will need to be in a position where they can emulate Direct Let's organizational structure, to achieve similar benefits. Competitors will incur huge start-up costs in acquiring such a national customer base.

2 Can IT induce switching costs?

As a result of their strategy Direct Let are able to offer commissions up to a maximum of 12 per cent. This compares favourably to an industry norm of 15–16 per cent. Therefore, if clients of Direct Let do switch to another agency they will forfeit 3–4 per cent of their rental income. Direct Let's marketing of property means that clients should also see a high proportion of their properties let (currently averaging 95 per cent), again comparing favourably with the competition. At the moment the client has a considerable amount to lose by switching management firms.

3 Can IT change the ground rules of competition?

We have argued that Direct Let's strategy will fundamentally change the basis of competition in the industry, from offering a highly personalized service, to offering a streamlined, standardized *product*. However, until Direct Let goes to market fully it will be difficult to gauge whether the basis of competition in the market will change.

4 Can IT change competition from cost to differentiation?

Before Direct Let, competition was based on differentiation of service as cost was fixed at the market rate. Although Direct Let competes on cost it has also considerably differentiated its product from the rest of the industry.

5 Can IT build links to suppliers?

No, because clients are gained by a process of negotiation and human interface.

6 Can IT be used as product?

No, because if Direct Let sold access to their information system they would be undermining their competitive advantage.

Conclusion

In conclusion we have managed to answer 'yes' to at least 3 of McFarlan's questions which suggests Direct Let have used IT to create a competitive advantage. However, there are improvements that could be made.

1 Since the introduction of PLMS lean management is prevalent throughout Direct Let. Administrative duplication has been eradicated by integrating all the business processes, e.g. PLMS is linked to the company's financial accounts package. However, lean management is not being practised in the payments department where double entry of data is necessary because PLMS does not have an integrated purchase ledger. Including this in the system will bring cost saving benefits and provide more useful management information.
2 On a more strategic level Direct Let could improve internal communications. For example it could provide their area managers with laptops and modems so that information, e.g. schedules, could be communicated far more effectively than verbally on their mobile phone. This would also enable the area manager to send e-mails and faxes back to the office communicating, for example, the result of a viewing, and therefore further centralize the administrative function.
3 The present security is too simplistic and should be tailored to the specific tasks and responsibility of each user. At the moment security on the system is layered depending on the seniority of the user but even the lowest level of access is far too trusting so that even temporary staff have sufficient access to cause potentially hazardous problems.
4 As this is the first version of PLMS it will itself require modification, as it is expected that users will identify problems and possible improvements as they experience working with the new system. This is not of any great surprise as virtually every new piece of software in the market has been upgraded. However, in its first edition PLMS has achieved its purpose.

This research has established that within the industry IT is perceived as purely an administrative tool. Pinnacle's position of management broker gave the group the unique vantage point from which to observe this opportunity. Their pioneering strategy has established them immediately as leaders in IT development within the property management industry. The business process within Direct Let and the structure and culture of the organization have never been seen before in the industry and it is probable that when Direct Let goes to market others will emulate their strategy.

Appendix A Questionnaire

Do you use an IT system to track/control your lets?
What information does it hold? How often is this data updated?
Are you happy with the security of data within the system?
What kind of hardware architecture do you have?
Do you have someone explicitly in charge of IT?
Is the system fairly simple to use?
Do you think your system gives you any kind of advantage? If so, what?
What are the disadvantages of your system?
Do you think it is important to your business?
Do you have an IT strategy?
Do you think IT is important to the industry as a whole?
How many properties do you manage and what rate of commission do you charge?

Appendix B Sample organizations

- Bath Apartments
- Black Horse Agencies
- Challenger International
- D C Elliot Newman
- Home Lets
- Local Lets of Bath

Bibliography

McFarlan, F. (1984). Information Technology changes the way you compete. *Havard Business Review,* May–June.
Venkatraman, N. (1991). IT-induced Business Reconfiguration. In *The Corporation of the 1990s.* (M. Scott Morton, ed.), Oxford University Press.

2 Demaglass Limited

Samantha Jones-Pritchard
School of Management, University of Bath

This chapter examines the strategic role of IT within Demaglass Ltd. First the organization is described, then the information systems used. The IS benefits are assessed which allows conclusions to be drawn on the strategic impact of IT.

Introduction to Demaglass Limited

Demaglass Limited has an annual turnover of £90 million and is a global supplier of glass components and glass making equipment. There are three operating divisions within the group; Demaglass Lighting and Pharmaceutical, Demaglass Tableware and Demaglass Technology. The head office is based in Harworth where glass shells and glass tubes for the lighting and pharmaceutical markets are manufactured. The tableware division is based in Chesterfield which manufactures glasses and stemware for the LV (licensed victuallers) trade and high-street retailers. The technology division manufactures and installs glass-making equipment throughout the world.

Demaglass is currently re-developing its whole IT infrastructure in order to provide the tools to assist major change and allow the organization to move further along the road to becoming a world class manufacturer. The main area of focus for the project is business excellence and the organization will undergo significant change in order to acquire the tools, skills and people to become a 'Class A' manufacturer. A major part of this is the implementation of a fully integrated business system. The lighting division system has been fully implemented and work has started on the systems for the tableware and technology divisions and is due for completion 1999.

The first phase of the implementation went live at the end of September 1997 at Harworth. The company has undergone an extensive business process reengineering exercise to enable it to maximize the benefits from the new business system and improve operational performance.

Methodology

The main thrust of the research was close observation, over a twelve week period, of the team (known as the 'Talisman Team' – **T**ableware **a**nd **L**ighting **I**nformation **S**ystems **M**anagement Information **a**nd **N**etworks Project) responsible for overseeing the implementation of the IT system. During this period the implementation programme was investigated and interviews with the personnel involved with the project were carried out.

The choice of information systems

The Talisman Team was set up in October 1995, six months after the new Chief Executive, Don Greaves, joined Demaglass. The team was given the objective of sourcing and installing a business system which had a total investment estimated at £3.7 million. A cost and benefit analysis showed that such a system would bring the group £74,000 in savings per month. Fourteen months later a contact was signed with JBA Limited for the purchase of System 21. Why did Demaglass let £1 million of potential savings be lost through the sourcing and preparation of purchasing a business system? It was because the logic of this loss wasn't made at the start of the project. The objective was to find the most suitable system and the work involved in this was comprehensive and also took longer than anticipated. The Talisman Team saw the implementation of the business system as an opportunity to make changes within the firm that would make it a world class manufacturer.

What makes some implementation projects more successful that others? Often management fails to realise the anticipated benefits because potential savings are not analysed and managed. 'Managers have focused their attention primarily on the technology of IT and not enough on gaining a sustainable advantage from IT' (Cecil and Goldstein, 1990, p. 74) . Equally it may be said that an IS system has brought savings to a company by providing reports on performance and reducing administration costs but the amount of savings that have been made is not known. However there are projects which have been able to demonstrate their success.

Such firms are Zeneca Colours who achieved a 70 per cent reduction in manufacturing lead times, 80 per cent reduction in lot sizes, with customer service improving to 90 per cent. Ciba-Geigy achieved a 70 per cent reduction in work in progress (WIP), 20 per cent reduction in inventory and a 60 per cent reduction in lead times. ICI Paints reduced their lead times by 40 per cent and increased customer service to 90 per cent. Finally, Pilkington Optronics improved productivity by 40 per cent and increased on-time delivery from 30 per cent to 98 per cent (Wight, 1996).

What did the management of these firms do to bring themselves the success other firms have not had? Often, the reason was that they used IT as a tool to bring significant change to the organization by putting more emphasis on people and processes rather than information processing. This was the focus of Demaglass.

The information system and its benefits

The JBA integrated business system is of modular design covering all functions of the business with each module being designed to run discretely or integrated into the full suite of functions. As System 21 is an 'off the shelf' package it was important to make sure the business cycle of Demaglass fitted in with the operation of the software.

The pedigree of System 21 lies predominantly in the core business functions, e.g. finance, sales, etc., therefore JBA have forged links with market leaders in the areas their software doesn't cover. The three 'bolt on' packages implemented at the lighting division are planned maintenance, finite scheduling and export documentation.

Before the final decision was made to purchase the system the financial implications were analysed. As well as the cost and benefit analysis, the Net Present Value was calculated and this gave a positive value (see Table 2.1).

Table 2.1 NPV of JBA

Capital cost	Year 0	Year 1	Year 2	Year 3	Year 4	NPV
JBA £816,504	£183,740	£186,188	£186,188	£186,188	£186,188	£1,590,434.91

Assumptions:
NPV at 10 per cent per annum
Capital cost – All capital costs incurred at date of delivery
Year 0 – Cost incurred at date of delivery, i.e. charges are pre-paid one year in advance
Years 1–4 – Cost incurred at beginning of period
Source: Systems Evaluation – Quantitative Assessment Model, Arthur Anderson

Nevertheless, it is difficult to evaluate the specific benefits the IS system will bring to Demaglass, as the system is primarily a tool to process and report information. 'It is probably true that many of today's businesses simply could not function effectively without automated information processing systems of some form or another … it is not certain that any benefits will accrue just because a computer is installed: far from it' (Martin and Powell, 1992, p. 4). The major benefits gained from an implementation of this nature seem to be generated from process simplification. The change initiative was led by the

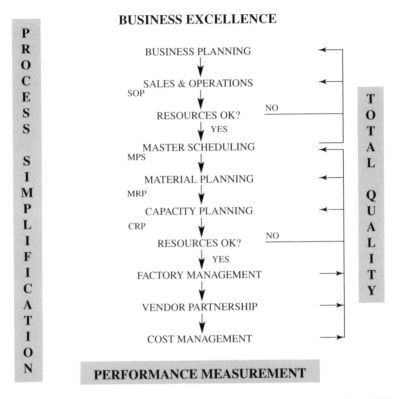

Figure 2.1 *Bringing the sales and operations functions together (M. R. Pitt, 1998 – Business Excellence Course Notes)*

Talisman Team who developed new working practices through extensive business process reengineering. This has resulted in a more streamlined flow of information through the elimination of non-value added activities.

Through various workshops and training sessions much emphasis was placed upon the people within the organization, as people are a key resource for improvement. For example, work was carried out to develop 'sales and operations planning' which is a formal method of bringing the sales and operations functions together, as shown in Figure 2.1, so that the two departments could work together as a team rather than as separate entities.

The reaction of Demaglass' employees to the system has been experienced by other organizations. Martin and Powell (1992) depict examples of reactions to change by users (Figure 2.2). These reactions can be seen in various personnel, with the majority being in the 'acceptance' box. Fear can also be evident. In this research there were examples of users physically breaking out in a sweat at the thought of using the system. Demaglass operates in a manner similar to how it did twenty or thirty years ago with staff who have been with

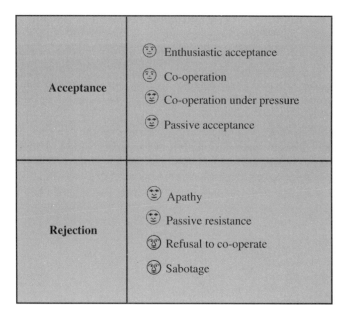

Figure 2.2

the company for the whole of that period. Some of these users are asking questions like 'why do we have to use the system and change what we are doing, we have worked this way for twenty years'. During training or pilot runs some users have clearly found it hard to understand the system and to move around the various applications.

The system implementation is going to enable Demaglass to maintain a position with their competition. The changes that are being made from the implementation of the system are going to enable them to provide their customers with a better service and have a lower cost base by streamlining the administration costs. It is these improvements which form part of the strategy of the firm; it is the business system which provides the opportunity for these changes to be made. However, the organization's philosophy is that the changes are not going to be made through the system *per se*, they are going to be made through the people who use the system. The system will provide the people with visibility on costs of products. This is information they have not had easy access to and it is the information that will enable them to make judgements and understand the value of their actions. It will also give management visibility on the performance of the firm. Users will have up-to-date information that will enable them to act upon it straight away, rather than having information from the previous twenty-four hours, which is often too late.

Business process, organizational relationships and change

The implementation of the system has been the driving force for change which will result in a change in individuals' roles, thus having a direct effect on the full business process. These changes will introduce more efficient work methods in order to remove the non-value added tasks and avoid duplication of effort.

Figure 2.3 shows how the network is set-up over the two sites. This network will allow users to share information, with reports being available to any personnel that require them. The intention is that this will streamline the business

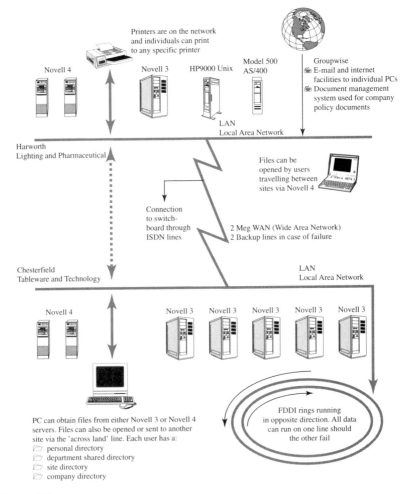

Figure 2.3

process, hence making it more efficient. It will also have an impact on organizational relationships as information will be available to more users. The
JBA system is loaded onto the AS/400 and data for Harworth can be obtained
from Chesterfield and vice versa via the megastream line.

Importance of IT

When asked about the importance of IT to Demaglass, Don Greaves, Chief
Executive, said that is was important, but put the emphasis on the words
'Information Technology' as opposed to 'Business System'. He explained that
the business system, although being an integral part of IT, is the start of it. The
developments and enhancements to the IT that will be introduced over time
will start to give Demaglass the competitive edge.

To reflect on this discussion with Don Greaves an understanding as to how
competitive advantage could be gained from IT is needed. To be able to do this
reference is made to McFarlan's six questions on competitive advantage
(McFarlan, 1984, p. 99), which are summarized in Table 2.2.

Table 2.2

McFarlan's six questions	Relation to Demaglass Limited
Can IS create defensible entry barriers	This IS is unlikely to create any barriers to entry. However, the high capital costs required when setting up a glass manufacturing business mean that high barriers do exist
Can IS induce switching costs?	It is unlikely that the IS will induce any switching costs
Can IS change the ground rules of competition? Can IS change competition from cost to differentiation	The current phase of the business system will not change either of these, however, the CEO spoke of enhanced CAD systems which will give them the 'quickest route to the market' with new product development. This will change the rules of competition by allowing them to have a differential advantage in a fast changing industry
Can IS build links with suppliers?	Work has already started in this area where their packaging suppliers are electronically linked to their production schedule and packaging stocks. From this information the supplier automatically maintains the packaging inventory levels
Can IS be used as a product?	It is unlikely that, due to the nature of the business, that the IS can be used as a product

It is apparent form this table that it is unlikely the system will bring Demaglass any great competitive advantage. However, Max Hopper (Hopper, 1990, p. 100) explained that 'by being the first to develop proprietary systems, pioneers could revolutionise their industries'.

Strategy

The management team have drawn up long- and medium-term plans which are five year and three year plans respectively. On a yearly basis there is a departmental 'policy deployment' where each department details their objectives with a plan on how they are going to achieve them. Each of these plans details the strategic objectives of the firm that will help Demaglass become 'best in class', as stated in the mission statement by the Chief Executive. Part of the strategy for being 'best in class' is for the firm to develop the tools to give them the strength required to meet this objective, the business system is one of these tools recommended by Andersen Consulting (Figure 2.4).

When analysing the financial implications of installing the information systems, the management team may have done well to also 'visualize their system in terms of a strategic grid' (McFarlan, 1984, p. 100) as shown in Figure 2.5

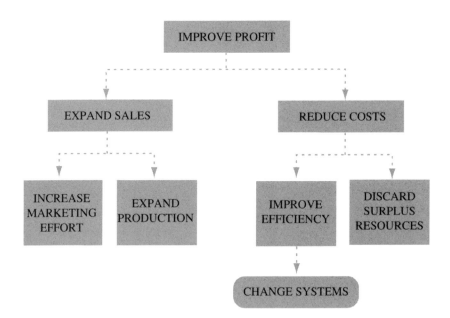

Figure 2.4 *Strategic objectives (source: Anderson, 1986; p. 12)*

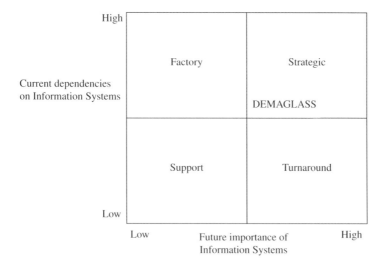

Figure 2.5 *Strategic grid*

Demaglass is placed in the 'strategic' quadrant. The IT, although being a supportive function which will assist in improving efficiency, is integral to the business and was implemented following a strategic decision.

The improvements will allow Demaglass to provide customers, internal and external, with accurate information and make realistic promises which will result in improved customer satisfaction. Through this information the management team will be able to improve business decision making. As Ian Gibson the MIS Manager stated, it will help 'enable Demaglass to achieve its corporate objectives, provide customers with a first class service and achieve and maintain a position of best in class'.

The goals set by the management team are going to be achieved through an educated workforce who are going through an environment where a culture of empowerment is being introduced. The management team is also going through change where they are now working to encourage empowerment.

Conclusion

The members of the Talisman Team are focused on the objectives set with installing the business system and defining new work methods. It is clear to the management of Demaglass that for them to be able to gain a competitive advantage within their market they need to make radical changes to the way the company operates. This chapter has discussed how Demaglass have made a decision to install a business system as part of an overall objective in improving the operation of the company.

As part of the research interviews were carried out with the Talisman Team, the Financial Director and the Chief Executive. They were asked for their thoughts on how IT would improve the overall performance of Demaglass. From the interviews it was clear that they all 'saw' the same advantages from the system, some of the statements made were:

- 'The system will provide information that is vital for the management'
- 'It will lead to efficient and effective running at a minimum cost'
- 'It will strip out the non value-added tasks'
- 'It is a catalyst for change, an opportunity to get the 'house in order''
- 'The system provides the potential, not the benefit, it is an enabler'
- 'The IT strategy supports the business strategy'
- 'IT uncomplicates manual tasks'

The decision to implement the business system was part of a strategic decision of the management team to make the company a world class manufacturer. With this sort of project carrying huge costs the implementation would have to be strategic with a positive NPV. It was part of the management's strategic decision to purchase the business system as they felt it would improve the efficiency of Demaglass, however, there is a danger that they believe the system will solve the operational problems currently experienced. As Mark Williams, a Talisman Team member, pointed out, the system is simply a control check that will force people to get their working methods right. It is these working methods that will bring the benefits to Demaglass and improve the business.

Bibliography

Anderson, R. (1986). *Management, IS and Computers*. Macmillan.
Cecil, J. and Goldstein, M. (1990). Sustaining competitive advantage from IT. *The McKinsey Quarterly*, **4**, pp. 74–89.
Hopper, M. D. (1990). Rattling SABRE – New ways to compete on information. *Havard Business Review*, May–June.
Martin, C. and Powell, P. (1992). *Information Systems: A Management Perspective*. McGraw-Hill.
McFarlan, F. (1984). Information Technology changes the way you compete. *Havard Business Review*, May–June.

Pitt, M. R. (1998) *Business Excellence Course Notes*, School of Management, University of Bath.
Wight, O. (1996) *Products and Services Directory.*

3 Johnsons News Limited

Miranda Back
School of Management, University of Bath

The purpose of this chapter is to explain and assess the implications of EDI (Electronic Data Interchange) to the company, looking at how it has used different EDI methods to share information in the industry and transform supplier/consumer relationships, enabling it to gain competitive advantage.

Methodology

The majority of the research was in the form of interviews with Andy Watkins, the Retail Technology Manager at Johnsons. He initiated the setting up of the project and has progressed it through every stage, he therefore has very in-depth knowledge about the system and the ideas behind it. Company literature and reports have also been used to assess the benefits of the system and the extent of competitive edge it has provided. Substantial secondary research has also been carried out, drawing from relevant books and journals.

Overview of company and industry

The newspaper and magazine market is a very complex market with a large variety of different customer needs. Johnsons is the fourth largest news wholesaler in the country supplying newspapers and magazines to approximately 10,000 retailers. The small cornershops account for approximately 50 per cent of Johnson's business, with the remainder coming from high street news suppliers, such as WH Smith Retail (30 per cent), the major multiples such as Safeway (15 per cent), and forecourts and airports (5 per cent).

The accepted method of trading in the industry is that wholesalers bid for contracts to supply certain areas with different publishers' titles. The retailer does not have any choice in which wholesaler delivers a particular title to them. In this industry, unlike most others, there is a heavy imbalance of power on the supplier's side.

Strategic significance of IT in the industry and within Johnsons

IT is fundamental to the industry due to the complexity and timeliness of the order and delivery functions. Millions of newspapers and magazines are sold in Britain each day and it would be impossible to operate the supply of these without the aid of IT. Using McFarlan's Strategic Grid (McFarlan, 1984) we can place Johnsons in the strategic section (Figure 3.1) as it has high current dependence on IT and its planned IT investments will have a high strategic impact. Recognition of the increasing importance of IT within the organization and industry, and the need for the information it can bring, has instigated the design and development of this project.

The problem

Both magazines and newspapers are very 'time sensitive' products. Obviously there is no demand for yesterday's news which means that waste is a major

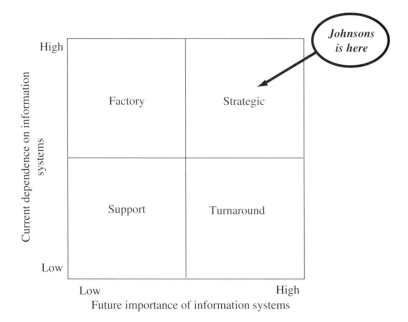

Figure 3.1 *McFarlan's Strategic Grid*

issue in this market. Johnsons wanted to use IT to maximize availability of titles whilst minimizing waste. There is also a demand for sophisticated information from the retailers.

Methods of EDI that Johnsons Uses

Johnsons now uses four methods of EDI: Newslink, Tradanet, Internet and Bespoke. This chapter will concentrate on the first two of these methods as these are the ones that are used most extensively by Johnsons.

Newslink

Newslink is a method of EDI which uses the SPEDI (simple protocol for electronic data interchange) system. This method is aimed at linking Johnsons to its smaller retailers using EPoS (electronic point of sale) technology. The Newslink system has been developed by Johnsons and various EPoS suppliers (Computer 100, YP Electronics, CTN Systems, Datasafe Systems, AND Systems and Adamsoft). Figure 3.2 shows how Newslink works.

Tradanet

Tradanet is the second method of EDI used. This is a standard network for transmission of EDI data in the EANCOM format. This format has been agreed worldwide and has set codes for the layout and barcodes, etc. This is

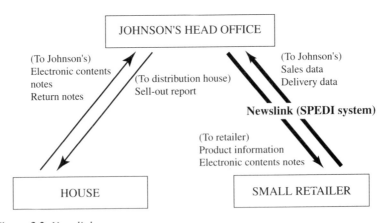

Figure 3.2 *Newslink*

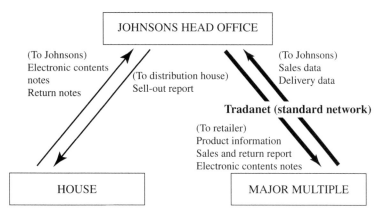

Figure 3.3 *Tradanet*

the form of EDI aimed at Johnsons larger customers – the major multiples. These companies would only use a worldwide 'standard' EDI method and hence use this system rather than Newslink. Figure 3.3 shows the links between the parties involved.

Processing information

At the end of every working day all of the sales data stored on the EPoS system in the stores is sent to Johnsons, either via Tradanet or Newslink. Johnsons' distribution houses send electronic contents notes (showing what has been delivered) and also returns notes (detailing what has been returned). At Johnsons head office the data is amalgamated to produce two reports:

1 Sell-out report – this is sent to the distribution houses and shows them which titles have sold out in which stores.
2 Sales and returns report – this is used by Johnsons and the retailer together. It shows which titles are being excessively returned, which titles routinely sell-out and how many copies of which titles go missing (known in the industry as 'shrinkage'). This information is shown in figures for each week and graphically to show trends over periods.

It is the evaluation and application of the information which these reports provide that is important. The benefits they can bring are discussed in the next section.

Benefits of the use of EDI

Sell-out report

By identifying which titles have sold out the distribution houses can then replenish stocks of titles on that day and improve availability in the store, thus sales are maximized. The aim is to increase availability of all titles to 100 per cent, although this has not yet been achieved the availability in some stores has increased quite dramatically from 70 per cent to 93.5 per cent.

Sales and returns report

The report identifies which titles are being over-stocked thus the standing order can be adjusted. This is particularly important for non-returnable titles. It is detrimental for both the retailer and Johnsons to overstock as they both have to process the paperwork and collection that is required. They also lose out on the profit they could have made from other titles occupying that shelf space.

Better recognition of which titles are selling and which are not (with fluctuations during months and seasons) allows Johnsons to improve its supply management and the retailers to better satisfy consumer needs, all of which increase the potential for greater profitability.

The smaller retailers can use the shrinkage information to evaluate the layout of their stores to best prevent theft. They can also use the sales information to identify which titles are not selling as well and possibly reallocate shelf space to more popular titles or extend the ranges of popular titles.

The major multiple chains can use this report to compare one branch with another. The report can be used to highlight 'trouble stores' in which newspapers and magazines are not selling well. This may be due to the position of these products in the store, in which case this gives scope to the store managers for improvement.

Competitive edge and organizational relationships

Johnsons now has a much closer relationship with its retailers, especially Martins, which was the first retailer to set up information links with Johnsons. The cooperation that has resulted from this technology has meant that retailers and Johnsons are now working together to achieve their common goal, namely maximizing sales and minimizing returns. Johnsons has identified value adding services that it can offer and recognized the mutual benefits these can bring.

Figure 3.4 shows the five levels graph (Venkatraman, 1991) from which we can establish the path that Johnsons has followed in developing this technology. Johnsons entered the first stage on the graph (localized exploitation stage) with Martins in March 1996 when it introduced the technology in six 'trial' stores. It has progressed through this stage to the internal integration stage, during which it has integrated the technology into its operational and managerial roles, for example action has been taken upon sell-out reports to alter standing orders. It is now entering into the third level – business process redesign – redesigning its business processes such as that of the introduction of the 'afternoon' replenishment service. It is becoming revolutionary as opposed to evolutionary. It is now maximizing its use of the system to incorporate electronic processing of contents and delivery notes, and product information, previously carried out manually and using the information gained from the system to maximize availability. As Figure 3.4 shows, as the degree of transformation increases and Johnsons has the possibility of entering Levels 4 and 5 of the graph, the range of potential benefits will also increase.

As McFarlan's six questions (McFarlan, 1984) illustrate, competitive advantage can be gained through companies using IT to induce switching costs. By introducing this technology Johnsons is encouraging its customers to rely increasingly on its electronic support, building it into their operational dependence and hence making switching to a competitor unattractive.

The true competitive edge for Johnsons however, comes from the way the

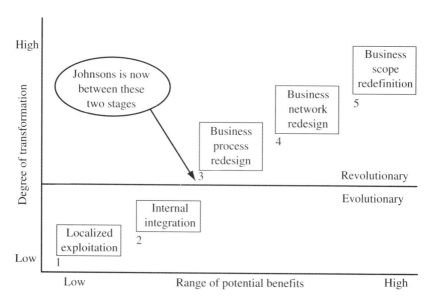

Figure 3.4 *Five levels graph*

publishers view their new activities. As explained earlier, Johnsons has to win contracts from the publishers. Consequently, impressing a publisher with their service quality is vital. Johnsons is now changing the basis of competition from price to differentiation. They are offering a new product feature in the form of a value adding service – this change in the base of competition is recognized by McFarlan as a way of gaining competitive edge.

The differentiation proves that Johnsons is showing initiative and offering an extra service which no other wholesaler is offering – a way of actively increasing availability and hence sales of publishers' titles. This makes Johnsons a much more attractive wholesaler to award contracts to. It has added benefits for Johnsons in that it puts them under less pressure to cut costs to compete with other larger wholesalers, who benefit from greater economies of scale, as they are competing via differentiation as opposed to cost.

The publishers also evaluate the performance of their wholesaler by retailers' comments and complaints. The initiative has allowed Johnsons to improve their relationship with their retailers, thus this feeling of co-operation has filtered through to the publishers and will help Johnsons to win future supply contracts.

This project requires a relatively small and extremely flexible wholesaler. The size and nature of Johnsons as a company relative to its competitors provides it with competitive advantage as this project would be extremely difficult, if not impossible for larger wholesalers such as WH Smiths to implement in the foreseeable future. This is due to the vast amount of information and the timeliness with which it would need to be processed and actioned.

Criticisms

Quality of data is dependent on the retailer

The retailer is responsible for the scanning in and out all the products. If this is not done correctly it can alter the results of the report and hence the value of the data. Retailers have identified problems due to the use of 'hot keys' (keys on the till marked for specific titles), as it is easy for the wrong button to be pressed, and also from 'double-scanning', which makes inventory checks inaccurate, thus leading to no sales based replenishment for sold-out titles.

Frequency

It is vital that the data be sent on a daily basis, within a given time-span to allow for a second delivery in the day to replenish sold-out titles. If data is not sent on time by the retailer and processed quickly by the wholesaler it becomes obsolete.

Politics and power

The limitations of this technology are predominantly accounted for by the 'social shaping' approach. This suggests that the capacity of the technology is equivalent to the political circumstances of its production. In Johnsons' case this involves the politics which surround its relationships with the publishers.

Information power gives them the 'ability to access and use information to defend a stance or viewpoint – or to question an alternative view held by someone else – and is important as it can affect strategic choices'. This 'information power' can also alter the balance of power in a supplier/buyer relationship as illustrated in Porter's Five Forces (Porter, 1985) theory. It is this change in the balance of power that Johnsons appears to be trying to gain through the concealment of this information from the publishers.

However, if the true benefits of this system are to be gained, this information needs to be shared with the publishers. They can then use it as market research, on which decisions regarding future line extensions and new product ranges can be based, which, if made successfully, will benefit publisher, wholesaler and retailer alike.

Conclusions

This project has a lot of potential for enabling Johnsons to gain 'real' competitive edge. However, the problems associated with the system need to be minimized, and if possible eradicated completely. The accuracy and timing of the data involved could be improved by better training of staff involved in input and transmission of the information, thus increasing the value of the data. The problem with the politics and power issue may not as easily be overcome however. This needs to be addressed by Johnson's top management, who need to realize that the full benefits of this technology and information cannot fully be gained unless there is more 'openness' with the publishers as to the results of the reports. Johnson's reluctance to share this information is understandable as they feel that they now have more power over the publishers. However, this stance will limit the true value of this project in the future.

There are several possible additions to the information exchange which could be developed in the future, these include the electronic transmission of invoices and receipt of payments – this would reduce the staffing necessary at present to carry out this function and hence increase Johnson's profit margins.

Johnsons is now planning its activities around its developments using the EDI methods detailed. The strategic significance of IT to Johnsons is increasing and will continue to do so in the future.

Bibliography

McFarlan, F. (1984). Information Technology changes the way you compete. *Harvard Business Review,* May–June.

Porter, M. E. (1985). *Competitive Advantage: Creating and Sustaining Superior Performance*. Free Press.

Venkatraman, N. (1991). IT-induced Business Reconfiguration. In *The Corporation of the 1990s – Information Technology and Organisational Transformation*. (M. Scott Morton, ed.), Oxford University Press.

Reports

Sell-out reports – Martins Newsagents
Source: Johnsons News Limited
Sales and returns reports – Martins Newsagents
Source: Johnsons News Limited
Project overview report
Source: Johnsons News Limited

4 Tesco

Niku Banaie, Simon Hogan, Kate McArdle,
Daniela Meier
School of Management, University of Bath

Over the last twenty years supermarkets have increasingly turned to IT (information technology) to help them to cut costs, combat failing margins, improve customer service and compete with their rivals. The industry has invested in several IT initiatives in a concerted effort to move away from the painful 'price wars'. The importance placed on IT investment is underlined by the latest survey by IBM showing that despite reduced market growth expectations companies in the grocery sector intend to increase their technology investment by up to 10 per cent (Price, 1997).

In addition, other evidence suggests that consumers are looking for more than just cheap food – a recent survey by Healey & Baker (Strachan, 1997) indicates that shoppers are predominantly looking for two things; the largest possible product range and convenience. Hence, today, the fierce competition between UK food retailers is based on non-price aspects such as quality and range of products, service and convenience. Tesco is at the forefront of this battle, being the first to introduce a loyalty card scheme, invest in internet retailing and improve customer convenience through its self-scanning checkout system.

Porter's Five Forces (Porter, 1985) can aid our understanding of the industry structure. The two main forces in this industry in the UK are buyer power and rivalry, i.e. the customer has the power to obtain bargains and decrease prices. Establishing switching costs by differentiating through IT is therefore essential. This chapter will evaluate if Tesco has succeeded in doing this and will assess the strategic business implications of its IT initiatives.

Loyalty cards

Tesco was the first of the major UK players (Tesco, J. Sainsbury, Safeway and Asda) to implement a loyalty card scheme, in February 1995, following a one-year trial at fourteen stores. Seven months later Sainsbury was toppled from its long-standing number one spot and by February 1997, Tesco had 9 million card holders, equivalent to a 71 per cent penetration level. At the time of writing they have over a million more card holders than their nearest rival (Wolf, 1997) and sales growth rates of 8.1 per cent in real terms.

Self-scan check-out system

Safeway was the first to introduce self scanning to the UK in March 1995. Tesco followed in January 1997 by testing the scanners in the Osterley store in West London. Today their 'smart shopper' can be found in several stores nationwide. Although data from Tesco is not yet available, 18 per cent of Safeway loyalty cardholders use the system regularly and the figure is increasing (Bagnall,1996).

Internet retailing

Tesco was the first supermarket to develop home shopping via the internet and has introduced it into six trial areas. Their site took six weeks from concept to full implementation, involving about five people. This work includes the efforts of their IT division, the BIT (Business Information Technology) group who designed the 'look' of the internet superstore and Microsoft Consultant services who provided the expertise in the merchant server application. Sainsbury estimates that about 20 per cent of its twelve million customers a week are interested in some form of surrogate shopping. Other food retailers have no concrete plans for such a service, but few are ruling it out (Cope, 1997).

Description of IT

Customers apply for membership of the ClubCard Scheme and are sent a card. They earn 'bonus' or 'reward' points on purchases which are stored cumulatively – one point for every pound spent. Methods of redemption include exchanging points for discount vouchers, Air Miles, donations to charity, or reductions on gas or telephone bills. All supermarkets are being innovative in ways to redeem reward points in order to add value to the scheme.

Tesco's self-scanning terminal is considerably more sophisticated than its forerunner at Safeway. In a joint development with Siemens Nixdorf Information System and Telxon (Ody, 1997), Tesco are introducing small terminals equipped with liquid crystal displays, radio communications, touch screens and possibly integrated swipe card readers. This unit will be used as a scanner but will also be able to display messages and could become a multi-purpose information device that works in conjunction with the loyalty card databases – special offers tailored to the individual customer can be displayed on the trolley.

A Tesco Loyalty Cardholder can now enter the store and swipe the card to obtain a specially equipped trolley. Special trolleys and boxes have been provided for this purpose and very basic controls allow the shopper to scan the goods as they shop. The scanned codes are turned into item details and the till receipt is printed out. Customers then take their receipt to the checkout where they can pay without the shopping load having to be unpacked and rescanned. In the future Tesco wants the customer to pay automatically with a credit or debit card without seeing a cashier.

In the first internet trial in Osterley, customers can either use a CD-ROM catalogue to compile a list and then e-mail it to the store, or they can use the Tesco direct website, which sells more than 22,000 products, the same as a normal store. ClubCard holders shop on-line in the virtual superstore and have the goods delivered to their home for a five pound charge. As expansion continues into other areas of the country you will get the product range of your 'adopted' home shopping branch. If you live outside a home shopping area then you get what is called 'the world store', a cross section of products from the general range.

Business benefits

Tesco's corporate strategy is one of 'customer focus', where 'anything to make the customer happy' is the axiom. This was a deliberate move by Tesco, and others in the industry, away from price competition. The company has applied its resources to increasing customer loyalty which Tesco defines as 'a high share of the customer's available expenditure and a strong commitment to the brand such that competitive pressure has little or no effect'.

Tesco are starting to tailor promotions to meet the needs and wants of the individual customer, using information derived from the loyalty card system which allows them to segment their market. It is *pushing* sales as Ann Treneman, of *The Independent* remarks:

> We only feel a little embarrassed as we stand in front of an industrial sized jar of mayonnaise wondering if we should get three for the price of two and 'earn' 100 bonus points. It is now one of my personal goals in life to 'earn' enough bonus points to pay for an entire week's shopping ... My loyalty has been bought, no sweat. (Treneman, 1997)

Research from Project Assist reveals that 'loyal customers spend 30–50 per cent more per transaction, visit three times the average, spend four times more a year and account for 50 per cent of sales' (*Marketing Week*, 1997). Through the use of IT Tesco are encouraging consumers to remain loyal. It seems that the ClubCard is a win-win game for both consumer as well as Tesco who are obtaining detailed information on customer buying behaviour.

A recent survey by NCR states that shoppers disliked queuing and were continually looking for ways to avoid checkout lines (Taylor, 1997b) – the self check out system was Tesco's solution to this customer dissatisfaction. An Andersen Consulting official has commented that customers who use the self check scan facility 'perceive that they save fifteen to twenty minutes per shopping trip when they may only save four or five minutes' (Oram, 1996). By allowing customers to scan their own goods in the self check-out system, Tesco has the potential to reduce its labour costs as fewer cashiers are needed. US research suggests that a supermarket checkout lane costs more than $100,000 a year to operate, 90 per cent of which are wage costs (Taylor, 1997a). By eliminating the majority of checkout personnel in the long term, a supermarket can therefore reduce its costs significantly.

Tesco are providing the opportunity to purchase weekly groceries for those who do not like the shopping experience or those who do not want to leave the comfort of their armchair, or simply those who do not have a lot of time. In essence Tesco are catering for those customers who are not ordinarily customers but are valuable even so. For example, the most likely user will be young affluent males, who do not like supermarket shopping; are computer literate; who prefer the higher margin branded products, and can afford to pay a premium for delivery. The economics of internet shopping are even more compelling. If a traditional retail outlet cost around £1.25 million to set up, a comparable internet site can be set up for under £50,000, according to Cap Gemini Sogeti (Goodwin, 1996), and maintenance costs are very low. A single website has the ability to take its goods and services to a global audience. Although small at the moment, the potential market is huge – £8.5 billion according to estimates from the Healey & Baker survey (Strachan, 1997). That is 16 per cent of the country's total grocery spend.

Utilizing data

The launch of the Tesco 'ClubCard' in February 1995 managed to 'build a six million name database', by July, 'in record time and at record cost' (Hawkes, 1995). As well as names and addresses, the information includes; the number of people in the household; the average weekly shopping budget; employment status and pet and car ownership. These details are cross referenced to information captured at the point of sale (EPoS), a process which is identical for self scan and internet shopping allowing 'every piece of information about your time spent at the check out to be stored' (Grayson, 1997).

Despite the huge volumes of information, retrieval is swift; for example, to check six billion records would take about half an hour using five processors on their dedicated IBM S/390 mainframe, working in parallel (Grayson, 1997).

The databases are used for sophisticated segmenting and targeting also known as 'stealth marketing' (Clarke, 1996) which is more efficient and effective. Tesco is gearing its £30 million advertising and marketing budget from above-the-line to direct marketing based on the information from its cards (*Marketing*, 1995). Tesco has over 1300 different mailshots targeting vegetarians, diabetics, students, pensioners, etc., (*Financial Times*, Nov 1996). The supermarkets are 'experimenting' with their information, using it to change their range of products, improve stock management and try different prices and layouts (Partingdon, 1995). Sophisticated data-warehousing techniques reveal trends in buying behaviour that may not be easily spotted. Customers are transformed into 'small tightly defined groups whose tastes and choices can be minutely described, predicted and most importantly of all, influenced' (Price, 1997).

The consensus seems to be that information about what customers are not buying is of equal importance. For example, 'they find that people who buy feta cheese and olives usually buy Californian wine. If you buy both the former but not the latter they send you an offer on Californian wine because they think you should like it and that you should be buying it' (Price, 1997).

Has Tesco's IT strategy created a competitive advantage?

Tesco's IT strategy will now be evaluated in terms of McFarlan's six questions (McFarlan, 1984).* The cost of developing and implementing IT is a definite barrier to new entrants, and is often a major problem for firms within the industry. Tesco spent between £10 and £20 million to set up its ClubCard program – a sum new entrants find daunting. Such costs have even dissuaded Asda from going down the 'loyalty path', preferring to invest in high margin products such as 'George' clothing. However, the internet and self checkout facilities are comparably cheaper and the cost of development provides no defensible entry barrier in the long run.

This can also be said about switching costs. Some shoppers become locked into a loyalty system, whilst others such as 'card junkies' and 'premium hunters'

---

* Which are:
– can IS create defensible entry barriers?
– can IS induce switching costs?
– can IS change the ground rules of competition?
– can IS change competition from cost to differentiation?
– can IS build links with suppliers?
– can IS be used as a product?

are able to manipulate the system to their advantage due to competitive replication by all stores. Although there is a limit to the number of cards consumers will carry, the benefits to these promiscuous shoppers are that they can continue their regular shopping whilst picking up discounts from other stores.

Self-scanning systems lead the customer to purchase store-specific packing boxes. In addition, the convenience factor of being 'used to' one system can be seen as a switching cost but as the various systems have major commonalities this aspect becomes less significant.

In relation to internet retailing, costs are quantified by the time it takes to familiarize oneself with a new site – the learning curve effect. When a consumer switches to a substitute product, the loss of customer specific pre-order data collated over time on the regular site has to be considered. IT does induce switching costs in this case, however these can be overcome if the customer is willing to invest time and effort.

Initially, the ground rules of competition in the industry changed from price to value added, including stronger emphasis on quality, a greater range of goods and providing better customer service – a change which has been facilitated by the use of IT. In the future competition will be based purely on information, leading data warehousing to play a key role. In this case IT will be crucial as supermarkets which do not have this data available, will be at a major disadvantage.

When first implemented the new IT has the desired effect of changing from price competition to differentiation, with customers able to distinguish between supermarket chains. This was short-lived, however, as close on the heels of the ClubCard, the ABC and Reward Card were implemented by Tesco's main competitors, a 'herd mentality' which cancelled out any differentiation resulting in 'a culture of sameness' (*Marketing*, Nov 1995). Not only this, but by failing to continually improve its system, Tesco allowed its competitive advantage to be lost as its competitors developed greater warehousing capabilities and better customer deals on their cards. In order to avoid competitive disadvantage, Tesco introduced self-scanning technology and had the advantage of learning from Safeway's errors, thus being able to implement a far superior system.

Internet shopping places Tesco again at the forefront of the industry. Though only of use to customers with a personal computer and a modem, the cost is hard to establish with a trade-off between the time spent shopping in store, the cost of being on-line and delivery premiums.

Therefore, IT can differentiate between stores, but only for a limited period of time until competitive replica have been established.

Tesco is using IT to build links to suppliers by transmitting the information gathered through scanning and checkout technology to them immediately and with the help of EPoS and EDI. This means forecasts and stock requirements have greater accuracy leading to increased sales, reduced ordering time, fewer shortages in stocks and wastage. On the other hand Tesco is not sharing the information gained by the use of IT with their suppliers to foster relations. They are more likely to use this to gain power over their suppliers as Ogbonna and Wilkinson (1988) have found from their research into the supermarket industry. Loyalty cards are a vehicle by which 'retailers evolve from distributor' to become the 'source of all knowledge', whereas manufacturers become 'the weaker pawns' (Foster, 1995).

One by-product of such advanced IT is that it can be a major profit generator for the company. Internally the advantage cannot be quantified but externally the market for carefully cross-referenced data is huge. Whilst Tesco's promise '... not to pass on customer's names and addresses to anybody else' (Tesco Home page) complying with the Data Protection Act, who is to judge the value of anonymous data with a going rate of £100 per 1000 names? Eighty per cent of the adult population are said to be concerned about how their data is protected and used (Wolf, 1997). It is foreseeable that there could be a consumer backlash if retailers are not careful about how this information is treated.

Detailed knowledge of the IT systems could also be seen as a potential product, especially in relation to internet retailing. The opportunities of consultancy are yet to be exploited but it is doubtless that they exist. Supplier advertising space on the site and on self-scanning screens is another possibility as well as specifically relevant vouchers to be printed off at point of sale. The implementation of IT has clearly been advantageous to Tesco if only for a limited period in some circumstances. The company realises that IT will play a vital part in food retailing in the future and is prepared to expand its present systems.

Has IT become strategic for Tesco?

Using McFarlan's strategic grid (McFarlan, 1984) in order to establish the role of IT, we can deduce that the industry has changed dramatically within the last twenty years. IT has evolved from being merely a support function (e.g. automatic cash registers) to playing a crucial part in the daily transactions of a company. Tesco is aware of the future importance of IT (as outlined above) and is at present reliant on IT for purchasing and sales, and increasingly for its marketing functions putting them on the 'strategic' quadrant of the grid. But, are they using their IT strategically? To help this analysis, we can apply the MIT90s framework (Scott Morton, 1991).

The first element to change was the corporate strategy with the move to 'customer focus' and non-price competition as a reaction to changes in customer requirements (external socio-economic environment). In order for this change to be implemented, technology had to play a key role. Innovations in this field facilitated and encouraged this change (external technological environment).

Having the technology in place and utilizing it appropriately are two different things. Tesco have the former but the latter will only be possible when the structure and processes evolve and become balanced. Cultural aspects are the hardest to change as the structure will have to become de-centralized to complement local marketing; the processes will need to be geared towards major distribution centres as a result of an increased number of internet shoppers; and job descriptions will have to be revised due to the use of the new self scanning technology (Hunt, 1997).

It is here that we see Tesco faltering. Whilst their corporate strategy has evolved over time, encompassing and exploiting technological advances, they have failed to be self critical and adapt their internal structure to suit their external environment. As a result they are not utilizing their rather costly IT to bring potential business benefits to fruition, thus prohibiting them from maintaining their role as market leader in the long run.

Bibliography

Bagnall, S. (1996). Supermarket customers check out delights of shop and go. *The Times,* 19 April.

Clarke, R. (1996). Customer loyalty today. *The Times,* May.

Cope, N. (1997. Sainsbury's on line to increase cyber shopping. *The Independent,* 7 February.

Financial Times, November 1996

Foster, P. (1995). *Marketing Week* February.

Goodwin, C. (1996). Shopping on screen: virtually upon us? *Accounting,* December.

Grayson, I. (1997). Checkout the facts. *The Independent,* 18 March.

Hawkes, P. (1995). *Marketing,* July.

Hunt, J. (1997). The big squeeze. *The Grocer,* June.

McFarlan, F. (1984). Information Technology changes the way you compete. *Harvard Business Review,* May–June.

Marketing Week, January 1997.

Marketing, November 1995.

Ody, P. (1997). Tesco test DIY scanner technology. *The Daily Telegraph,* 28 January.

Ogbonna, E. and Wilkinson, B. (1988). Corporate Strategy and Corporate Culture: The Management of Change in the UK Supermarket Industry. *Personal Review* **17**(6), pp. 10–14.

Oram, R. (1996). Safeway shoppers to tally own bills. *The Financial Times,* 27 April.

Partingdon, R. (1995). *The Times,* August.

Porter, M. (1985). *Competitive Advantage.* Free Press

Price, C. (1997). Survey – UK retailing: loyalty cards. *The Financial Times,* 13 March.

Scott Morton, M. S. (1991). *The Corporation of the 1990s – Information Technology and Organisational Transformation.* Oxford University Press.

Strachan, J. (1997). Multiples target the home front. *Marketing Week,* February.

Taylor, P. (1997a). Survey – UK retailing. *The Financial Times,* 13 March.

Taylor, P. (1997b). Self service rings change at supermarkets. *The Financial Times,* 12 May.

Treneman, A. (1997). Supermarkets 2007. *The Independent,* 28 February.

Wolf, P. (1997). Have supermarkets gone bananas. *The Birmingham Post,* 16 January.

5 Department of Health

Julie French
School of Management, University of Bath

This chapter examines the role of IT within the Department of Health. The research is based on personal experience, observations from within the organization and interviews. The work allowed conclusions to be drawn about the business aspect of a new office information system.

The OIS system

In pursuit of a system which would improve the flow of information within the Department of Health (DH) and the National Health Service (NHS) an initiative was designed and implemented at the start of the 1990s, known as the OIS (office information system). A key objective of the system was to support the relocation of 1000 staff from London to Leeds, in particular to provide effective communications between senior staff in Leeds and Ministers. This objective was met (ISD, 1991). It introduced comprehensive, straightforward office automation services to approximately 4000 users across the Department. It proved to be a successful system, achieving excellent tangible and intangible benefits such as increased efficiency due to time-savings, cost-savings and improvements in communications. A degree of common standards for e-mail, document exchange and file sharing which is unusual in UK public sector systems has also been achieved. No one definition fully explains the role of office automation but it can generally be defined as the use of technology to help achieve the goals of the office. OIS performs different functions depending upon the nature of the office and the organization.

The impact of the OIS

The step to a full standardized office information system is quite a dramatic one, especially as the DH and, indeed, other Government departments are

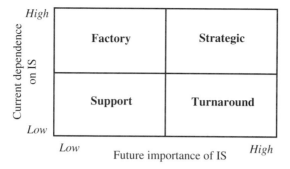

Figure 5.1 *McFarlan's strategic grid*

becoming increasingly under pressure to provide fast and efficient information across the nation. One theorist, McFarlan (1984), has designed a 'strategic grid' which assesses the importance of IT in organizations. This is shown in Figure 5.1.

The axes on the grid indicate the organizations current dependence on information systems, and the estimated future importance of information systems. It is fair to say that when the decision was made to introduce OIS to the DH, the organization had low dependence on any information system. However, it was predicted that IT would become greatly important in the future and so the investment was made. Therefore, from this analysis the DH can now be defined as being in the 'turnaround' phase of the strategic grid, and is currently going through an important revolutionary business transformation.

There are clear technology pushes which have led to the Department reengineering its business, using modern information technology to radically redesign its business processes in order to achieve a dramatic improvement in performance. The price of IT over recent years has fallen quite considerably leading to the uptake of information systems in the work place. The introduction of OIS by the DH has resulted in huge cost savings in comparison to costs which would have been incurred had they kept responding ad hoc to business pressures (see Appendix A for cost breakdown). Also, connectivity capabilities allowed the process to go ahead, with improved communications between the DH, the NHS and the eight regional offices (DBI, 1996).

To enable managers to understand the new opportunities and threats presented by information technology in the 1990s the Massachusetts Institute of Technology designed an applicable framework. This is known as the MIT90s framework, and outlines the role of five variables which influence the impact of IT on an organization. Figure 5.2 illustrates this concept (Scott Morton, 1991).

The five variables – strategy; structure; technology; individuals and roles; and management process – must be in balance if an organization is to be successful. Relating this framework to the DH we can first speak of its overall

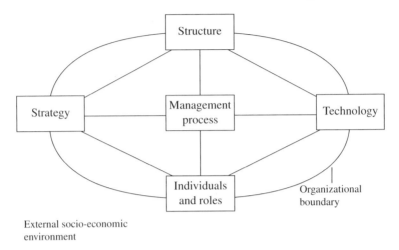

Figure 5.2 *The MIT90s framework*

strategy, which had to change as a knock-on effect of changing technology. The strategy is fundamentally to provide quality information to aid the needs required for a healthy nation. In recent years, as technology has been modified, the DH has been able to develop the strategy further to include providing information speedily and efficiently. As the strategy changes, so must the other variables. IT can be viewed as a new engine for an organization, such a powerful tool that it should be deployed by those with enough vision to see what consequence it can realistically have on the organization. Thus, the management processes have been affected by IT. The employees and their roles within the DH have had to change and adopt new work practices in a new cultural setting.

Without some flexibility in these variables, the implication of the MIT90s framework is that IT would have a negative impact. One example which was experienced by the DH was individuals' resistance to change in response to the implementation of OIS. Resistance to change may occur for a number of reasons including uncertainty in relation to the future (if they will still have a job), the need to learn new skills, and perhaps the loss of power due to the removal of discretion in the performance of tasks. At the DH, management tried to minimize resistance to change by forming working groups and holding regular meetings and presentations to inform employees of the current situation. Employees are encouraged to air their views and management feel certain that this involvement has reduced barriers to change. Changes in actual working practice have also had to run alongside the implementation of OIS.

The research has found that users who had resisted change initially came to be happy with the benefits that the system had brought. This finding is reflected in the post-implementation survey which the Statistics Division carried out which showed that 99 per cent of users did not wish to change back (DBI, 1996).

If the individuals' roles had remained as they were prior to OIS whilst other aspects of the organization had changed, the forces would have been in disequilibrium. It can be said that the implementation of OIS resulted eventually in the five forces acting in harmony, signifying the positive implications of the system and thus indicating success. But more importantly here perhaps is the idea that the introduction of IT in an organization requires changes in working practices, and is not a simple, straightforward process. Thus, the flexibility of the organization will shape the strength of the information system.

Before examining the success of OIS, it is important to outline the modifications of the system since its first implementation. Only then can the overall success of such a system be assessed, and its business impact analysed.

In 1994 two projects were launched – to enhance OIS with new desktop products and to extend the OIS network and services to the eight new regional offices. The first objective of the OIS II desktop project was to achieve a 1 per cent improvement worth £1.34 million per annum by 1997/98 in individual and group productivity, from increased ease of communication and speed and effectiveness of information searching. The second objective was to deliver direct financial benefits of £28,000 per annum from savings in information systems department (ISD) support, through the rationalization of products and improved management tools, and on non-manpower budgets such as postage and distribution.

Evaluation of performance

To evaluate the performance of OIS the SWOT method of analysis can be helpful; that is, the examination of the system's strengths, weaknesses, opportunities and threats.

Strengths

In the years prior to OIS implementation, the Department had introduced IT piecemeal in response to business pressures, with no corporate infrastructure. This approach addressed all the Department's business needs, particularly the need for efficient communications underpinning the announced relocation of the NHS Management Executive to Leeds. However, in particular, it did not address the need for standardization which is very important in the business of IT as it allows cost savings if everybody coordinates effectively. Standards provide a framework for how data is transmitted and they must be constantly updated in response to communication systems development.

The DH has introduced a number of standards alongside the implementation of OIS. The fundamental standards for OIS and the applications that run on it relate to the user workstation, the operating system, the network operating system, the user software, and the applications support software. Problems with conversion of documents have been minimized since the introduction of standards. The mere existence of standards is one strength associated with OIS. Management seemed to be in the same school of thought as Hammer (1990) in respect of the relocation issues, treating these geographically dispersed resources as if centralized.

The cost-efficient nature of OIS in comparison to the business pressures approach can be categorized under the strengths of the system. The introduction of OIS has resulted in huge cost savings in comparison to costs which would have been incurred had they kept responding ad hoc to business pressures (see Appendix A for cost breakdown). These cost savings have amounted to approximately £11.4 million over a seven year period which has enabled investments into modifying the system (OIS II & OIS III).

OIS has achieved a faster and more convenient means of communication, reflected in the success of the decentralization of the Department. Productivity has increased enormously since OIS has achieved improvements through time savings with the new technology. For example, particular gains will be by secretaries and those whose jobs involve text processing.

Smaller innovations with the system have also had a significant impact on business practices even if these may be perceived as relatively unimportant revelations. For example, OIS has provided users with the ability to print longer documents at will and allow the local development of information such as address books and local reference material.

The Office Information System is generally a stable system with few equipment failures and quick resolutions of minor problems by ISD. This is particularly important as users become more and more dependent on word-processing and e-mail facilities to carry out their business. Another important strength is the on-site support from ISD.

Weaknesses

The weaknesses of the system centre around the lack of an integrated suite of products and the facilities that come with such a suite. For example, with an integrated suite of products users would have trouble-free copies of graphs and tables from a spreadsheet to a word processed document. Many users commented that e-mail tends to generate more paper not less. As it is easy to use the temptation is to send more documents than really necessary, and to send them to people who do not need them.

There is a difficulty with the system in linking paper and electronic documents together. Users also experience difficulty in printing graphs.

The system is inadequate for managing large and volatile collections of documents, and there is no electronic equivalent of the archiving file store. Thus, the use of paper files still exists more than ever, as IT fails to replace them electronically.

These weaknesses are being addressed by OIS II, implemented during 1998, which introduces an integrated suite of desktop products and facilities for managing electronic documents.

Opportunities

Opportunities available to OIS focus mainly on its future development. OIS is continuously reviewed as the IT industry becomes more and more advanced and the need for modification becomes apparent. Changes must occur for, in the long-run, if the DH continues to use existing technology the industry will be unable to provide support for the system due to components becoming out dated and difficult to find.

Between now and the year 2000 the next phase of the IT strategy will be introduced within the DH – OIS III. The driving force behind the OIS III strategy is the pressure from the IT industry. The modifications which are being considered for OIS III are the possible change of word-processing software, introducing an integrated suite of programmes and looking at video-conferencing access from desktop PCs.

From March 1997, all Regional Offices were connected to the Department's existing video conferencing service. In the OIS III strategy there are plans to introduce the accessibility of VC from some desktop PCs. The demand exists mostly among the senior officers in the DH, especially since the senior officers' posts were split between London and Leeds during the relocation of the NHS Executive Management. Thus, there is demand for a cost-saving means of communication, rather than having to travel to Leeds from London for meetings every fortnight, for example. It is estimated that the VC facility from desktop PCs will not cost much to implement.

Although there are a number of possibilities which could improve the system, ideas will always exceed resources and so the concept of priority becomes important. The Information Services Directorate have worked hard to computerize existing office practices and now they are in a stage of new ideas which could revolutionalize the way in which the DH functions in the new millennium.

Threats

It is probably fair to say that the threats that may surround the OIS are related to the IT industry itself. The IT-driven nature of the Government is putting pressure on the civil service to modify and develop for the future. The Government is currently keen to launch the Government Secure Intranet soon, with the possibility of introducing an extranet (a closed system available to selected external customers rather than to just one's own employees). Developments such as these do provide valuable opportunities for the civil service as a whole but unfortunately provide risks as well, mainly those involving unauthorized users. The system is undergoing 'live penetration testing' as an IT security group (IT-SEC) tries to hack into real systems in real operational situations to unveil weaknesses in the system.

Conclusion

From the facts and information conveyed throughout this chapter, it is possible to evaluate the business benefits that OIS has brought to the DH, and to summarize how business processes and organizational relationships have transformed.

The principal business benefit that OIS has been responsible for is the improved communications link between the different areas of the Department. This was essential following the relocation of the NHS Management Executive to Leeds from London; speed and efficiency were the key requirements for communication. The system has provided a standard e-mail service, document exchange and file sharing service. Over 4000 users now communicate effectively.

Business processes and organizational relationships have had to be flexible during the implementation of OIS enabling the process to be integrated relatively smoothly. The influence of the IT industry forced the DH to rethink its present technology and then reengineer its business. The strategy and structure of the organization were modified. In terms of the organizational relationships, management incurred initial problems from employees in the sense of resistance to change. This conflict and the resulting anxieties were largely resolved by management who have introduced working groups to inform and involve workers in future OIS developments.

OIS looks set to continue improving work practices and productivity, especially with exciting new developments planned. The impact that services such as video-conferencing will have on business is not certain but the introduction of the Government Secure Intranet should work to the Department's advantage, providing greater scope for information.

To progress into the next century, consideration should be given for a move to an integrated package of software to allow cross communications between the different Government departments. However, it is very difficult to standardize working practices because of the different budgeting systems.

On the negative side there were some initial inhibitors to the OIS implementation, particularly concerning the management of change. Users have been trained in the use of OIS tools and facilities but when, why and how to use them and any resultant changes in working practices has had to be left to user divisions to decide.

It is probably fair to say that as long as there is no remit to manage the impact of change, visions such as the 'paperless office' will remain unattainable dreams. The Department needs to allocate responsibility for issues in which business may change. This is a strategic concern which should be shaping the future plans for technology.

In summary, from the evidence provided, the OIS has been a very important development to the organization. The benefits which IT has brought have transformed the business in a positive and strategic manner. The flexibility and ability of management has allowed the OIS implementation to be successful as contributing factors are kept in balance.

Appendix A Budgets and costs

Two costs are shown. First, there is the business-pressures approach which is an estimate of the costs of responding to individual business pressures, without an OIS strategy. The final column shows the costs of implementing OIS by Summer 1993. Costs are calculated over a seven-year period.

Cost £000	Business pressures	OIS implementation
Staff (implementation management, systems support, etc.)	20,931	12,894
Equipment (hardware, software, maintenance, etc.)	18,766	16,122
Contractors (systems implementor, consultants, etc.)	–	3,205
Training	1,307	1,818
Other (furniture, consumables, Telecom Gold, etc.)	6,358	1,910
TOTAL	47,362	35,949

This table shows that by implementing the OIS strategy it would cost £11.4 million less over the seven year period than continuing to respond, ad hoc, to business pressures. Furthermore, it would enable the Department to:

● respond to business demands for new OA systems;

- establish a corporate OIS infrastructure facilitating future business applications;
- provide the communications needed to support relocation.

Bibliography

DBI Associates Ltd. (1996). *OIS II Desktop and Regional Office Implementation: Post Implementation Review – Final Report*. Internal document.

Hammer, M. (1990). Reengineering work: don't automate, obliterate. *Harvard Business Review*. July–August, 104–112.

ISD (1991). *Business Case – Office Information Systems for the Department of Health*. Internal document.

McFarlan, F. (1984). Information Technology changes the way you compete. *Harvard Business Review,* May–June.

Scott Morton, M. S. (1991). *The Corporation of the 1990s – Information Technology & Organizational Transformation*. Oxford University Press.

Pollard, J. (1997). Just in case. *Link* (the internal DH newspaper), July.

IT sources

OIS Noticeboard – DH programme
Analysts' Bulletin Board – DH package on Lotus Notes
Public Health Bulletin Board – DH package on Lotus Notes

6 Technology opportunities for the music industry

David Cooke
Cranfield School of Management, Cranfield University

This chapter was originally written for publication on the World Wide Web. It was published on the Cranfield Intranet as part of the full time MBA assessment in information systems. In order to comply with the restrictions of printed media some modifications have been made. All words that had a hypertext link are emboldened in the text that follows. References to Scarlet Music indicate a major player in the industry such as Warner Music or EMI but do not relate to any specific company.

Introduction

Much of the conventional wisdom underpinning IS/IT planning is based on the notion that the business strategy informs the IT strategy. The business strategy is generally thought to be the right starting point. Some authors have written about a two-way bridge between the business and IT suggesting that IT provides opportunities for the business as well as the business driving IT. However, it has remained unclear as to how the 'traffic' from IT to the business is to flow.

This chapter argues that developing an information infrastructure is critical for business success and forms the beginnings of understanding this 'traffic flow'. An information infrastructure framework is introduced as a way of thinking about IT infrastructure in a wider context. It is claimed that the information infrastructure necessary goes beyond the conventional concern with the technical elements to include skills, processes and other factors.

The purpose of this chapter is to develop on the analysis of the main influences and trends affecting the UK pop music industry for Scarlet Music.

Environment   Scenarios   Assumption   Technology   Conclusion

Figure 6.1

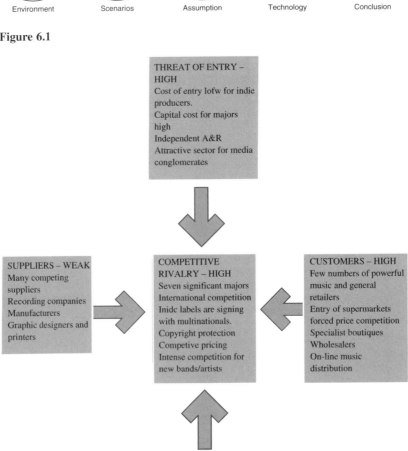

THREAT OF ENTRY –
HIGH
Cost of entry lofw for indie
producers.
Capital cost for majors
high
Independent A&R
Attractive sector for media
conglomerates

SUPPLIERS – WEAK
Many competing
suppliers
Recording companies
Manufacturers
Graphic designers and
printers

COMPETITIVE
RIVALRY – HIGH
Seven significant majors
International competition
Inidc labels are signing
with multinationals.
Copyright protection
Competive pricing
Intense competition for
new bands/artists

CUSTOMERS – HIGH
Few numbers of powerful
music and general
retailers
Entry of supermarkets
forced price competition
Specialist boutiques
Wholesalers
On-line music
distribution

SUBSTITUTES –
INCREASING
All other forms of pop
music i.e.; ratios, MTV, live
acts, festivals
Other consumer durables
i.e. Sony Playstations,
computer, domestic
multimedia

Figure 6.2 *Porter's five forces*

Through the identification of the main drivers to change, analysis of the **environment** and changing consumer tastes and rapid **technological** advancements.

Three **scenarios**, have been developed to provide Scarlet Music directors a view of the future.

The chapter **concludes** on how Scarlet Music should adapt to the changing consumer expectations and new technology in order to retain a position of competitive advantage.

Competitive pressures

Rivalry

Competitive rivalry between the majors is extremely high with each music company vying to find the next Oasis.

Threat of entry

Barriers to entry to the industry for an indie are not high. With new technology it is possible to produce music – especially dance music – from a bedroom and many small labels operate precisely in this way.

Entry into the major league requires considerably more investment, however the threat of new competition here is still high. The collapse of traditional industry boundaries has caused a flurry of alliances, acquisitions and deals between companies trying to exploit potentially lucrative, yet risky business opportunities in the redefined global information industry. Existing media conglomerates such as Spielberg's Dream Factory and Walt Disney are known to be interested in expanding into the music industry.

Suppliers

Most of the suppliers to the music industry, recording studios, graphic designers, CD manufacturers are numerous and small scale, so pose little competitive threat to the majors. Artists and bands, also a source of supply, are a scarcer resource, hence the importance of strong A&R in a successful music business.

Substitutes

Music substitutes for singles and albums are very limited. Music companies should recognise however, that they are competing with other types of entertainment media such as Sony[1] Playstations. Consumers have an increasingly diverse range of options in terms of how they spend their disposable income.

Customers

Music companies have no direct relationship with the consumer. All sales are dealt with through intermediaries, the retailers who have significant power in determining music sales. In 1996, specialist and general multiples (such as WH Smith) handled 74 per cent of single and 83 per cent of album sales.

The most important retailing development in the last couple of years has been the entry of the major supermarket chains. Some critics have argued that their presence may damage the long-term viability of the market by their common practice of aggressive price-cutting. However, supporters have noted that supermarkets have been successful in attracting lapsed buyers back into the habit of buying records, especially women.

Scenarios

The **scenarios** developed for the short-, medium- and long-term have been based on the analysis of the music industry, its environment aligned with **technology** drivers and a series of assumptions outlined below.

Changing consumer tastes are only one concern for music companies. Music companies survive and profit by forming the value chain between musician and retailer. In the next five years, rapid advancements in IT will enable consumers to choose new ways of buying and listening to music, which will dramatically change this relationship.

Short term

- Customer demand exists at a commercially viable level, for the purchase of Scarlet Music records directly from the company using the internet[2], to substantiate the cost of development, support and logistics.
- Existing retailers, do not feel threatened by Scarlet Music direct sales to customers.
- An online A&R, attracts sufficient numbers of talented new artists, to justify the increased administration required to filter an increased volume of unsolicited new bands and artists.
- Alliances can be established with indies that have the talent to discover new bands with the potential to attract overseas sales.

Table 6.1

Short Term (6–18 months)	Medium Term (18 months–3 years)	Long Term (3 years onwards)
• Launch interactive web site, to allow the purchase of catalogue records, through secure e-commerce. With postal delivery of media direct to customer. • Establish on-line A&R (see Taxi) to provide new bands better access to music company. • Establish alliances or agreements to distribute records for Indies.	• Push the emerging technologies of media storage e.g. DVD. Utilise extra storage capacity, to provide enhance fidelity, e.g. surround around sound, videos, interactive media. • Increase sales and distribution over the internet, direct to customers. Provide access to artist interactive interviews, videos of concerts, music on demand. • Provide stores with the facilities to enable the in store creation of CD on demand.	• Supply music, film, concerts on demand direct to houses, through cable modems with high band widths and satellite communications. On pay as you listen basis. • Direct sales to customers, allowing the development of customer preference databases, to improve direct marketing on an individual basis. • Music on demand kiosks, located in shopping centres, stations, stores to enable customers to create CDs.

Environment Scenarios Assumption Technology Conclusion

Short Term Assumptions Medium Term Assumptions Long Term Assumptions

Medium term

- Emerging technologies such as DVD can offer customers sufficient perceived benefits to persuade them to swap from existing media such as CDs to a new media.
- Demand increases for e-commerce over the internet, in preference to traditional retail shopping.
- Customers demand interaction and multi media from music offerings.
- Retailers and customers welcome the increased flexibility of custom CD creation and technology enables the cost effective production of CDs in low batches.

Long term

- Scarlet Music are not out-manoeuvred by direct selling from artists, indies or retailers.
- Increased demand for in-house entertainment, through cable modem, digital TV. Customers are prepared to pay on demand for entertainment, rather than purchase permanent copies.
- People without direct access to the internet or interactive cable facilities, demand more permanent media such as CDs.

Technology

The future of CDs

In 1977, the digital recorder was introduced in Japan – 77 years after the first recording studio opened in New York City. In the following years, artists, producers and the entire music industry were revolutionized by digital recording and distribution. In a survey of five of the experts in the field of digital recording technology, *Wired* asked them to predict the timetable for various types of digital technology. The results were are shown in Table 6.2.

Custom CDs on demand

Although existing compressions schemes degrade the audio quality, increased storage capacity and improved compression techniques mean that CDs on demand are becoming a reality. The greatest use for CD on demand will be for new albums and artists with unpredictable sales potential and for 'difficult-to-find albums, which at present would not be profitable to release'.

Table 6.2

Technology	Timetable
Custom CDs on demand	1998
Digital studio recording	2002
Affordable home CD recorders	1997
Online shopping for CDs	1998
Death of audio CDs	2010

Source:
http://www.wired.com/wired/2.12/departments/reality.check.html

Digital studio recording

Specific sonic qualities and low price of analogue tape – and the large amounts of non-linear digital storage space needed for audio – will keep magnet tape in the recording loop except in the worlds of film and advertising.

Affordable home CD recorders

While these are now on sale for around £300, it is thought that it will face the some controversy as digital audio tape recording, 'the problems with protecting copyrights'. However, the 5-inch CD is set to become popular among home-computer users to create CD-ROMs, and as hardware sales increase, the recorders will drop in price enough to break into the home audio market.

Online shopping for CDs

It is believed that 'alternative music could be revolutionized by emerging technology'. The primary issue is getting the consumer wired with the high bandwidth necessary to download music at reasonable rates.

Death of audio CDs

CD-ROM format is likely to remain for a while, but electronics and record companies could 'push a next generation technology with greater revenue potential'. Whilst in the future 'data densities in memory cards will be higher enough and cheap enough for mass storage'. Today DVD[3] have already entering the market, promising higher capacity (17 GB) giving the flexibility to store full-length feature films and high fidelity sound.

The UK pop music industry is a mature industry with strong competitive pressures in the form of rivals, new entrants and customers. Major music companies have particular strengths in managing and promoting bands, whereas the indies have a strong track record of developing new talent. The industry however, now faces formidable challenges from rising customer expectations and the rapid growth of the internet and cable channels as a

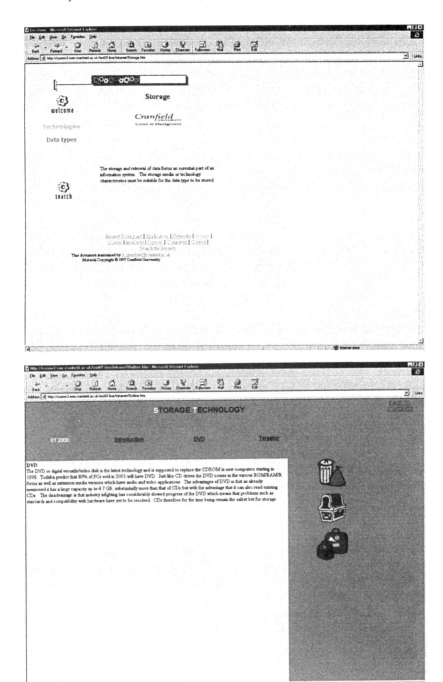

Figure 6.3

replacement for the music companies' and retailers' sales and communication interface.

Scarlet Music's survival as an intermediary between artists and consumers will depend on its ability to adapt to these challenges, to engage in potential new forms of electronic commerce and to build new direct relationships with consumers and infrastructure providers.

Music companies are particularly vulnerable because of the lack of a face-to-face relationship with the end consumer. Relationships in the industry have been driven by managing bands and selling to retailers. Development of a better understanding of customer needs however, could reduce the risk of launching new bands, help improve the length of product life cycles and provide myriad opportunities for cross-marketing of products, thereby significantly reducing overall business risk.

To maintain a competitive advantage, it is recommended that Scarlet Music utilize the opportunities provided by technology to develop closer links between the artist and the consumer, through maximization of the market space and adopting the short- and medium-term scenarios outlined in this chapter.

Particularly:

- Sell direct to customers via the internet.
- Facilitate access between artists and A&Rs.
- Establish alliances with indies.

To avoid these problems, Sony has adopted a flexible approach with each independent, with the only common theme being that Sony has the right to distribute the independent's music outside their domestic markets. This saves the independent from having to assemble ad hoc licensing deals in different countries. Source: *Financial Times*, 6 March 1998

Within seconds after the songs are posted, Netheads from Poughkeepsie, NY, to Pakistan can download songs like Toast by Plasma Boy Scott Brookman's When I Die You Can't Have My Organs' or more … (*Rolling Stone*, September 1994).

Supported by the world's leading multimedia computer developer, Silicon Graphics, IUMA is built on the internet's graphic user interface known as the World Wide Web. With this visual interface, users can browse as they do in a record store: by artist, genre, location, and date uploaded. Throughout the site, users will find music, biographies, lyrics, photos, artwork, and even videos. In addition, fans can contact the artist through e-mail, post public reviews, and order music and other artist products on-line.

'IUMA is a kind of digital club where the bands play for free, there's no cover charge and the owners are just happy to come' (Mondo 2000).

Source: http://www.iuma.com/

References

Bower, J. L. and Christensen, C. (1995). Disruptive technologies: Catching the wave, *Harvard Business Review*, Jan–Feb, 43–53.

Broadbent, M. and Weill, P. (1997). Management by maxim: How business and IT managers can create IT infrastructures, *Sloan Management Review*, Spring, 77–92.

DeLamarter, R. T. (1988). *Big Blue: IBM's Use and Abuse of Power*, Pan Books, London.

Earl, M. J. (1989). *Management Strategies for Information Technology*, Prentice-Hall, London.

Acknowledgement

The authors would like to acknowledge the contributions made by the MBA Learning Team – Blue 7 – during the work on the group assessments leading up to this work. Specific thanks go to Richard Hinchliffe, Dirk Nold, Andre Von Steiger, Isabel Wade and Debra White.

Notes

1 Sony Music distribution deals with independent labels could become a model for other creative industries. In the past when Sony scouts spotted new acts they often found that they were already signed up with an independent record label. Sony's solution was negotiate with the independents, leaving them free to run their own business but giving Sony the rights to sell their music in other countries. Traditionally, relationships between independent labels and multinational music groups have been fraught. Many have sold out to multinationals, only to find that their old owners have had difficulty in adjusting to corporate life. PolyGram closed the GO! Discs label after a row with its founder and was recently embroiled with a disagreement with Island Records.

2 The Internet Underground Music Archive is the first and largest high-fidelity internet music outlet, setting the standard and creating the future of music distribution right now. As of July 1995, IUMA receives in excess of 300,000 accesses per day, and offers the works of over 800 independent musicians to an estimated 30 million internet users. This on-line community includes a global audience of fans, radio station programmers, club promoters and music industry A&R representatives who have already signed bands from IUMA to major labels.

3 The DVD or digital versatile/video disk is the latest technology and is supposed to replace the CD-ROM in new computers starting in 1999. Toshiba predict that 80 per cent of PCs sold in 2001 will have DVD. Just like CD drives the DVD comes in the various ROM/RAM/R forms as well as extension media versions which have audio and video applications. The advantages of DVD is that as already mentioned it has a large capacity of up to 4.7 GB, substantially more than that of CDs but with the advantage that it can also read existing CDs. The disadvantage is that industry infighting has considerably slowed progress of the DVD, which means that problems such as standards and compatibility with hardware have yet to be resolved. CDs therefore, for the time being, remain the safest bet for storage.

Part Two
Information Systems Planning

David J. Grimshaw

The main purpose of IS/IT planning is to formulate a policy within which a business can make informed decisions about IT investment. Information systems' planning has been a major issue in most recent surveys of management issues undertaken worldwide. This part of the book identifies several key themes within the overall topic.

This part contains four chapters. The first two chapters are a case study of a multinational computer vendor and a case study of BP Acetyls. The third chapter is not a case study; rather it analyses the experiences of several UK companies in adopting business process reengineering (BPR) initiatives. The fourth chapter provides an overview of the BPR concept, addresses the role of IT in business process redesign and discusses pertinent management issues. The first chapter is about improving information systems strategy in a large multinational IT organization. The chapter discusses the findings, which emerged from a project conducted within a large business unit. The primary objective of the project was to identify ways of improving the information systems strategy. The project highlights seven major themes, which represent key areas of concern for information systems practitioners.

These practical themes, discussed below, are a useful starting point for this part because they will be picked up in each of the succeeding chapters.

1 The need to agree a common understanding of what an information systems strategy is.
2 The need for a strong relationship between the business and information systems communities.
3 The argument for a strong linkage between business planning and strategic information systems planning.
4 The difficulty of identifying IT ideas which supply competitive advantage.

5 The need for a balanced systems portfolio.
6 The difficulty of implementation.
7 The difficulty of applying a single information systems strategy framework.

The second chapter outlines a strategy proposal for the European division of BP Acetyls. This proposal is based on a thorough understanding of the business requirements, gained by an analysis of the value chain and process modelling. The scope of the analysis is confined to the supply chain of the existing business and developing relationships with customers. Recommendations address issues of people, accountability, benefits management, prioritization and cost.

The third chapter in this part reviews three UK organizations that have undertaken business process reengineering. The motives, manoeuvres and outcomes are examined in a manufacturer, a building society and an insurance company. The authors state that IT and BPR have a recursive relationship and emphasize the importance of ensuring a close alignment of IT with the business strategy.

The final chapter looks at theoretical foundations, examples and critical assessments. Examples from different business sectors show how IT has been used to redesign customer-driven processes. Product and service quality has been improved and, in some cases, innovation capabilities have been increased.

7 Improving the development of IS strategies in a large multinational

Greg Holba and David Targett
School of Management, University of Bath

Traditionally, companies have struggled with IS/IT (information systems/information technology) strategy development. Often they have assumed that it is heavily reliant on technical knowledge and therefore the domain of the IT professional – the IT 'anorak' as they might say. Recent literature, however, has pointed to the need for the whole organization to actively participate in, and own, IS/IT strategy development and implementation (see, for example, Scott Morton, 1991).

In this context, research was conducted within a large business unit of a multinational corporation with the objective of identifying ways to improve the IS strategy process. It involved thirty managers representing a balance of IS, IT and business managers. The findings revealed a number of learning points for IS strategy practitioners. By presenting these learning points and useful models and frameworks from the literature, the authors aims to provide food for thought and assist practitioners in increasing the likelihood of successful outcomes.

Research approach

The research was conducted in two main phases. The first phase entailed interviewing an equal balance of IS managers, IT managers and business managers. (IS managers were responsible for the development and maintenance of information systems; while IT managers were responsible for the IT infrastructure, namely hardware, networks, corporate software and tools.)

The interviews were semi-structured, with open questions, and were designed to obtain information about the managers knowledge and current practice of IS strategy work, along with their thoughts about areas for improvement.

The second phase involved running workshops with a random cross section of the managers interviewed. The purpose of the workshop was to:

- verify the interview results through feedback presentations;
- familiarize managers with published models which deal with IS strategy practice;
- explore possibilities for practitioner improvement.

Organizational background

The business unit investigated serviced a worldwide marketplace and comprized numerous divisions. The organization to which the business unit belonged, had a strong corporate culture based around the organization's values of diversity, autonomy and team-based work. Flexible ways of working were encouraged and project work predominated. The organization's area of business is a broad range of computer products and services.

The organization's business planning was very advanced, providing for long- and short-term planning. The business unit's long-term planning was conducted in a 3–5 year cycle and was strongly based on market and competitor analysis. The short-term planning was conducted yearly and was based around business objectives which are derived and implemented at many levels in the organization's hierarchy.

A number of internal IS/IT groups served the business unit. The IS services were decentralized and reported directly into the business. The IT services were centralized at the corporate level for decision making purposes, and programmes were rolled out by regionally-based teams.

Useful strategic IS models

During the workshops a number of strategic IS models were used. The most fruitful models are now summarized before the learning points are discussed. It is hoped that IS strategy practitioners will find them useful frameworks for diagnosis and intervention.

Earl's notion of three levels of IT strategy (Earl, 1989)

Many managers find the notion of IS/IT strategy is confusing. Earl (1989) argues that this confusion is due to a number of factors and suggests that a

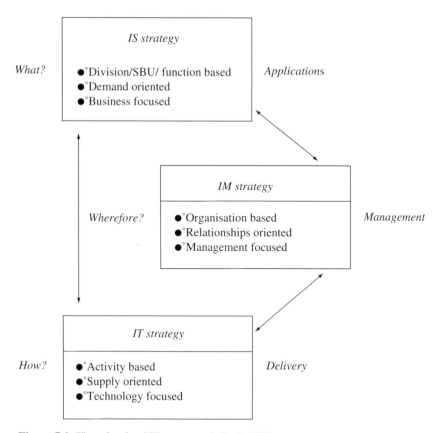

Figure 7.1 *Three levels of IT strategy (© Earl, 1989)*

clearer distinction should be made between information systems (IS) strategies, information technology (IT) strategies and information management
(IM) strategies. Such a distinction is summarized and explained in Figure 7.1.

In this schema Earl explains that an IS strategy is concerned with the
issue of *what* should be done with technology. For this reason it is primarily
concerned with aligning IS with business needs. An IT strategy is concerned with the issue of *how* technology can be used to deliver requirements.
It is primarily concerned with technology policies (e.g. architecture, risk attitudes, vendor policies and technical standards). An IM strategy's main focus
is the IS/IT organization and management, and therefore comprises 'policies,
procedures, aims and actions' required – *wherefore* is Earl's less happy
terminology.

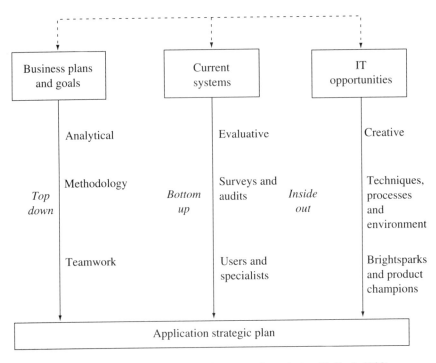

Figure 7.2 *A multiple methodology for IS strategy formulation (© Earl, 1989)*

Earl's multiple methodology (Earl, 1989)

Another useful model provided by Earl (1989) suggests that the development of IS strategies can take place in one of three fundamentally different ways. These are shown in Figure 7.2. The 'top-down' approach typically translates business objectives into IS requirements, and can be viewed as requirements from a vision of the future. The 'bottom-up' approach typically looks for opportunities from the current position, and can be viewed as requirements to improve. The 'inside-out' approach typically looks to innovative ideas to generate IS requirements, and can be viewed as requirements from innovation. Earl argues that all three approaches have a valid role to play in generating strategic IS.

The application portfolio grid (Peppard, 1993, Ward and Griffiths, 1997)

Peppard (1993), and Ward and Griffiths (1997) advocate the use of an applications portfolio grid as a high level strategic tool for mapping information

STRATEGIC	HIGH POTENTIAL
● Applications which *are critical to* sustaining future business strategy	● Applications which *may be important* in achieving future success
● Applications on which the organization *currently depends* for success	● Applications which *are valuable but not critical to* success
KEY OPERATIONAL	SUPPORT

Figure 7.3 *Application portfolio grid (© Ward and Griffiths, 1997)*

systems and providing a management approach for each quadrant. The grid is shown in Figure 7.3.

Peppard's description of how applications, categorized according to the four quadrants, should be managed, is as follows (Peppard, 1993, p. 69):

- *Strategic* Given that the objective of these systems is to lever IS/IT to deliver and sustain business advantage, strategic applications require the commitment and involvement of senior management. Very often these systems require large investments and thus central coordination of requirements is paramount. Investments will often be evaluated based on business benefit rather than return-on-investment criteria.
- *High potential* Applications in this quadrant need an environment that accepts risks. It involves expenditure on research and development that may not produce results. The theme therefore is experimentation. Given that applications are high risk, the underlying assumption is that today's high potential applications may create competitive advantage in the future. Senior management need not be too involved, however, they must endorse the concept and commit funds and resources.
- *Key operational* Investments in key operational applications are primarily to avoid business disadvantage. Risk reduction is the cornerstone of any management strategy to manage applications in this quadrant. It is important that systems in this quadrant be reliable and robust, thus only proven technology should be used. All user requests must be capable of being satisfied which requires excess capacity to be available to respond to urgent needs.

- *Support* Given the support nature of applications in this quadrant, direct senior management involvement is not usually necessary. However, policy guidelines will normally be set requiring tight budgetary control. The justification for investment in this quadrant is financial, perhaps using cost-benefit analysis or discounted cashflow.

Venkatraman's IT-induced reconfiguration model (Venkatraman, 1991)

IS/IT is increasingly seen as an enabler of business change, where the real benefits of strategic IS come from its role as a mediator for organizational change, business process reengineering, business network redesign and spawning new enterprises. The most notable contribution to such thinking has come from Venkatraman (1991), who describes five levels of IT-induced business reconfiguration. He argues that the first three levels are mainly to do with internal efficiency and effectiveness benefits, and levels four and five are about changes which are visible from outside the organization. These five levels are illustrated and described in Figure 7.4.

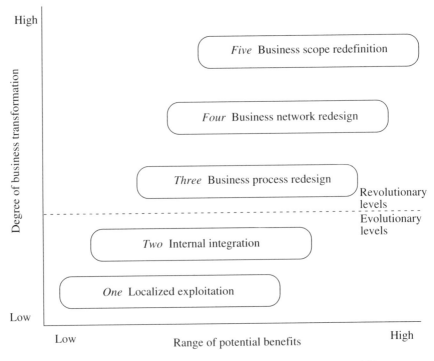

Figure 7.4 *Five levels of IT-induced reconfiguration (© Venkatraman, 1991)*

- Level 1 – Localized exploitation only effects isolated pockets of the business.
- Level 2 – Internal integration is about linking the isolated pockets together or introducing corporate infrastructure systems.
- Level 3 – Business process engineering redesigns business processes within the company to make them more effective in achieving what is required of the business.
- Level 4 – Business network redesign achieves the same as Level 3 but also links in elements of the business value chains of other companies.
- Level 5 – Business scope redefinition alters the range or type of business undertaken.

Venkatraman also describes Levels 1–2 as 'evolutionary' in nature being achieved through incremental activities; whereas Levels 3–5 are more 'revolutionary' and radically alter the organization's business practices.

The index matrix

Hunt and Targett (1995) point out that benefits derived from information systems can be classified according to a matrix developed by the Index Group and this is shown in Figure 7.5.

The index matrix describes the development of IS applications as falling into three eras. The first era represents the time where IT was first applied to functional areas bringing efficiency and later effectiveness to business functions, for example accountancy, sales ordering. The second era represents the next stage when IT impacted the individual. This era saw the arrival of personal computers. The third era represents the latest move of IT in playing a key role in transforming activities and extends its arm to include the whole organization.

Earl's empirical SISP survey (Earl, 1990)

Earl (1990) has also carried out a survey into SISP (strategic information system planning) approaches employed in UK organizations. From this work he has developed a typology which suggest that organizations employ one of a number of types of approaches (Figure 7.6). He favours the 'organizational approach' as it exhibits an emphasis on the process of SISP within a context of team-based working and learning.

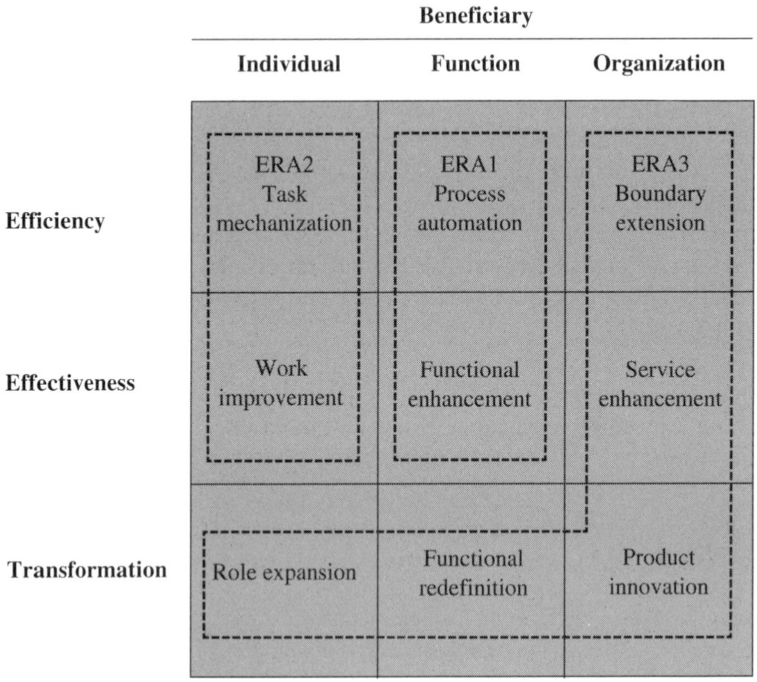

Beneficiary

	Individual	Function	Organization
Efficiency	ERA2 Task mechanization	ERA1 Process automation	ERA3 Boundary extension
Effectiveness	Work improvement	Functional enhancement	Service enhancement
Transformation	Role expansion	Functional redefinition	Product innovation

Figure 7.5   *The index matrix (adopted from Hunt and Targett, 1995)*

	Business led	Method driven	Administrative	Technology	Organizational
Emphasis	The business	Technique	Resources	Model	Learning
Ends	Plan	Strategy	Portfolio	Architecture	Themes
Relation to business strategy	Fix points	Derive	Criteria	Objectives	Look at business
IS role	Driver	Initiator	Bureaucrat	Architect	Team member
Metaphor	It's common sense	It's good for you	Survival of the fittest	We nearly aborted it	Partnership
Method strength	Low	High	Low	High	Medium
Process strength	Low	Low	Medium	Low	High
Implementation	Medium	Low	High	Medium	High

Figure 7.6   *Earl's classification of SISP approaches (adopted from © Earl 1990)*

Practitioner learning points

An analysis of the interview transcripts revealed over 450 unique discussion threads. There appeared to be very little variance of opinion between the different stakeholder groups (namely IS managers, IT managers and business managers). Where variance was found this is highlighted.

These discussion threads, along with the information gathered from the workshops, have highlighted a number of major learning points for practitioners of IS strategy work. These are presented below in the light of literature on (i) IS/IT strategy formulation and implementation literature and (ii) SISP (Strategic Information Systems Planning).

Learning point 1: Business planning provides the context for strategic IS work

The managers interviewed strongly voiced the need for IS strategy work to be 'linked to', 'aligned with' or 'integrated with' the business strategy. The most popular understanding was to see IS/IT strategy being linked back to a business plan or business strategy. Representative quotes included:

> What I would like to see is a clear linkage between an IS/IT strategy and business planning. (Business manager)

> I think the thing that needs to be done with an IT strategy is the alignment of IT investment and direction with the business. (IS manager)

> To my mind it should be done along with the business strategy formulation. But I guess it could be a second step. But it must be closely linked. (IS manager)

In a similar fashion to the managers interviewed, numerous authors have agreed that IS strategies should be linked to an organization's business plan (Camillus and Lederer, 1985; Earl, 1989; Goldsmith, 1991; Scott Morton, 1991; Dutta, 1996). To use Galliers' (1991) words:

> It is almost a truism to suggest that SISP should be closely linked to business planning.' (Galliers, 1991)

This disquiet is recognized in empirical literature which reveals that the linkage of IS plans with organizational objectives have been among the top problems reported by IS managers and business executives (Galliers, 1987, Lederer and Mendelow, 1986).

Building on Earl's view of IS strategy and IT strategy interrelations, Ward and Griffiths (1997) illustrate the relationship between business, IS and IT strategies in the manner shown in Figure 7.7. They conclude:

We should treat IS/IT like any other normal part of the business ... like marketing, production or purchasing. ... This implies an approach to developing strategies for information systems and technology that are derived from and integrated with the other components of the business strategy. (Ward and Griffiths, 1997)

Unfortunately, the managers interviewed described numerous occasions where previous SISP had not been linked back to a business strategy. This feature of past attempts is not uncommon in other organizations (Galliers, 1991).

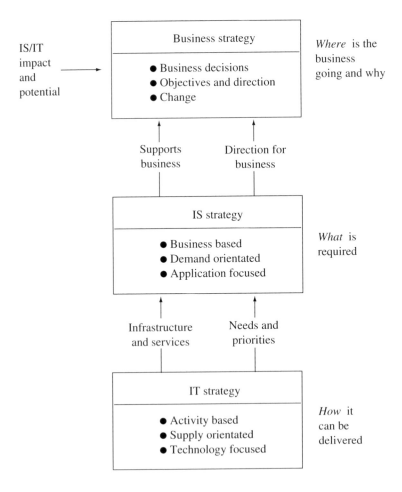

Figure 7.7 *The relationship between business, IS and IT strategies (© Ward and Griffiths 1997)*

Earl's empirical SISP survey (1990) proved very useful in identifying the reasons for the organization's past failures. In some cases, the previous SISP process had been 'technology driven' with, to quote an interviewed manager 'pie-in-the-sky thinking', undertaken by IS/IT professionals without active participation from the business community. In other cases the process had been 'method driven' by external consultants, who conducted one-off formulations based on their own prescriptive methodologies. Earl (1990) argues that such SISP approaches do not involve the business community enough. They may consult with business managers for the purpose of information gathering and opportunity identification, but they do not represent a truly collaborative effort. From the details described by Earl, one would expect that such approaches result in outputs that Piercy describes are 'seen as an unavoidable burden imposed on managers, which is merely an irrelevant distraction from the real job of running the business' (Piercy, 1991). Unfortunately, this is exactly what had happened to past strategies described by the managers – they had been consigned to the business unit shelf!

Having argued that SISP should be carried out after business planning, there is growing body of recent literature which suggests that innovative business strategies are increasingly coming from innovative strategic IS/IT work. In such cases technologically based ideas can lead the way (e.g. Silk, 1995, Scott Morton, 1991). Unfortunately, the managers interviewed did not appear to be aware of this notion and expressed the view that IS work should be used only to support the business. With this stance it becomes hard for IS/IT strategy workers to be involved in, or feed into, processes that could generate innovative technology-led business strategies.

To reconcile the need for IS/IT led business planning with the need for SISP to follow business planning, the authors suggest that SISP practitioners become involved in the business planning. Acting as equal participants makes it possible for innovative IS/IT ideas to enter the early stages of strategic work and later drive out technologically led business strategies. Such proactive interventions over business improvements from IS/IT managers will remove what Synott (1987) calls 'hurdles to the use of IS/IT as a potential competitive weapon'.

Learning point 2: Sustainable competitive advantage is unlikely to be obtained from IS strategy work which focuses on efficiency and effectiveness gain

When discussing issues of IS/IT strategy work, some managers suggested that such work could provide the organization with a means of identifying competitive advantage. The predominant view of managers interviewed was that seeking competitive advantage could be found in securing efficiency and effectiveness gains. Typical quotes included:

> It has a particular goal of finding ways of creating a competitive advantage. Efficiency and effectiveness is key to this. (IT manager)

> That is what we don't see happening in [the organization], a clear vision of how we can use IT to position ourselves at the head of the pack, particularly with improved effectiveness and efficiency. (Business manager)

This view agrees with the management, strategy and technology literature of the 1960s and 1970s, which argued that IS/IT could support the business through increased efficiency and improved effectiveness (Robson, 1997, p. 183). By considering the index matrix presented by Hunt and Targett (1995) it is possible to identify efficiency and effectiveness as benefits from the first and second eras of IS development. However, there is more to strategic IS work than improving efficiency and effectiveness.

In the early 1980s articles began to appear which described successful cases in which the use of IS brought companies competitive advantage by changing the basis of competition against rivals (e.g. Parsons, 1983). This was a departure from the 'conventional' use of systems at the time, namely to improve productivity and performance (Earl, 1989, p. 39). Typically, advantages were identified where SIS provided an organization with generic business strategies, such as cost leadership, or differentiation. However, other benefits were also heralded, such as the ability to change industry structures (e.g. Hopper, 1990). The age of searching for competitive advantage through SIS was born!

More recent literature suggests that organizations have to move beyond efficiency and effectiveness to consider the development of applications designed to affect the organization as a whole and/or to generate transformational benefits. This latter category should include possibilities of business network redesign and business scope redefinition. The authors direct readers to Venkatraman (1991) if they wish to explore such benefits further.

Some writers recognize that situations do exist where a first mover cannot be copied, and a sustainable competitive advantage can be obtained through strategic IS work. Such scenarios rely on a gap of capability between the first mover and its competitors (Coyne, 1986), the ability to create long-lived barriers to entry (Porter, 1980), or a continued updating of a competitive system to maintain the competitive edge (King, Grover and Hufnagel 1989). However, some authors have attempted to dispel the euphoria by describing the transitory nature of any competitive advantage achieved. By the mid-1980s articles began to recognize that successful strategic IS automatically become a necessity for every player in the industry sector. As Ciborra and Jelassi (1994) put it '...whereby strategic applications represent a sheer competitive necessity'. Therefore, any advantage can only be maintained as long as competitors do not possess similar systems and as Ciborra and Jelassi (1994) point out 'it is dangerous to believe that an information system can provide an enduring business advantage.' For this reason, Feeny and Ives (1989) suggested that to obtain a long-term advantage from investments, companies should carefully analyse the lead time of competitors in developing similar applications before embarking on SIS work. In a similar fashion, Silk suggests that:

> there is an important lesson here about the strategic benefit gained from technology (especially IT): if it works, it will be imitated, and if it is imitated, you have to be ready with the next enhancement of the system and the service to give the customer.' (Silk, 1995)

The search for strategic competitive advantage through IS continues today. However, the new emphasis from the literature is on the construction of sustainable competitive advantage obtained by building up intangible assets such as strong IS/IT staff, reductions in the gaps between IS/IT and internal business communities, and organizing for effective IS/IT work (e.g. Ross, Bearth and Goodhue, 1996; Mata, Fuerst and Barney, 1995). As a result, this has opened up new areas of research into the softer areas of IS/IT, such as the influences of socio-political, psychological and cultural aspects of IS planning, and implementation (e.g. Reponen, Parnisto and Viitanen, 1996).

In summary, while the debate rages about how sustainable competitive advantage can be achieved using strategic IS, one issue appears to have emerged as fact. Companies undertaking strategic IS work need to look beyond just efficiency and/or effectiveness to get ahead of the competition.

Learning point 3: Managers benefit from sharing a common language for IS/IT strategy work

The interviews revealed a lack of agreement about what an IS/IT strategy is and what outputs should be expected from the process of strategy formulation. To some degree such a lack of understanding is not surprising as the IT field is rapidly changing, bringing with it new ideas and ways of thinking. Mirroring this, the literature does not provide a common definition of IS strategy work, reflecting the changing concerns of practitioners and academics. For example, Earl (1990) suggests that in the late 1970s much IS strategy was concerned with how to manage IT, and then this notion was later relegated in favour of concepts such as competitive advantage, infrastructure and business transformation.

Approximately twenty-five different phrases were used by the managers to explain what they thought an IS/IT strategy should address. The most common phrases were broad definitions and included:

'Processes', 'Data', 'Environment', 'Applications', 'Infrastructure', 'Tools' and 'Hardware'

As a result, the managers had difficulty establishing a common language for dialogue and they recognized that this inhibited progress. For example, the IT infrastructure professionals expressed difficulty in obtaining cooperation from IS and business manager counterparts when defining infrastructure principles, as the language of technology acted as a barrier to communication.

At the heart of this issue lies the distinction between IT and IS. Therefore, in order to assist the managers in finding a common language, Earl's three levels of IT strategy model (1989) was discussed in the workshops. From the comments received it appeared that all participants understood and agreed the delineation between IS (demand for systems) and IT (supply of technology), and the sort of strategic work that each would undertake. Following the workshops a number of the managers commented that it helped them understand the differences in responsibilities of different IS/IT groups in their organization.

Readers should note that the apparent ease with which this model was understood, may be due to the fact that the organization's IS and IT services were already organized on the basis of supply and demand. For this reason, other organizations may find other models more appropriate in securing a common language for dialogue. However, such a language is needed.

Learning point 4: IS strategy work benefits from a collaborative approach

The managers interviewed expressed a desire for strategy IS work to exhibit wide participation. This notion is in line with the literature relating to change management and the need for commitment from all relevant stakeholders (Beer, Eistenstat and Spector, 1990; Scott Morton, 1991). It was also congruent with the statement of the organization's published values and the observed culture of the business unit.

The use of a collaborative approach is increasingly seen in recent literature. Writers such as Scott Morton (1991) describe the need for strategic IS work to be owned by the business as a whole. Without the senior executives understanding and driving, or at a minimum buying into the work, it is unlikely that it will succeed due to priorities being misaligned across the whole organization. Similarly, Earl (1990) identifies that the most successful SISP approaches adopted in UK companies are heavily reliant on cross-functional team-based activities – the 'organizational approach'. Here, methods are employed in which the purpose and process of strategy implementation is emphasized in a collaborative ethos.

In practical terms, the need to adopt a collaborative approach during SISP entails encouraging joint working throughout the IS strategy formulation and implementation. In large worldwide strategy developments, a joint diagnosis requires significantly longer time due to a larger number of stakeholders. To reduce long time-scales, it is vital that strong relationships exist between the business and IS/IT communities. One of the best ways of strengthening such relationships is to equip IS/IT managers with skills which assist them in their dealing with other managers. Therefore, organizations should consider IS/IT manager development programmes which increase managers' understanding of the business and develop their ability to grow cross-functional and third-party relationships.

Learning point 5: Using a single IS strategy framework is not always appropriate

In order for a company to identify, develop and implement IS which provide competitive advantage, or fulfil a competitive necessity, it is generally agreed it must construct appropriate IS/IT strategies (Currie, 1995, p. 51; Earl, 1989, p. 62; Peppard, 1993, p.76; Ward and Griffiths, 1997, p. 242). In addition, IS/IT strategic work is recognized as a means of rationalizing technological investment and ensuring identification and exploitation of appropriate new technology (Peppard, 1993, p. 79; Mills, 1989, p. 9).

For these reasons, the authors' initial intention was to recommend a single IS strategy framework for the organization to use. Unfortunately, the attempt to select a single SISP framework encountered practical difficulties. First, the number and variety of plausible SISP frameworks is very large. This meant that the search became a non-trivial activity.

Second, selection entails ensuring a good fit with the organization, the way it does things and any specific initiatives it is currently undertaking. By analysing the interviews, it was observed that the business unit exhibited a number of factors which mitigated against the successful adoption of a specific framework

- It exhibited a strong culture based on the published organizational values, where an emphasis on diversity, autonomous activity and team-based work dominate.
- It was undergoing a major business process reengineering programme.
- It exhibited a very complex and changing organizational structure. (It had recently reorganized and was still 'bedding-down'.)

● It had an established business planning environment which overlapped (in tasks) with a number of the SISP approaches.

To make matters worse, numerous authors suggest that, in general, the use of strategy frameworks is incongruent with real-world planning:

> It does not adequately or validly represent the human or organizational realities that we and others have experienced in the practice of planning. (Piercy, 1991)

> What Argyris found was a radical cleavage between the benefits people professed ('espoused theories') and the beliefs people actually acted out in the moment of truth ('theories-in-use'). (Caulkin, 1997)

> ...because of their time pressures, managers tend to favour action over reflection and the oral over the written. (Mintzberg, 1994)

Similarly, formal-rational frameworks have been criticized as too prescriptive and intellectually restrictive, leading to inhibited creativeness and a lack of innovation in strategists:

> Strategy making needs to function beyond the boxes, to encourage the informal learning that produces new perspectives and new combinations. (Mintzberg, 1994)

> Frames can become cages. (Doyle, 1991)

Also, Doyle (1991) argues that the greatest benefit of employing a framework is obtained by the 'first mover'. Therefore, subsequent users do not generate new innovation through a used framework. They merely copy the innovation originally secured by the first user.

The practitioner difficulties encountered and the anti-framework arguments suggested that the selection and utilization of a single SISP framework would be inappropriate for the situation encountered in the organization under study. Nevertheless, disregarding the notion of selecting a specific framework should not result in disregarding the tools and techniques attributed to them. SISP frameworks provide a rich resource of tools and techniques which find profitable use in IS strategy work. For example, by considering value chain analysis it is possible to improve channel management in the business unit. By considering critical success factor analysis it is possible to generate IS requirements aligned with business needs.

For this reason, it was recommended that a more flexible approach be adopted by the organization in its use of SISP frameworks. It was suggested that the organization select a wide range of SISP tools and techniques and trained its managers in their use. In this manner the managers could choose which tools to use on the basis of:

- the situation encountered;
- the individual manager's preferences and abilities.

Such an approach would be particularly suited to a flexible organization in a rapidly changing marketplace, as it avoids a prescriptive use and allows for innovation. Robson (1997) provides a comprehensive itemization and explanation of various tools available.

Learning point 6: Systems portfolio management can increase the contribution IS can make to the business

The interviews revealed that no consensus existed among the IS managers regarding the management of new and existing systems, and no regular coordinated approach to system planning was taking place. As a result, the IS service's ability to make reasoned contributions to the business was hampered. In addition, with no common view, it is reasonable to suggest that system identification, development and implementation may be sub-optimal, with individual managers concentrating on their own priorities in an uncoordinated manner.

When presented with the applications portfolio grid (refer back to Figure 7.3) (Peppard, 1993; Ward and Griffiths 1997), the managers recognized that it would provide them with a coherent framework for capturing and deciding on system priorities. A number of the managers commented that it would be possible to consider different management strategies for each quadrant of the application portfolio grid. This view is echoed by Peppard (1993, p. 69): 'An application should be managed in relation to the contribution it makes to the business.' By way of example, those applications that fall in the 'high potential' quadrant need an environment that accepts risk and involves research and development expenditure, which may or may not produce positive results. To put it another way, one manager stated:

> ...if you follow my approach, funding would be invested in what the business needs and doing speculative research to showcase new ways of doing things.

While discussing the applications portfolio grid, most managers raised a concern that their organization lacked 'strategic' systems. Following further investigations it became apparent that significant 'strategic' systems funding was taking place, but only on one major strategic system. The author suggests that this discrepancy is due to the fact that the application portfolio grid's usage does not define or measure a 'system'. For example, Peppard (1993) recommends that one merely identifies the systems that should lie in each quadrant to provide a view of the portfolio. Unfortunately, the definition of an application can be subjective, and merely counting the number of applications provides a biased picture of the portfolio. (As was the case in the workshops.)

Therefore, the author recommends that practitioners enhance the application portfolio grid to include the resources (financial or human) deployed for each IS project identified and then represent such amounts relative to each other as circles in the grid. This can be shown as in Figure 7.8.

Another idea practitioners may wish to explore is to classify the importance of individual business processes according to the four quadrants and then decide which applications to develop on the basis of which ones support the critical business processes.

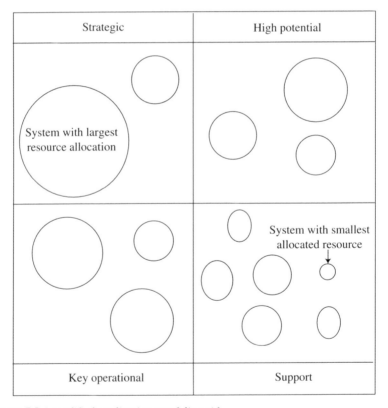

Figure 7.8 *A modified application portfolio grid*

Learning point 7: Implementation practice can be improved by following the example of some Japanese firms

Most of the managers interviewed commented that the implementation of strategies, and in particular the implementation of projects resulting from strategies, were problematic as implementation issues in the business unit were disconnected from strategy formulation. They stated that this disconnection was seen in:

- lack of coordination over implementation resources;
- problems business managers face trying to meet operational performance targets while being impacted by the implementation of projects.

A common aspect of the formal-rational frameworks proposed by strategy writers is that they put forward strategy formulation and strategy implementation as two distinct processes. This can be seen in most of the commonly available frameworks, and the way many of the management consultancies organize separately for formulation and implementation work. It reflects a common Western approach whose influence can be found in leading management texts, and is typified by the following quote:

> The distinction is that strategy formulation is the process of deciding on new strategies, whereas strategic planning is the process of deciding how to implement strategies. (Anthony and Govindarajan, 1995)

This traditional view asserts that creators of strategy are then responsible for obtaining business buy-in from the relevant parts of the organization to begin the process of implementation which is carried out by others. As a result, Currie points out that in most companies 'implementation often bears little relationship (if any) with the formal-rational strategy process' (Currie, 1995, p. 76).

Currie (1995) has identified that one approach to overcoming this problem is to follow the example set by Japanese firms, who differ from Anglo/American firms by:

- Developing three-year strategies for IS development with detailed implementation plans as part of strategy work.
- Linking target setting and measurement to implementation.
- 'Relentlessly pursuing' technology strategies until they are fully operational.

It is clear that the first two points could be used to address the concerns raised by the managers interviewed. By developing strategies that include implementation plans the overall coordination of implementation would no longer be piecemeal. In addition, by developing targets alongside the implementation activities it becomes possible to reduce the budgetary dilemma faced by business managers. This could be achieved through the provision of short-term relief from performance targets during implementation periods.

Learning point 8: Diversity issues faced by transnational organizations introduce extra implementation complexity

Almost all the managers interviewed commented that the implementation of strategies, and in particular the implementation of projects, is often very complex as the organization was committed to diversity. Diversity was a highly valued element of the organization and was seen as core to its corporate identity. It accommodated individual and group differences, and provided it with the capability for original and creative flexibility in organizational work and customer facing activities. The main diversity factors which managers identified as inhibitors to success were:

- The late discovery of local requirements which invalidated worldwide process design and application development.
- The favouring of small IS developments based on local needs rather than worldwide requirements.
- The ability of regional business managers to delay or obstruct implementation on the valid grounds of reduced short-term national level performance.

Unfortunately, due to the paucity of IS implementation literature it is not possible to use literature to shed light on these issues. However, general change management literature does provide insights which the organization could learn from. Due to the prominence and desirability of diversity in the organization, it can be argued that any change management must utilize diversity rather than attempt to overcome or by-pass it. According to Dunphy and Stace (1988), this entails applying a collaborative mode of work. Such work consists of a gradual, often bottom-up change, which utilizes consultation, collaboration and participation involving group problem-solving and win–win seeking. Its strengths include achieving win–wins, having a continuity of change and leveraging competencies.

The down side of adopting an implementation approach based on diversity is that it inhibits strategic global developments which bring advantages such as economies of scale and common global business processes. For example, if multinationals decide to manage their customer services in different ways, dealing with key global corporate customers in a homogeneous manner becomes a problem.

According to the strategy literature the balance that multinationals strike between meeting national markets and global coordination is best achieved through flexible organizations which Bartlett (1996) has named 'transnational organizations'. Unfortunately, the issue of organizing to provide transnationals with IS/IT has not yet been addressed. Therefore, until such work is carried out, it is recommended that multinational IS services should be developed in line with the organization's corporate strategy.

Summary

The major learning points discussed in this chapter provide practitioners with numerous insights into ways of improving IS strategy work in large multinationals. Their validity as practitioner concerns has been confirmed by the IS strategy and SISP literature across a wide variety of organizations.

However, the research made it clear that the process of establishing the learning points was as important in determining how the organization approaches future IS work as the points themselves. For this reason, it is suggested that practitioners employ tools and techniques from SISP frameworks to provide a context for exploring avenues for improvement in other organizational settings. A sound starting point would be to use the strategic IS models presented in this chapter.

References

Anthony, R. N. and Govindarajan, V. (1995). Management Control Systems, eighth edition. Irwin US.

Beer, M., Eistenstat, R. A. and Spector, B. (1990). Why change programs don't produce change. *Harvard Business Review*, **68**(6), pp. 158–166

Bartlett, C. (1996). Building and managing the transnational: The new organizational challenge. In. *Competition in Global Industries* (Porter, ed.), Harvard Business School Press, Boston.

Camillus, J. C. and Lederer, A. L. (1985). Corporate strategy and the design of computerized information systems. *Sloan Management Review*, Spring, **26**(3).

Caulkin, S. (1997). The Gurus – Chris Argyris. *Management Today*, October, pp. 58–9.

Ciborra, C. and Jelassi, T. eds (1994). *Strategic Information Systems (A European Perspective)*, John Wiley & Son.

Coyne, K. P. (1986). Sustainable competitive advantage – what it is – what it isn't. *Business Horizons*, January–February, pp. 54–61.

Currie, W. (1995). *Management Strategy for IT*. Pitman.

Doyle, J.R. (1991). Problems with strategic information systems frameworks.

European Journal of Information Systems, **1**(4), pp. 273–280.

Dunphy, D. C. and Stace, D. A. (1988). Transformation and coercive strategies for planned organisational change. *Organisation Studies*, **9**(3), pp. 317–334.

Dutta, S. (1996). Linking IT and business strategy: The role and responsibility of senior management, *European Management Journal*, **14**(3), pp. 255–268.

Earl, M. J. (1989). *Management Strategies for Information Technology*. Prentice-Hall.

Earl, M. J. (1990). Approaches to strategic information systems planning experience in twenty-one United Kingdom companies. *Proceedings of the International Conference on Information Systems*, December, pp. 271–277.

Feeny, D. and Ives, B. (1989). In search of sustainability – reaping long term advantage from investments in information technology. *Journal of Management Information*, **5**(1), pp. 36–50.

Fried, L. and Johnson, R. (1992). Planning for competitive use of IT, *Information Strategy*, **8**, pp. 5–15.

Galliers, R. D. (1987). Information Systems Planning in Britain and Australia in the mid-1980s: Key Success Factors, unpublished PhD, University of London, London, UK.

Galliers, R. D. (1991). Strategic information systems planning: Myths, reality and guidelines for successful implementation. *European Journal of Information Systems*, **1**(1), pp. 55–64.

Goldsmith, N. (1991). Linking IT planning to business strategy. *Long Range Planning*, **6**, pp. 67–77.

Hopper, M. D. (1990). Rattling SABRE: New ways to compete on information. *Harvard Business Review*, **68**(3), pp. 118–25.

Hunt, B. and Targett, D. (1995). The Japanese Advantage? Butterworth-Heinemann, Oxford.

King, W. R., Grover, V. and Hufnagel, E. H. (1989). Using information and information technology for sustainable competitive advantage. *Information and Management*, **17**(2), pp. 87–93.

Lederer, A. and Mendelow, A. (1986). The co-ordination of information systems plans with business plans. *Journal of Management Information Systems*, **6**(2), pp. 5–19.

MacDonald, K. H. (1997). Personal communication during MBA, Bath University.

Mata, F. J., Fuerst, W. L. and Barney, J. B. (1995). Information technology competitive advantage: A resource-based analysis. *MIS Quarterly*, December, pp. 313–335.

Mills, M. (1989). Information strategy planning. *Administrator Journal*, April, pp. 9–11.

Mintzberg, H. (1994). The fall and rise of strategic planning. *Harvard Business Review*, January–February, pp. 107–114.

Parsons, G. L. (1983). Information technology: a new competitive weapon. *Sloan Management Review*, Fall, pp. 3–14.

Peppard, J. (1993). *IT Strategy for Business*. Pitman.

Piercy, N. (1991). *Market-Led Strategic Change*, Thorsons.

Porter, M. E. (1980), *Competitive Strategy*, Free Press.

Reponen, T., Parnisto, J. and Viitanen, J. (1996). Personality's impact on information management strategy formulation. *European Journal of Information Systems*, **5**, pp. 161–171.

Robson, W. (1997). Strategic Management and Information Systems, second edition. Pitman.

Ross, J. W., Bearth, C. M. and Goodhue D. L. (1996). Develop long-term competitiveness through IT assets. *Sloan Management Review*, Fall, pp. 31–42.

Scott Morton, M. S. (editor), (1991), *The Corporation of the 1990s, Information Technology and Organisational Transformation*. Oxford University Press.

Silk, D. J. (1995). *Harnessing Technology to Manage Your International Business*. McGraw-Hill Europe.

Synott, W. (1987). *The Information Weapon – Winning Customers and Markets with Technology*. John Wiley and Sons, USA.

Venkatraman, N. (1991). IT-induced Business Reconfiguration. In *The Corporation of the 1990s* (M. Scott Morton, ed.), Oxford University Press.

Ward, J. and Griffiths, P. M. (1997). *Strategic Planning For Information Systems*, Wiley & Sons.

8 An IS strategy proposal for the European division of BP Acetyls

Lucy Jackson, Karen Hart, Philip Moore, Philip Reid,
Duncan Scarr-Hall and Mike Stoller
Cranfield School of Management, Cranfield University

Executive Summary

Introduction

The purpose of this chapter is to recommend ways in which information systems can help the European division of BP Acetyls meet its key business objectives.

Business strategy and market needs

This business faces a number of key challenges:

- It is a joint leader in a mature and increasingly competitive market.
- It is in a business where products are undifferentiated and development of relationships with customers is paramount.

We have identified four areas that are key in maintaining and building BPA's competitive position in the face of these challenges:

1 product quality;
2 price;

3 availability, and
4 customer service.

Information systems and Business Needs

The current systems are strong in managing product quality, and BPA have also initiated a range of projects to improve relationships with customers. However, BPA's ability to be competitive on price, and to ensure a ready supply of product, are undermined by poorly co-ordinated production management systems and poor demand forecasting.

Recommendations

Our key recommendations are to:

1 Develop improved demand forecasting systems, based on both market data and information currently held about historical order trends by customer. This should be used to provide production plans more closely matched to demand.
2 Contribute to improving the relationship of trust with customers by providing them with on-line information about product quality, availability, and delivery, as well as HSE and other generic information. This should make them more warmly disposed towards BPA but should also enable BPA to start discussions about other meaningful forms of partnership.
3 Develop further extensions of electronic data interchange (EDI), and pilot the provision of guarantees of product availability in return for closer co-operation on developing demand forecasts.
4 Provide further internal data links so that production and demand are ever-more closely linked and kept in step.

Costs and benefits

Our indications are that this package of proposals can be achieved for costs in the order of £450,000, plus the costs of developing further EDI links with customers. In addition, we must point out that in order to realize the benefits, BPA staff – in particular the production managers and sales teams – must assume different roles in order to convert the potential benefits into quantifiable returns on investment.

We do believe though that properly managed, these developments will keep

BP Acetyls at the forefront of the European market in terms of market share and value generation.

Introduction

Background to the Assignment

In this chapter, we consider how development of information systems could help the European Performance Unit of BP Acetyls (BPA) achieve its goals. We analysed BPA's position in the world-wide acetyls market, the changing nature of this position and resulting strategies for the European business, before assessing current information flows and the ways in which these could be improved for the benefit of the business. The data for this chapter was gathered by interviews with key personnel, feedback from internal meetings, from customer research, and from internal BP information sources.

Scope of this chapter

While technology control and asset management play crucial roles in this business, where cost leadership is crucial for success, we have confined the scope of this chapter to the supply chain of the existing European business and developing existing relationships with customers.

Note on terminology:

In this chapter, we use the terms 'information systems' and 'information technology', each with specific meaning. Information *systems* refer to the transfer around the business of information essential to its success. Information *technology* is the software/hardware which actually enables this information to be provided to the individual desks.

Business context and BPA's strategy

Scope of the market

Acetyls is one of the largest of the seventeen business units within BP Chemicals, accounting for around 25 per cent of the company's capital employed. The business manufactures and sells chemicals related to acetic

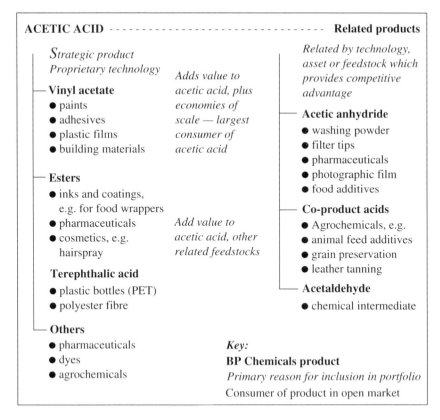

Figure 8.1 *111: Acetyls product portfolio*

acid – synthetic vinegar. Figure 8.1 outlines the product portfolio and indicates the very wide variety of ultimate uses for these industrial chemicals.

The world market is valued at more than $5000 million per annum, and while real growth is expected in the Far East, the European and North American markets are not expected to grow faster than GDP. BPA is a close number two in the acetyls world behind Hoechst Celanese, and within Europe, BPA is the main or second largest supplier in all major markets.

Generic in Market trends

BP has controlled the process technology in acetic acid – the crucial barrier to entry – since 1986, and this has been a key success factor for business growth since then. However, the turn of the century sees this grip loosening, an issue already being countered by major technology and asset developments.

In addition, while the 20 per cent of customers that buy 80 per cent of the product already enjoy considerable power, this is increasing further, especially in the developed markets, with:

- the trend for global deals to maximizse purchasing power;
- the increasing strength of the ultimate customer, often a major retailer; and trends towards greater supplier disclosure.

BP Acetyls strategy and market needs

Strategy for BP Acetyls Europe

BPA has an ambitious global goal which calls for faster than GDP growth and value generation.

> To secure world leadership in acetic acid and a strengthened derivatives position, ensuring long-term growth and value generation.
> Source: BP Acetyls.

This places the following imperatives upon the core European business:

1 Retain the 20 per cent top customers accounting for 80 per cent of the revenue, strengthening the relationships for the long term to:
   a) increase customer loyalty;
   b) win their new demand;
   c) reduce costs to service.
2 Win a disproportionate share of any business above GDP through preferred supplier status and customer service innovation.
3 Manage the supply chain for increasing efficiency:
   a) to achieve maximum reliability of supply;
   b) at lowest cost.

European customer needs

The most important factor for acetyls customers is *product quality*, since impure product could shut down their plant: the product must meet an internationally agreed standard even to be acceptable. While this therefore is not a source of differential advantage, it represents the first major challenge for BPA.

	Competitive factor	Order winner or qualifier
1	Product quality	Qualifier
2	Tanker cleanliness	Qualifier
3	Price competitiveness/flexibility of price negotiations	Winner
4	On-time delivery/accuracy of delivery documentation	Qualifier
5	Availability of supply	Qualifier
6	Speed of response to market changes in price	Qualifier
7	Forewarning of problems (of supply)	Qualifier
8	Understanding customer needs	Winner
9	Emergency response arrangements	Qualifier
10	Partnership	Winner
11	Punctuality of delivery	Winner
12	Flexible lead times	Winner
13	Authority of sales contact	Qualifier
14	Responsiveness of salesman/sales office to customer needs	Winner
15	Communication of market (price) trends	Winner

Figure 8.2 *BPA's competitive factors (source: Acetyls European Customer Survey)*

Competition is based on *price* and *availability*, but service factors are becoming increasingly important, as shown in Figure 8.2; the second key challenge for BPA is to develop service so far ahead of the competition that the customer loyalty it seeks can be satisfied.

The external supply chain

The ready availability of supply is a key issue for customers and, therefore, for BPA in managing the supply chain. The business must constantly balance the risks of holding too little stock, possibly letting down key customers, against the costs of holding too much stock, with an additional risk of enforced plant shutdown if demand slackens unexpectedly. As Figure 8.3 shows, BPA is far removed from the final consumer: and as the Forrester effect reflects, the further the manufacturer from the end user, the greater the volatility in demand for their product. The third major challenge therefore is to manage supply cost-effectively in the face of volatile demand.

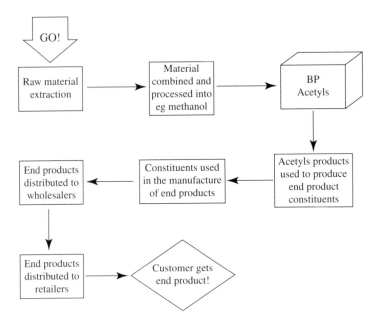

Figure 8.3: *BP Acetyls external supply chain*

Summary of competitive factors

Both in BP strategy and in customer needs the key factors that dominate are:

- product quality;
- price;
- availability;
  and
- customer service.

The next step in the analysis is to understand how well current IS supports these factors.

Information systems and the key business issues

Current information systems

In order to analyse BPA's current systems, we have used the four categories of the 'applications portfolio', as shown in Figure 8.4 (further details of individual systems are given in Appendix A1). This helps show the role of each system in use, and their potential in supporting business objectives.

Fit between IS systems and key strategic requirements

BPA already have highly developed systems for managing *product quality*, and current developments in on-line quality testing systems look set to keep BPA at the leading edge in this arena.

The issue of *price* ultimately revolves around the extent to which supply meets demand, and the price sensitivity of customers – which in part revolves around the strength of the relationship with those customers.

The issue of how well current IS supports the key business issues therefore actually rests on how well IS supports:

1 the way product availability is managed, through the management of the supply chain; and
2 the development of relationships with customers.

We will focus on these in the next two sections.

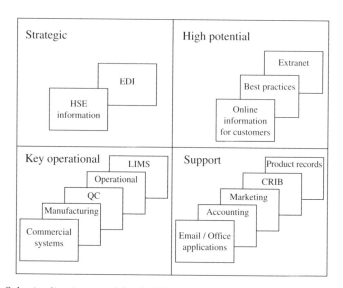

Figure 8.4 : *Applications portfolio for BPA*

Supply chain management
The major purpose of supply chain management is be to make product available on-demand and at the lowest cost, by:

1 a) avoiding excess stocks;
2 b) avoiding unplanned plant shut-downs ;
3 c) reducing the need to buy in finished product during stock shortages.

In addition, the need to build greater, stronger and more mutually dependent relationships with key customers may call for a capability to *guarantee* supply, so that the need to predict demand becomes doubly imperative.

1 How do the current systems measure up?
The way in which the process makes product available for customers and supports forward planning is illustrated shown in Figure 8.5, but the process is rife with double keying, manual reconciliation of spreadsheets, data graves and manual adjustments. Demand forecasts are received from several sources by several destinations and integrating this information is a time consuming task.

The *strategies* we suggest to facilitate the supply chain objectives can largely be carried out through the enhancement and linking of existing information systems to achieve:

● better forecasting of demand;
● more integrated control of your internal commercial and production processes.

2 Demand forecasting
More accurate and useable demand forecasts should introduce both greater certainty and greater flexibility into production planning and avoid the periodic need to either over-produce or under-produce. Three new processes are required:

1 Formal market forecasting at a macro-level.
2 Systematic forecasting of the demand from individual customers based on:
   a) past histories and known changes in the variables that impact each customer's demand; and
   b) current information about tentative and firm orders.
3 Better quality demand-forecasts from the customers themselves.

Customers cannot be expected to provide the latter information without some incentive, and this is will be one of the objectives of the relationship development initiative.

However, the remaining two initiatives can be generated internally, and Appendix B2 provides details of the processes, data and systems and technology required.

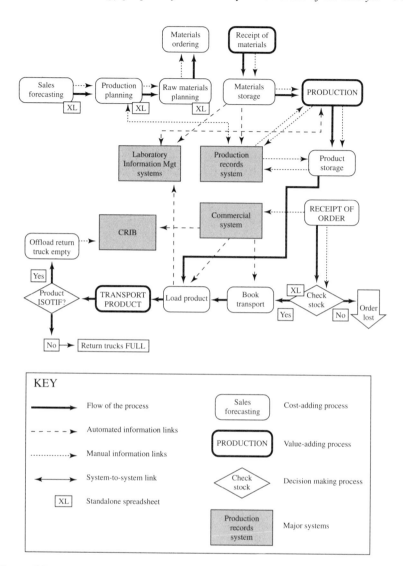

Figure 8.5 *Internal supply process*

3 Integrating the production and commercial processes

Improving demand forecasting itself will achieve most benefit with better integration of the internal processes. As we saw from Figure 8.5 there is:

1 little connection between the commercial and production processes;
2 excessive manual data transfer;
3 a large number of *independent* spreadsheets.

We suggest that an integrated 'sales forecasting and production planning module' (SFPP) is developed (see Figure 8.6), which combines:

- staged demand forecasts (projected macro-demand→tentative orders→ firm orders);
- projected plant shut-downs;
- existing stocks of raw materials, production rates and finished product
- Figure product.

This integrated SFPP would be such that the volume of production can be managed more effectively, adjusted more easily and potentially completely automated. Ultimately, orders for raw material supplies could be produced. The benefits of providing *continuously up-dated*, accurate information on how

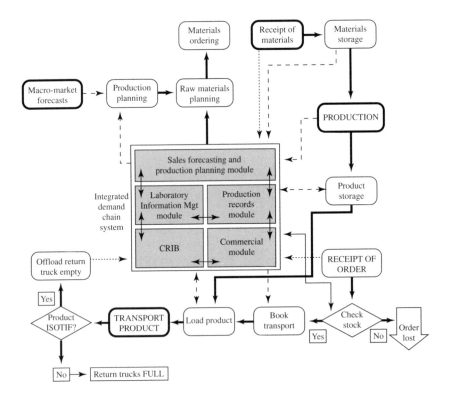

Figure 8.6 : *Proposed new process*

much raw material, goods-in-production and finished product there is in the system at any one stage *now and in the next week and next month* will enable production planning with more certainty. Less time spent on gathering data will enable swifter action in the now unlikely event that stock becomes too high or too low and we expect it will be possible to carry less stock once the accuracy of forecasts is developed and proven.

Customer relationship development
BPA cannot fully achieve the supply chain objectives without active co-operation from customers, but to obtain that co-operation it first needs to establish a relationship of trust. IS can help develop that by helping BPA to 'open its books' on key issues of product quality, availability, and delivery, as shown illustrated in Figure 8.7. In this way BPA can win complete customer confidence and reap the associated benefits of secure outlets and increased transparency of demand changes.

We believe the existing high potential and strategic systems which touch the customer can be extended to assist this aim of closer relationships.

1 ISOTIF
BP could provide extranet links to allow customers to obtain information on-demand on product quality, and the location, volume and estimated time of arrival of their current delivery. The former is already underway, the latter would involve substantial changes by contracted hauliers who would need to

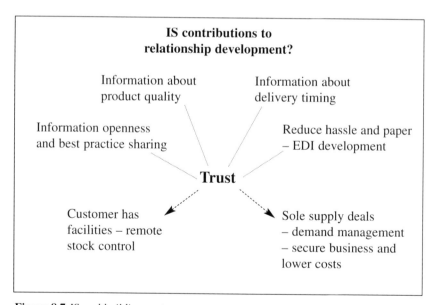

Figure 8.7 *IS and building customer trust*

adopt the kind of tracking systems widely used in parcel delivery.

2 Development of EDI

Last year BPA Europe's largest customer received a staggering 1700 invoices, and extending EDI facilities would not only reduce costs for both BPA *and* the customer, but provide an ideal, low risk opportunity to pilot demand forecasting and stock management.

3 Generate openness and trust, share best practice

BPA could extend the extranet information to give privileged information to key customers on HSE, supply chain management, product quality trends and best practices in manufacturing. However, free information can be undervalued by customers and the business must develop a strategy to manage this perception.

General information could also be freely and easily available on the internet fostering better relations towards pressure groups and promoting an image of openness.

4 Customer snapshot

This initiative will develop a one-page view of customers available to anyone who could impact a customer. This would be a crucial tool in fostering and tracking the links between functions in the customer and BPA functions and anticipate the opportunities and threats as customers consolidate their purchasing effort.

Recommendations

Introduction

The above suggestions will help to:

- develop an even more robust and cost effective internal supply chain;
- better manage capacity to meet demand; and
- foster even better relationships with customers.

We now address issues of people, accountability, benefits management, prioritizsation and costs.

People

There is no doubt that customers buy from suppliers they like to deal with, and the proposals should allow individual efforts to be re-focused to meet customers' needs more effectively and at lower cost, and enable them to anticipate changes in these needs. The provision of more accurate information will enable faster, better decisions to be made.

Success depends on the pro-active contributions of key people in these areas and we need to be clear that they are not making themselves redundant in so doing, but the key challenge is that people will need to take on *new dimensions* to their role, for example:

- sales staff must be convinced that developing meaningful demand forecasts with their customers is contributing to BP's competitive thrust;
- production planners will work with buyers of raw materials to ensure smoother and more reliable supply *to* BP, which will require a new, externally-focused role;
- production planners will need to become accustomed to relying on automated production plans rather than their self-designed spreadsheets.
- performance measures must reflect the new roles and methods, for example, plant performance must not be measured on utilizsation in isolation, but in conjunction with demand generated in the market.

Management:

These issues will all need careful preparation, training and support. Given that a key outcome will be the closer integration of commercial and production processes we believe that each half of the programme should be managed by a senior manager from the appropriate area. However, they will be charged with working as a team to ensure the timely interlinking and effectiveness of the two programmes working in parallel.

Benefits management

Providing better information, via IS to production managers and clients will not of itself deliver benefits. Production planners will have to use that information to fine-tune delivery of product to the strength of demand, and sales teams will have to educate customers to exploit the information provided to their – the customers' – benefit. To ensure that benefits do emerge, clear targets need to be set and monitored.

1 Supply chain management

The objectives of this initiative are improved availability and reduced costs. Key measures that need to be monitored after implementation are:

- reduction in stock days of:
  - raw materials
  - finished product
- reduction in the:
  - number and severity of stock-outs
  - number and value of lost sales
  - value of finished product purchased to fulfil orders during stock-outs.

Not all of these are carefully monitored now (e.g. sales are often deflected when sales staff know that stocks are low) so the monitoring processes should be defined and implemented *now* so that like with like can be compared before and after implementation.

2 Relationship development

The objectives of this development are to secure existing customer relationships, increase the propensity of customers to move to sole supplier deals, and increase their willingness to share information about their own demand and move towards remote tank monitoring. Therefore, some of the key measures are likely to be subjective. They will include:

- the speed and success of simplifying processes due to good relationships;
- the progress of customer relationships, e.g. from combative to partnership;
- the costs of servicing individual accounts;
- increases in the value of orders from key clients;
- progress towards stronger EDI links;
- success in attracting the desired disproportionate share of new business.

Priorities

In developing the prioritized action plan we have considered three factors:

1 Developing confidence in, and support for, the mission needs early successes.
2 Low cost initiatives that we can control internally.
3 Balancing low cost with visible benefits.

Therefore we recommend the following broad priorities:

1 Develop the *internally-based* demand forecasts outlined in Appendix B2. Comparisons with systems of comparable complexity suggest that this would cost less than £100,000, given that the data already exists with CRIB (the consolidated repository of information for businesses).

2 Progress openness with selected customers by making available key information on-line. This is comparatively low cost, does not require customers to change existing systems and starts the process of establishing a relationship of openness and trust.

The extranet pilot cost in the region of £20,000, but with the inclusion of additional information, admittedly from existing data sources, one has to assume that costs could reach £200,000 for an extended pilot.

3 Start talks with key customers about extending EDI, and about providing guarantees of product availability in return for closer co-operation on developing demand forecasts. This programme would have to be progressive: it would not be possible to guarantee availability to all customers initially without the demand forecasts that you would get in exchange. However, as more key accounts work with you to develop demand forecasts so supply should progressively become more predictable.

The costs of extending the EDI project will largely depend on the system's infrastructure at the client end, but would not be prohibitive.

4 Providing the last data and processing steps to integrate the internal production and commercial processes.

This project would largely involve building data links between systems, and comparison with similar systems suggest a cost in the region of £250,000.

We are confident that progress on these fronts will keep BP Acetyls at the forefront of the European market in terms of market share and value generation.

Appendix A1: BP Acetyls systems – the applications portfolio model

1 Key operational

The commercial system (CS)

Provides order processing, automatic booking of haulier, despatch records, delivery documentation, invoicing, payment records, accounting. This also includes a system to purchase any finished product which might be bought and can be used for stock control although stock controls are generally done using spreadsheets.

The laboratory information management system (LIMS)

This system is used to sample and store the analysis information on the products made. This system provides a feedback loop to the production system ensuring that any process deviations are minimized.

Site manufacturing systems

Most chemical plants are controlled using a 'desktop control system' (DCS). An operator can see all measurements of what is going on in the process, e.g. pressure, temperature. If the operators want to change something they touch a touch screen which sends an electronic signal to open valves, etc. This system is essential to run the plant and is cared for accordingly.

Site quality control and systems

Holds data based on the analysis of the product at the plant. The analysis must be done to ensure that the product is in specification and is therefore fit for sale. The statistical data is also used for support of process development and with key customers for use in their process control.

Other site operational systems

There are other smaller operational systems, e.g. stock reporting, ship movements advised by brokers and agents, etc.

All of the key operational systems also provide the data source for management information systems. They are designed first to be effective and then to enable cost reduction, and there is transfer of experience across the chemicals business through existing networks. Duplication is avoided in the sales area as all the major chemicals businesses subscribe to 'CS'.

2 Support

Consolidated repository of information for businesses (CRIB)

CRIB is the database to which data from CS is downloaded. It uses Oracle Forms to enable analysis of sales data and trends and provides information down to individual customer level, including analysis of contribution. It can analyse by end use provided the right code is on the order in the first place!

CRIB also has the budget control and analysis mechanism for distribution cost reporting showing the costs associated with every physical movement of the product are downloaded directly.

It is also used to service various other information needs, e.g. exchange rates, invoice details, debtor reporting.

Also in this category are **accounting systems** and **office applications** (including e-mail).

A 'standard' desktop has been specifically designed for use throughout the BP Group. This is based around Microsoft software and applications. Spreadsheets are heavily used for market analysis, budgeting, forecasting and sales records.

Marketing/visit report systems

There are two different systems in use in BP neither are particularly customized to the requirements of BP Acetyls.

3. Strategic

EDI

Acetyls has access to, and used, BP Chemicals' expertise in EDI with major customers, reducing transaction paperwork. Some interfacing problems exist with customers ordering systems which have prevented the true potential of this system to be realized. The main problems have been costs to customer if their systems require double keying or changes render the links unusable. In addition, in the case of electronic order transmission, removing a telephone could sever a vital informative and relationship building link with the customer. Further integration with customers ordering systems could be possible together with a increase in the number of customers using EDI systems.

Extension to management of customers' stocks is just beginning across the company and has, for example, helped keep a crucial customer 100 per cent with BP Chemicals and secured sole supply contracts from majority supply positions. Internally, the Quality Management Team at one of BPA's manufacturing sites has recently developed, with an equipment supplier, a novel, in situ, flexible 'easy test' system for plant operators. These strategic systems are mostly localized within business areas and become more widely available where there is an existing network for communication.

HSE information

Another business has made extensive use of diskettes to provide customers with advance information and advice on health, safety and environmental (HSE) legislation.

4 High potential

On-line quality information

Provision of product quality information to customers on-line, so that they have direct information about the quality of the product they are receiving. This avoids the previous need to show a certificate of product quality to the client on delivery.

On-line best practice information

As above except that data given to customers is for best practices in HSE and plant operations in order to demonstrate openness to customers.

Extranet

Using the technology and systems developed for use on the internet, BP has set up a private network with suppliers in the shipping industry. The system allows shipping agents to update information directly into a BP hosted system on the availability and movements of tankers. The system has reduced the amount of paperwork between companies and gives more accurate and timely information to BP personnel.

Appendix B2: Proposal for internal demand forecasting process

Construction of the demand forecasting model would require BP to:

- Develop, at the market level, for each product, a computer model of how demand for the downstream products is altering over time; this will depend on a variety of independent variables many of which can be tracked with ease. This model can then provide the first estimate of demand for each product, and will be up-dated as an enhanced weekly or monthly report to support mid-term production planning.
- At the level of each *customer* BP can also develop a model of *their* demand based on the macro-market data and the actual history of orders from that customer; the model can of course be tested and refined with each new order. This process will gradually be rolled-out for each of the 20 per cent of our customers that provide BP with 80 per cent of demand.
- Step 2 will provide a detailed short-term demand forecast for each customer and product. As each new tentative and firm order is placed it is compared with the assumed orders for that product and customer and the demand forecast adjusted accordingly. In this way the production plan will be constantly fine-tuned.

Currently there are no systems capable of driving such a process, but CRIB does provide the detailed history of orders by customer that is the key input to Step 2, and can also automatically up-date any new system with individual orders as they are placed.

The new requirements to support the process are detailed below.

a) Data

Historical and constantly up-dated data on all economic variables affecting demand for each of the major acetyls-using products.

b) Systems

- Regression model for calculating and recalculating predicted demand for each product based on the value of the economic and other underlying variables.
- Regression model for calculating and recalculating, by customer, demand based on the same information plus actual order data.
- Model for comparing tentative and new orders for each customer (a new output from CRIB) with predicted demand (as output from Step 2) and adjusting predicted demand both at the customer level and at the aggregate level for the product. This system will provide automatic output to a production planning model.

It is proposed that these all form part of an integrated sales forecasting and production planning module that will itself exchange information with CRIB, LIMS and the production planning system.

9 Strategic aspects of business process reengineering (BPR) – UK experiences

Emma Visick and David Avison
Department of Management, University of Southampton
Philip Powell
Warwick Business School, University of Warwick

Introduction

The aim of this chapter is to assess the driving forces behind business process reengineering (BPR) initiatives, the procedures adopted to instigate change, the benchmarks used to measure success, and the degree to which success has been achieved in three organizations.

The chapter is in four sections. The first introduces business process reengineering. In the second section, the application of BPR in three UK organizations is examined; Boiler Ltd who manufacture heating appliances; The Society, a building society; and Insco, an insurance company. The identity of the organizations has been disguised but this does not detract from the analysis of their experiences. The third section examines the experiences gained and the lessons that can be drawn from them. The fourth section provides a comparison of these and other experiences of evaluating BPR. Finally conclusions are drawn.

Business process reengineering

The essence of BPR is a radical change in the way in which organizations perform business activities; 'the fundamental rethinking and radical redesign of business processes to achieve dramatic improvements in critical, contemporary measures of performance, such as cost, quality, service, and speed' (Hammer and Champy, 1993, pp. 31–32). The model of business process reengineering created by Hammer and Champy describes the characteristics of reengineered processes as follows. Several jobs are combined, performed by a 'case worker' responsible for a process. 'Case team' members are empowered to find innovative ways to improve service, quality, and reduce costs and cycle times. Due to process integration, fewer controls and checks are necessary, and defects are minimized by an entire process being followed through by those ultimately responsible for the finished product. Workers make decisions according to the requirements of the whole process. The steps in a process are performed in the order decided upon by those doing the work, rather than on the basis of fragmented and sequential tasks, enabling the parallel processing of entire operations. Differing customer requirements may dictate that several versions of a product are created in one process; teamwork reengineering enables easier product customization.

Organizations reengineer for four main reasons:

1 They face commercial difficulties and have no choice.
2 Competitive forces present problems unless the organization takes radical steps to re-align business processes with strategic positioning.
3 Management in the organization regard reengineering as an opportunity to take a lead over the competition.
4 Publicity about BPR has prompted organizations to follow the lead established by others.

Clearly, when referring to their BPR programmes in public, organizations tend to use euphemisms rather than making general references pertaining to strategy. Consequently, the distinction between information presented for public consumption and that for internal analysis has tended to cloud the issue of why organizations reengineer, and the changes which occur as a result.

UK Experiences of BPR

The following case studies assess the experiences of three UK organizations undertaking BPR; Boiler Ltd who manufacture heating appliances; The Society, a building society; and Insco, an insurance company.

Boiler Ltd

Based in Northern England, Boiler Ltd are a leading supplier of gas heating boilers, and gas and solid fuel fires. Employing 1000 people, Boiler Ltd became a partnership in 1983 following its transfer into employee ownership by the chairman. In 1993 turnover exceeded £70 million.

In 1983, a combination of a lack of investment, poor manufacturing methods, and no functional integration had contributed to a relatively backward, yet profitable, organization. Facing an uncertain future, Boiler Ltd relied on the domestic market for its prosperity. However, during the recession of the early 1980s, rather than reduce the workforce, the company continued manufacturing which led to a stock overflow as production exceeded sales.

During 1985 the domestic market began to improve and Boiler Ltd were able to release the accumulated stock. At the end of 1986, record profits were earned, share price soared, and Boiler Ltd became the market leader in gas boilers. As the property market accelerated towards a peak in 1989, the company faced a dilemma; its main products were 'stars' (high market share in a market with a high growth rate), yet the company was over-staffed. Four manufacturing sites remained, but sales had been mainly from stock. Probably because the company could afford not to, a reduction in the workforce had been resisted. By 1989, a downturn in the UK economy was evident. The 'star' became a 'cash cow' as demand fell; and the opportunity presented by the availability of cash was taken to modernize manufacturing, invest in new plant, equipment and training, and restructure the organization.

Redundancies and trade union conflict created considerable problems during the early phases of modernization. With a policy of employing local labour, recruitment had been conducted on an ad hoc basis; no controls operated with respect to selection, and training had been minimal. As processes were modernized and new plant installed, a number of tasks were eliminated and working practices reformed. A reduction in the workforce was met with hostility by the trade unions, and strike action was balloted. However, negotiations between workforce and management via a Partnership Council averted a strike, and the changes were agreed on the basis of a long-term commitment to growth and stability. Although, on reflection, it would appear that the authority of the trade unions was undermined, a combination of staff involvement and financial briefings to the Partnership Council enabled the workforce to participate in strategic decision-making. Following the changes and conflict of the early 1990s, the role of the trade union at Boiler Ltd has not diminished; their practices and attitudes have been modernized.

Boiler Ltd initiated change within the 'traditional internal structures and cultures' which had been 'incapable of responding fast enough' to a changing competitive environment. Focusing on the needs of its major customers – British Gas, local authorities, and builders' merchants – Boiler Ltd redesigned its processes along core business lines. A functional hierarchy comprising six levels – Finance, R&D, Manufacturing, and Sales and Marketing – was replaced by three-tiered, cross-functional SBUs, based on product groups, market segments, customer services, engineering services, sheet metal and paint plant, and the foundry; each with its own profit responsibilities; and all backed-up by a redesigned MIS.

In addition to the close involvement of major customers, the reengineering programme achieved initial direction following evidence gathered during a tour of Japan, the USA and the UK aimed at finding out about best practice. A JIT system and a Kanban system for small components, which functions through the close cooperation between the production and assembly teams and suppliers, were started immediately. Lessons learned from observing others have been drawn upon since; and regular contact with organizations such as Toyota and Rover enables a comparison of experiences. Consultants were appointed to appraise the processes at Boiler Ltd, and this led to a 'company improvement programme' starting in 1987, via a pilot scheme in part of the factory. The scheme illustrated the benefits of JIT, group decision making, and teamwork. Training programmes encouraged the workforce to influence the change process and participate in decision-making.

Following the success of the pilot, the practices were rolled out into the rest of the manufacturing operation. Initial suspicion, especially from the unions following redundancies, was overcome as the benefits became apparent. A reward system was negotiated based on a scaled wage rate plus a bonus attributable to team productivity.

The continuous improvement (CI) programme, which Boiler Ltd had been undertaking prior to reengineering, revolved around work cells. Viewing CI as the basis for 'beating customer expectations and thereby raising the competitive stakes continuously', Boiler Ltd has aimed to promote the philosophy as a 'natural part of ... day to day activities', in order to 'deliver total value to the customers beyond just product and price'. Internal suppliers were created through process teams and assembly line groups, and backward integration has incorporated vendor improvements. For example, five years ago 96 per cent of goods were inspected at goods in; now the figure is 1 per cent.

Within teams, a 'keys' approach to achieving excellence has given rise to the assessment of improvements. The keys comprise activities associated with improving:

- working conditions;
- skills;
- value adding activities;
- internal and external supply chain management;
- production scheduling.

These are driven and assessed by each team. Activities such as organizing the work area, maintaining machines and equipment, health and safety, and work in progress are the responsibility of all team members; achievements are assessed subjectively; and suggestions made for improvements are internally driven. As the source of competitive advantage, Boiler Ltd concentrated on reducing the time taken to perform value-added activities, through the application of JIT, CI, and TQM; and treating everyone in the organization as a change agent able to raise the competitive stakes by contributing to customer satisfaction.

The basis of reengineering was established through a teambuilding approach, continuous improvement, and training programmes. The creation of SBUs in 1990, and consequent workforce empowerment, however, exposed the inadequacy of IT systems which undermined communications. In one respect, the lack of sufficient IT forced people to manage relationships and develop new ways of performing tasks. However, the need for central control over the eventual development of suitable systems, led to the creation of MIS teams working directly with the process teams. Starting in finance and administration, systems are spreading into manufacturing and distribution; although misunderstandings by MIS personnel concerning manufacturing requirements delayed the proceedings.

According to the CEO, BPR was undertaken to gear processes more closely to customer needs in an industry facing structural and ownership changes; and, where the means of achieving competitive advantage have changed. With 24 per cent of the market and a strong brand name, Boiler Ltd are an independent organization, functioning solely as a manufacturer of heating appliances. Its competitors are owned by diversified organizations which use vertical integration to supply a variety of products to the public and private housing markets. Although currently confined to supplying the UK, Boiler Ltd are researching overseas markets with new product designs and distribution networks, particularly in Eastern Europe.

Evaluation of the reengineering programme's progress has largely used financial measures:

- net profit;
- return on sales;
- return on capital.

After two years, the expected results have not appeared. However, in terms of the manufacturing process, cycle time, stock levels, and work in progress have fallen, and the quality of finished goods has improved. The poorer than anticipated financial performance has been due to factors such as capital investment, new product development and launches, early retirement expenses, and training commitments.

The reengineering of processes at Boiler Ltd was the culmination of a series of change initiatives promoted since 1983 by management and the Partnership Council. However, individual personalities, notably the CEO and external consultants, have been largely responsible for the continued promotion and success of BPR. With the financial resources to undertake a widespread programme of change, the management presented the workforce with considerable incentives – a restructured reward system, a more flexible working environment, greater self-determination, and an 'open' training programme. A commitment by management to staff welfare has contributed to greater mutual understanding and open management has reduced the likelihood of conflict obstructing future changes.

The Society

Based in the Midlands, The Society is a small building society, with an annual turnover approaching £100 million. Over a thirty-month period, a reengineering programme led to a 40 per cent reduction in staff numbers to 1500 and a substantial improvement in its competitive position.

According to the CEO, BPR was undertaken to ensure 'survival'. During the recession of the early 1990s, income was falling, so early objectives were to improve the organization's earnings, while reducing expenses. The outcome shows that 'competitive edge and quality targets have been surpassed beyond what was thought possible'. Although the CEO argues that, due to the legacy of the original operations, reengineering is not necessarily an appropriate term to explain the changes, the consultants appointed agree that it adequately describes what happened.

Under the BPR initiative, sequential operations involving reporting lines and rigid procedures were rationalized into parallel processes. Concentrating on value adding activities, critical business processes were automated, and a number of activities eliminated. The procedures governing eight strategic systems were amended in the early stages; leaving the realignment of core business systems at the centre of later stages. The automation of sales, estate agency, and mortgage lending followed the redesign of manual processes, which identified key elements and reduced 'unnecessary tasks'. For example, at the mortgage lending front-end, a 'totally paper-driven business with a decentralized underwriting process in the branches' was transformed into 'a centralized, optical-disk-driven workflow' (Classe, 1993). Enabling a reduction in staff numbers, this led to a more rapid document turn around, and improved credit control.

In the design of IT systems, The Society transferred the initiative to system suppliers, with the brief to produce a system capable of enhancing the reengineered processes, and which was ahead of the competition. For example the IT system installed to control arrears currently operated at 30 per cent capacity. Also, the mortgage lending and investment systems were scrapped, as they had been operating for seven and ten years, lacked adequate documentation, had been designed to accommodate centralized control, and automated faulty processes. The new systems were designed to automate the reengineered processes; providing decentralized control via a centralized database.

The decision to reengineer was driven by a senior management team headed by the CEO; of these, only the CEO remains. Arguably, the incumbent management had been inhibitors to plans; the CEO argues that 'it was not their fault … they were unable to see a way forward'. Change teams, comprising cross-functional staff, are now responsible for strategy formulation and implementation. Aware of the corporate plan, these teams are responsible for deciding how to tie processes to it. In addition, plans originating in approximately sixty departments are reviewed by the executive team, and then approved following consultation. Continuous improvement training and feedback via staff questionnaires provide the organization with information on the efficiency and effectiveness of operations.

Critical success factors, used to evaluate the success of the reengineering initiative, comprise:

- customer satisfaction;
- net profit and return on capital;
- expertise in credit and risk management;
- staff satisfaction;
- asset valuation.

Based on mailshots, customer satisfaction since reengineering began has increased from 88 per cent to 96 per cent. Highly bureaucratic and paper-driven procedures had produced the highest cost–income ratio amongst the top twenty UK building societies before reengineering; profit per head is now in the top ten. Expertise in credit and risk management is based on arrears figures which have improved from 70 per cent worse than the industry average to 25 per cent better. Staff satisfaction has consistently improved, despite the loss of 1000 jobs.

The CEO attributes success in achieving support to the care taken in reducing staff numbers. Once the reengineering process had been explained, cooperation was forthcoming; implying that, had time not been taken to explain the radical approaches necessary, the programme would either have failed, or not reaped the returns achieved. To ameliorate the harmful effects of large-scale redundancy upon the remaining workforce, the society commissioned consultants to counsel staff before and during the early stages. As a result of a gradual approach to job losses, only 300 staff were made redundant involuntarily, the remainder accounted for by natural wastage.

The organization aims to be 'the first choice for customers … growth is not the be all and end all', neither is being number one in the industry, according to the CEO. Instead, the objective is to sustain a competitive edge by outperforming the competition in meeting market requirements; which entails maintaining operating performance above the industry average, and broadening their customer portfolio by purchasing the mortgage books of outgoing concerns. In addition, mergers and acquisitions will be aimed at extending the organization's network.

Insco

Based in Scotland, Insco are a UK subsidiary of a US insurance company, with a turnover of £100 million, employing 250 staff in the UK and 60,000 worldwide. Specializing in corporate healthcare, Insco started its reengineering initiative two years ago. Acknowledging that more reengineering projects fail than succeed, the head of IT attributes Insco's success to its total approach, involving 'heavy artillery, total organizational restructuring, and a change in the way people think ... quantum leaps' designed to improve efficiency and increase profit levels, not 'tinkering' with aspects of business activity. The achievement of these objectives was vital to success. During the reengineering programme, IT was regarded as only part of the overall plan. Other considerations included: how the company was organized; the manner in which work was conducted; and existing operational systems. Failure to address all these concerns simultaneously would have led to problems. For example, an internal focus on the sale of insurance cover and claims processing had largely ignored the requirements of customers beyond providing these services. However, during consultation with customers, it transpired that delays and errors had undermined the quality of service. A reorganization was conducted around outputs, rather than inputs, and the focus changed from internal to external measures of performance.

A clean sheet approach to job design enabled process activities to be configured in the most logical manner. From a hierarchy of managers and staff, cross-functional teams were created to concentrate on providing value-added service. A functional sequence of operations comprising sales, sales support, quotes, underwriting, and typing were merged into two teams; based on pre- and post-sales activities. Each team is responsible for 'logical groupings of customers', and deals with all requirements as a single process.

A new computer system was designed in-house to control work via a central database. New technology, based on Windows, a graphical user interface, local- and wide-area network, and client/server architecture, has been integrated with the reengineered processes. Manual, paper-driven activities, with no single information source for market research, quotations and strategic planning, have been linked by a network of operations, with a back-office system. A customer information system (CIS) resides at the centre, holding information on clients, future prospects, and competitors. Within the CIS, a workflow programme tracks the movement of quotes; and a rule-based underwriting system has been designed for pricing new business and conducting 'what-if' analysis. The combination of user-friendliness and flexibility enabled Insco to build the database and design an integrated system in a shorter time, using a prototyping approach. However, experience gained during these early stages illustrated that hardware requirements were greater than anticipated; and expertise, as a necessary ingredient during systems development, was understated.

Performance success is evaluated on the basis of service levels and relates to the quality of output, such as the turnaround time of sales and claims and the number of returns made by customers due to errors. For example, the number of claims processed per day increased from 35–40 to 75–90, and the days required to give a quote was cut from 17 to 2. Bonuses calculated on performance figures are paid quarterly; and, since reengineering began, efficiency levels have increased by 30 per cent.

According to the head of IT, a change in culture was expected to be one of the most difficult tasks during reengineering. However, circumstances meant that the experiences in Scotland were different to those elsewhere. Prior to reengineering, Insco relocated the majority of its insurance operations to a green field site in an Enterprise Development Area. In accordance with the regulations, 90 per cent of staff had to be recruited locally. As a result, Insco benefited from a young, available, flexible labour force, many of whom were technically trained, having taken further education following redundancy from shipbuilding and associated activities (Butler, 1992). Added bonuses include lower wage rates and a willingness of the workforce to experiment with and contribute towards change. Arguably, the improvements in performance were not so much the result of reengineering, but of designing processes, in a new location, with a compliant workforce.

Despite the special circumstances, cultural change was inevitable, creating a flatter structure, customer-focus, teamwork, coaching rather than directing, and a facilitative style amongst teams, which led to a more widespread understanding of others' roles. However, 'getting senior management to change was very difficult' and approximately 10 per cent of middle management lost their jobs. Although driven from the top, the remaining management lacked the capability to conduct a full reengineering programme. An initial feasibility study by consultants (involved at the US company), with a brief to work with management and sell the concept to the organization, was followed by the recruitment of a reengineering team. The team consisted of business and IT strategists, business analysts with computer skills, organizational development specialists and an organization and methods expert. Although just three of the original reengineering team remain at Insco, the legacy has been a newly-recruited senior management team committed to the BPR programme. Customer service teams have been created to maintain and develop the focus on future business. Team facilitators coach team members, resolve conflicts, and rectify operational problems. Continuous improvement remains the prevailing philosophy and empowerment of the workforce has pushed responsibility downwards.

After three years, Insco are reassessing their strategic direction. Private healthcare has become increasingly popular. Inflation affecting medical products and services currently stands at 25 per cent per annum and, companies are endeavouring to contain the cost of healthcare offered to their employees. In light of these, Insco aim to follow a new approach to healthcare management. The company has enlisted the support of customers to find out about the features of the services they offer, and to use the feedback to design new products. The BPR philosophy of internal efficiency and external customer focus drives the new strategic direction.

Assessing experiences

The context and reasons for the reengineering initiatives examined are all different. At Boiler Ltd, changing competitive forces were reshaping competition, and they regarded a radical approach as the best way to meet the challenges. In the case of The Society, the prospect of commercial failure presented few alternatives; reengineering achievements have been significant in bureaucratic financial organizations, and senior figures in the organization regarded reengineering as the only way in which The Society could survive. Insco, on the other hand, had experienced the benefits of reengineering in the US and reengineered to gain competitive advantage.

Similarities exist between the reengineering programmes of the three organizations. However, the history of each played a significant role in determining the ease with which the programmes were managed, and created differences in the reasons why BPR was adopted, how it was implemented, the problems, the measures of success, and the scope for the future. For example, the industrial history of Boiler Ltd created an interesting basis for change. The relationship between management and workforce was forged, in part, by unionization; and, cultural barriers complicated the change process. The Society experienced less resistance to change, due to a bureaucratic financial environment comprising predominantly male managers and female staff. Arguably, significant management control remains, even after reengineering, and workforce empowerment operates within relatively rigid guidelines. In the case of Insco, experience of reengineering overseas, combined with a flexible workforce and favourable contractual terms, created a relatively solid foundation.

In each case, consultants conducted a feasibility study and analysed the business processes. At Boiler Ltd, the CEO was appointed following early involvement as a consultant. The CEO of The Society initiated the BPR programme and changed the management team in order to force changes. The head of IT at Insco had been a consultant, although appointed to head the reengineering team before the BPR programme commenced. Consultants who had been involved in the BPR programme in the US were involved at the outset to sell the concept.

Critical processes were not dealt with simultaneously when reengineering began. Each organization decided on priority processes on the basis of the following criteria:

● Those experiencing the severest problems;
● those with the greatest impact on customers;
● those with which success was likely to be achieved most quickly.

However, reengineering remains a continuous programme; once the organizations started to reengineer and achieve success, the process of continuous improvement became a constant focus.

IT has been an important feature of the three reengineering programmes. The Society and Insco have embraced 'state of the art' IT capabilities. The practicalities behind Hammer and Champy's assertion that if the technology can be purchased by all organizations, 'a company will always be playing catch-up with competitors who have already anticipated it' (Hammer and Champy, 1993, p. 100) presents restrictions on organizations such as Boiler Ltd who have invested heavily in large-scale information systems linked to functional activities. An existing MRP system controls the overall manufacturing processes; although the MIS department are gradually redesigning systems. On the one hand, new systems have been more common in the administrative functions involving sales, marketing, finance, and customer service, which maintain geographical separation from the product line processes at the manufacturing end of Boiler Ltd's operations. On the other, the effort required to integrate Boiler Ltd's IT systems, coupled with the apparent caution over capital expenditure on indirect manufacturing equipment, have led to the relatively slow adoption of a common computerized MIS.

Reengineering projects fail primarily because senior managers lack the ambition for organizational change (Hammer and Champy, 1993). Furthermore, many fail to comprehend the degree of change required, not only in business processes, but also in managerial behaviour and organizational structure. Piecemeal approaches mean that gains in individual processes fail to translate into improvements in the performance of the organization as a whole. Top management often fails to clearly define future operations, and the extent to which competitive edge requires superior customer service, manufacturing efficiency, or innovation. Reengineering often addresses non-critical business activities. Only when the 'value proposition' has been set – 'a statement of the distinctive value the organization proposes to deliver to customers' – can the core business processes be accurately defined. Arguably, therefore, some BPR initiatives are being adopted either to gain publicity, or to further the careers of senior managers acting as the change agents. In addition, Champy (1993) cites a number of early-warning signs of failure: inadequate management attention and a lack of direct involvement by senior management; inadequate urgency leading to a lack of delivery; inadequate focus on core processes – any greater subdivision than five could lead to cross-functional performance improvements being missed.

Management leadership skills, knowledge, and ability are regarded as key success factors (Hammer and Champy, 1993). A number of common errors explain why an estimated 70 per cent of reengineering programmes fail to achieve the desired results. For example, by automating existing processes, organizations may avoid the total expense of having to redesign and reengineer. Work processes remain the same, down-sizing takes place, and the remaining workforce undergo temporary training aimed at motivating them. On the other hand, organizations may attempt to reengineer without anticipating that resistance to change will be likely. This, combined with the tendency of organizations to concentrate on process mapping rather than redesign, can lead to reengineering taking longer to implement than the one year recommended.

Management may confuse reengineering with other business improvement programmes such as TQM and quality circles. Consequently, processes may not be accurately identified; and organizations may tinker with aspects of business considered easier to change, and from which performance improvements are easier to measure (Hammer, 1990). Often aligned with BS5750 (ISO9000), process rationalization and automation have not yielded the dramatic improvements organizations expect.

Short-run financial pressures on management mitigate against the longer term returns of reengineering; profit and earnings per share take precedence over market share and competitive positioning. Consequently, many BPR initiatives experience the twin problems of a lack of allocated resources (Moad, 1993), and pressure to abandon the programme. By implication, resources include senior management time. Without guidance and direction from the top, change is unlikely to be forthcoming (although, some reengineering programmes have been successfully initiated by the IT department, when senior management is receptive to change and encourages bottom-up decision making). Reengineering requires consideration of jobs, structures, values, beliefs, and management and measurement systems, in addition to process redesign. Unless all the features of the 'business diamond' are considered equally, reengineering will not achieve change throughout the organization. Similarly, a lack of focus on specific reengineering projects distracts people from the main objectives of the organization.

A narrow problem definition, arising from management myopia, empire building, or cultural barriers to change, limits the scope of reengineering. Senior managers, insulated from day-to-day operations, and unable to envisage the processes of change, are unlikely to be capable of 'championing' a reengineering programme. Unless other managers can persuade their superiors of its value, organizations will not reengineer; reengineering cannot be driven from the bottom, due to the need for a broad view of the organization, and top-level guidance to promote cross-functional involvement.

Evaluating business process reengineering

Success equates not only with profit and shareholder earnings, but with market share, image, and external perceptions. Organizations aiming to reposition products and services in the market use BPR as the means not only for achieving the requisite change, but also to promote corporate achievements internally and externally. Current interest in BPR has been triggered by widespread media interest. In addition, conferences to advise organizations on how to initiate and run BPR programmes have eliminated myths and exposed the benefits of starting over and reassessing corporate strategy. Although organizations are increasingly involved in analysing the strategic manoeuvring of competitors, the role of consultants as promoters of BPR should not be underestimated. As in the cases of BS5750, TQM, and other trends, consultancy firms receive indirect publicity and gain vicariously through the success of clients. Advertising campaigns, coinciding with media publicity and conferences, have contributed to the high profile of BPR in promising a panacea for postmodern industrialization.

Western organizations have been critically analysing their business processes following a relative decline in commercial performance. Whether BPR will provide them with the means to sustain a competitive advantage depends, to an extent, on whether management is intelligent in initiating and implementing it. Irrespective of how promising BPR appears to be, management must dispense with its prejudices and aims towards self-aggrandizement. BPR programmes should not provide a means for empire building. Yet, BPR requires top-level leadership able to inspire the management and workforce to achieve higher returns and greater flexibility and efficiency by increasing customer orientation. However, if customer focus determines the direction of reengineered organizations, and financial targets remain the bases for performance evaluation, agreement must be reached on resource allocation if BPR is to be successful. Consistently, the commitment and authority of management is required to ensure that the necessary changes are made, and that the course does not deviate when success is not instant.

Clearly, a balance must be struck between maintaining the authority of management and empowering the workforce to make decisions and become more self-sufficient and self-determining. In many cases, a substantial change in the senior management team has been necessary during reengineering. Unable to envisage a way forward, and perceiving a personal threat to status and authority, senior managers have consistently balked at the extent of the changes necessitated by BPR. Conversely, however, BPR has significantly enhanced not only the image of organizations but also the personal images of the champions.

Measuring the success of reengineering has proved problematic. Whether organizations who say they are undertaking BPR are actually doing so is a matter of subjective assessment – publicity should not be taken at face value, particularly if fact and opinion both suggest that BPR is a flash in the pan, and merely aimed at enhancing the profile of organizations and consultants. However, if reengineering is a long-term phenomenon, the results of which may take ten years to become apparent, the results of UK initiatives are too early to evaluate.

Conclusions

This chapter has investigated the experiences of three organizations undertaking BPR and has focused on the role of IT in their programmes. According to Davenport and Short (1990), IT and BPR have a recursive relationship. On the one hand, IT usage should be determined on the basis of how well it supports redesigned business processes. On the other, BPR should be considered within the realms offered by IT. The combination of IT and BPR presents commercial organizations with the opportunity to radically change the way in which business is conducted. The increasing complexity of the environment has presented organizations with new threats and challenges. The need to maximize the performance of interrelated activities rather than individual business functions, combined with the opportunities offered by IT, has meant that a new approach to the coordination of processes across organizations is necessary to achieve a sustainable competitive advantage. Consequently, organizations need to ensure the close alignment of IT with business strategy; the latter being derived in the context of the changing commercial environment.

The following steps of process redesign are crucial to the success of BPR:

- develop business vision and process objectives;
- identify processes to be redesigned;
- understand and measure the existing process;
- identify IT levers;

- design and build a prototype.

However, without the strategic vision and substantial resource commitment from senior management, the success of reengineering will be limited. Following reengineering, organizations have encountered further problems which require resolution to ensure the long-term impact of BPR:

- Continuous process improvement is vital to the future of the organization;
- Changes are necessary in organizational structure;
- New skill requirements arise as a result of extending the scope of workforce activities and responsibilities;
- The responsibility of monitoring IT-enabled BPR should remain in the hands of process owners, but should be coordinated by IT strategists;
- The future direction of IT infrastructure should be ratified at the highest levels to ensure that an adequate commitment of financial resources is made.

As shown here, the long term and radical nature of BPR has resulted in a diversity of experiences. The interpretation of BPR within each organization determines the pace and impact of changes; BPR has been particularly successful in service and financial organizations, which have traditionally relied on IT. The role of IT differs in accordance with the ambition of management to utilize IT capabilities in the reengineered processes, as well as the extent and sophistication of IT application prior to reengineering. Organizations need to keep abreast of changes in technology which could improve their ability to compete – in many cases, the pre-emptive and ambitious use of state of the art and breakthrough technology has rendered a competitive advantage which, when applied to reengineered business processes, places the organization ahead of the competition.

Whether some organizations are reengineering or not is difficult to evaluate – only with insight before, during, and after can an accurate assessment be made. Scepticism about BPR has developed largely as a result of excessive emphasis being placed on publicity-seeking organizations. It is arguable that BPR is regarded by many organizations as a means of gaining external influence. If BPR proves to be a short-term phenomenon, such publicity will probably have been of benefit, as organizations will have nothing to prove. On the other hand, if BPR becomes a popular long-run approach to aligning IT and business strategy, organizations will have to prove their assertions are genuine. Whether BPR will have a significant impact on the prosperity of organizations will not be known for some time. Analysis of organizations currently undertaking BPR provides material for future research, especially with respect to the availability and application of advanced technology in the development of information systems. In addition, reengineered organizations may provide the opportunity to develop models and frameworks applicable to specific business domains.

References

Butler, D. (1992). A soft option for investment. *Management Today*, November, pp. 100–101.

Champy, J. (1993). Sculptors in Jelly. *Financial Times*, 28 July.

Classe, A. (1993). Don't tinker with it: BPR it! *Accountancy*, July, pp. 64–66.

Davenport, T. H. and Short, J. E. (1990). The new industrial engineering: Information technology and business process redesign. *Sloan Management Review*, **31**(4), pp. 11–27.

Taking it from the top. *Financial Times*, 5 July 1993.

A clean break with tradition. *Financial Times,* 12 July 1993.

Culture Vultures. *Financial Times,* 23 July 1993.

Hammer, M. (1990). Re-engineering work: Don't automate, obliterate. *Harvard Business Review*, July–August, pp.104–112.

Hammer, M. and Champy, J. (1993). *Re-engineering the Corporation: A Manifesto for Business Revolution*. Nicholas, London.

Moad, J. (1993). Does re-engineering really work? *Datamation*

10 IT Based-business process redesign: theoretical foundations, examples and critical assessment

Claudia Loebbecke
University of Cologne
Philip Powell
Warwick Business School

In order to cope with an increasingly turbulent business environment many organizations are rethinking their management and their business processes. They aim to simplify working procedures and improve their communications and co-ordination both internally and with their business partners. Information technology (IT) is used increasingly as an integral part of such business process redesign (BPR) efforts. Beyond simply supporting existing processes, it is applied to create new process design options. Despite many failures, there are numerous organizations especially those that have used IT to redesign customer-driven processes, which have benefited enormously. They have improved their product/service quality, respond faster to customer demands and to competition and, in some cases, have increased their innovation capabilities.

This chapter provides an overview of the BPR concept, addresses the role of IT in business process redesign and discusses pertinent management issues. Selected illustrative examples from different business sectors are presented. Finally, a critical assessment of the BPR concept and its practical impact are provided.

Introduction

The increasing complexity of the business environment presents organizations with new threats and challenges. The need to maximize the performance of interrelated activities rather than individual business functions, combined with the opportunities offered by IT, means that a new approach to the co-ordination of processes across organizations is necessary to achieve sustainable competitive advantage. Consequently, organizations need to ensure the close alignment of IT with business strategy; the latter being formulated in the context of a changing commercial environment.

Organizations have initiated change in traditional internal structures and cultures that are incapable of responding fast enough to a fluid competitive environment. Focusing on the needs of major customers, they redesign their processes along core business lines. Functional hierarchies are replaced by cross-functional business units based on product groups, market segments, or customer services, each with their own profit responsibilities. These are backed by redesigned information systems.

BPR: what, why, how

Business processes are sets of logically related tasks performed to achieve a defined business outcome. They have two important characteristics: they have customers, who may be internal or external to the firm; and they usually cross organizational boundaries, that is, they occur across or between organizational subunits. Examples of business processes include the development of a new product, the ordering of goods from a supplier, the creation of a marketing plan, and the writing of a proposal for a contract. A set of such processes forms a business system.

The essence of BPR is a radical change in the way in which organizations perform business activities; 'the fundamental rethinking and radical redesign of business processes to achieve dramatic improvements in critical, contemporary measures of performance, such as cost, quality, service, and speed' (Hammer and Champy, 1993, pp. 31–2). The model of business process redesign developed by Hammer and Champy describes the characteristic of redesigned processes as one in which several jobs are combined, with a 'case worker' responsible for a process. 'Case teams' develop innovative ways to improve service, quality, and reduce costs and cycle times. Process integration means that fewer controls and checks are necessary, and defects are minimized by those responsible for the finished product participating in the entire process.

Under BPR initiatives, sequential operations involving reporting lines and rigid procedures are rationalized into parallel processes. Concentrating on value adding activities, critical business processes are automated, and a number of activities eliminated. Customer service teams are created to maintain and develop the focus on future business. Team facilitators have a role in coaching team members, resolving conflicts, and rectifying operational problems. Continuous improvement is the prevailing philosophy, and empowerment of the workforce pushes responsibility down the organizational hierarchy. Frequently, the basis of redesign is established through a team building approach, continuous improvement, training programmes, and resultant workforce empowerment.

Bui (1995) outlines the integration of three 'redesign' efforts currently being undertaken:

1 Business scope redesign' represented by business networking activities, frequently resulting in more or less virtual enterprises.
2 'Business network redesign' following the notion of any time and any place and leading to electronic market places.
3 'Business process redesign' which he characterizes as capability teaming, resulting in lean, agile and robust companies.

Venkatraman (1990 and 1994) places IT-based BPR as the third level of IT-induced business reconfigurations which range from localized exploitation, internal integration, BPR, business network redesign, through to business scope redefinition. As a major BPR success factor he stresses the need for aligning the IT infrastructure and business process.

According to Oesterle (1996, p.16), business engineering is a 'method-based approach to transformation with the goal of incorporating the transition to the networked enterprise within the business strategy, as well as implementing the strategy within processes and providing it with information support systems'.

In general, organizations redesign for four reasons:

1 They face commercial difficulties and thus have no alternative.
2 Competitive forces present problems unless the organization takes radical steps to re-align business processes with their strategic position.
3 Management sees redesign as an opportunity to steal a lead over the competition.
4 Tremendous publicity about BPR prompts some organizations to attempt that which has purportedly been undertaken successfully by others.

To achieve BPR-objectives, Davenport and Short (1990) suggest the following steps:

● *Develop business vision and process objectives*
Instead of simple task rationalization, a redesign of entire business

processes should be considered with a specific business vision and related, prioritized objectives. Such specific BPR objectives may be, but are not limited to, cost reduction (important in combination with others, but insufficient in itself), time reduction, quality improvement, and/or employee empowerment, learning, and improved quality of work life. It is rarely possible to optimize all these objectives simultaneously. However, tangible and measurable benefits can and have to be achieved in order to make any BPR exercise successful.

- *Identify processes to be redesigned*
  Organizations should select a few key processes for their initial BPR efforts. They may decide on those experiencing the severest problems; those with the greatest impact on customers; or, those in which success is likely to be achieved most quickly. However, redesign remains a continuous programme; once the organization starts to redesign and achieve success, the process of continuous improvement must be a constant focus.

- *Understand and measure existing processes*
  The major reasons for understanding and measuring processes are:

  1 That problems must be understood so that they are not replicated.
  2 That accurate measurement can serve as a baseline for future improvements.

- *Identify IT levers*
  The common traditional approach consists of, first, determining the business requirements of a function or a process and then developing appropriate IT systems. However, an awareness of IT capabilities can and should influence the process design.Therefore, the role of IT in a process needs to be considered in the early stages of its redesign. IT is a powerful enabler and thus it deserves its own step in the process redesign. IT can create new process design options beyond just simplifying or supporting existing ones.[1]

- *Design and build a prototype of the process*
  The idea is to design and implement a prototype of a new process, perhaps first in parallel with existing processes. The prototype should then be examined for problems and achievements, and modified as necessary. Only as new process approaches broad acceptance and measurable improvements will it be phased into full implementation.

The role of IT in BPR-initiatives

According to Davenport and Short (1990), IT and BPR have a recursive relationship. On one hand, IT use should be determined on the basis of how well

---

[1] For the organizational impact of IT capabilities, see Davenport and Short, (1990) p.17.

it supports redesigned business processes (that is, IT as tool and infrastructure to support BPR). On the other, BPR should be considered within the realms offered by IT (that is, BPR as a management approach to improve IT). The combination of IT and BPR presents organizations with an opportunity to change radically the way in which business is conducted (Bjorn-Andersen and Chatfield, 1996; Cash et al., 1992).

Table 10.1 presents an overview of IT-based changes to the work process as suggested by Hammer in 1990. Many of the aspects – old rules, disruptive technologies, and new rules – have in the meantime been discussed in-depth, experimented with, fully implemented, and perhaps already eliminated (for example, expert systems have never or not yet achieved their promise). Nevertheless, the table provides a valuable starting point by outlining the concepts and technologies to consider in potential BPR projects: maturity in the literature does not necessarily imply the same issues are outdated in practice.

Pertinent management issues

Management leadership skills, knowledge, and ability are regarded as key success factors (Hammer and Champy, 1993). However, the estimated 70 per cent of redesign programmes that fail to achieve the desired results (Bashein et al., 1993) should serve as a warning to those organizations that may attempt redesign without anticipating the many potential problems, not least that resistance to change is likely.

Following redesign, organizations have encountered problems which require resolution to ensure the long term impact of BPR. These include that: continuous process improvement is vital to the future of the organization, changes are necessary in organizational structure; new skill requirements arise as a result of extending the scope of workforce activities and responsibilities; the responsibility of monitoring IT-enabled BPR should remain in the hands of process owners, but should be co-ordinated by IT strategists and; the future direction of IT infrastructure should be ratified at the highest levels to ensure that an adequate commitment of financial resources is made (Visick, Powell and Avison, 1999; Davenport and Short 1990).

General management and human resource management are key issues concerning both employee groups – those having to cope with the redesigned business processes and the IT personnel. 'Business as usual', a poor selection of key managers, group pathology, and low morale endanger the success of IT-based BPR (Bui, 1995). To avoid such problems in striving for the long term success of BPR efforts, organizations therefore need:

● To have BPR assigned as a top priority by senior management.

Table 10.1 *Changes in work through IT (adapted from Hammer, 1990)*

Old rules	Disruptive technologies	New rules
Information can appear in only one place at a time	Shared data bases	Information can appear simultaneously in as many places as it is needed
Only experts can perform complex work	Expert systems	A generalist can do the work of an expert
Businesses must choose between centralization and decentralization	Telecommunications network	Businesses can simultaneously reap the benefits of centralization and decentralization
Managers make all decisions	Decision support systems, data base access, modelling software	Decision making is part of everyone's job
Field personnel need offices where they can receive, store, retrieve, and transmit information	Wireless data communication and portable computers	Field personnel can send and receive information wherever they are
The best contact with a potential buyer is personal contact	Interactive video disk, world wide web	The best contact with a potential buyer is effective contact
You have to find out where things are	Automatic identification and tracking technology	Things tell you where they are
Plans get revised periodically	High-performance computing	Plans get revised instantaneously

- Leadership; exhibited as ownership of responsibility, intelligence, commitment to a shared vision.
- Repeated and thorough communication and discussion; involving future directions – risks and opportunities, expectations of people and organization(s), and clear management plans, even when things go wrong.

- To create a team of winners; requiring increased discretionary decision making authority, increased access or control over resources, and improved opportunity for upward mobility.
- To select good leaders; these need vision and proper priorities, sufficient interpersonal fit, to promote team work – participation, to promote productive empowerment.
- To design and implement a monitoring process.

Examples of IT-based BPR-initiatives

The long-term and radical nature of IT-based BPR has resulted in a diversity of experiences. The role of IT differs in accordance with the business sector, the ambition of management to utilize IT capabilities in the redesigned business processes, as well as the extent and sophistication of IT application prior to redesign (Visick, Powell and Avison, 1999). This section presents illustrations from three IT-based BPR initiatives that differ in these three dimensions (see Table 10.2).

Table 10.2 *Examples of IT-based initiatives*

	Business sector	Management ambition to utilize IT	Extent of previous IT-application
CompuNet	System services	high	high
Gerling	Financial services	medium - high	medium
KHD	Manufacturing	high	low

IT-based BPR in the service sector: the example of CompuNet[2]

CompuNet is the leader in reselling, networking, maintaining and supporting personal computers in Germany. With nineteen subsidiaries in eighteen locations, operating under the umbrella of a holding company, CompuNet has a turnover in excess of DM1 billion (1996). Around 75 per cent of CompuNet's approximately 1200 employees work in service-related positions, including the technical customer service division. Since CompuNet clients increasingly consider their IT infrastructure as a competitive necessity (a quasi commodity), the company pursues a strategy of cost leadership, focusing on delivering quality service at low cost.

---

[2] For a more detailed discussion of CompuNet's BPR efforts see Loebbecke, C., Jelassi, T. (1997a), an in-depth company background is provided in Loebbecke, C., Jelassi, T. (1996).

As a multi-vendor system integrator and maintenance company, CompuNet has recently managed several BPR efforts to prepare itself proactively for the competitive environment in the fast developing system service market. As Jost Stollmann, CompuNet's Chief Executive Officer, states 'the goal of our business process redesign effort is to provide top-quality service in system support as a standardized, industrialized product.

The baseline: SAP, Lotus Notes and competitive pressure

In 1988, CompuNet first installed SAP, and soon after this application package was turned into a company-wide IT platform for all business processes (accounting, inventory control, invoicing, purchasing, etc.). The system's ability to provide real-time information on all relevant business processes tremendously enhanced the transparency of corporate transactions.

Further, CompuNet was one of the first extensive Lotus Notes users in Germany. All employees use the package as the basis for their inter-office communication. Crucial for CompuNet's decision to implement Lotus Notes was its ability to support integrated work processes (document management, process monitoring, and 'workgroup computing'). Hence, geographical dispersion loses importance and departments are turned into logical units.

In order to compete in a demanding business environment, CompuNet recognized the need to streamline its business processes not only internally, but in relation to its customers and suppliers. They realized the potential of providing customers of multi-vendor systems with a comprehensive guarantee and efficient support management.

Rebundling customer service processes

In early 1992, CompuNet started to redesign completely its value chain through simplification of its core service activities. The approach consisted of redesigning business processes to follow standardized SAP procedures for all business transactions. The central concept was to purchase all products without any guarantee rights at lower prices in order to remove CompuNet's obligation to process individual reimbursements of guarantee claims with the manufacturer, and to introduce the concept of 'guarantee bundling'. Since October 1992, all CompuNet products have been delivered with a new 'Life Cycle Guarantee'. It runs for 48 months, which corresponds to the expected life cycle of the hardware and covers repair, travel expenses for technicians, spare parts and all other costs related to equipment damages. When CompuNet's service centre agents key in a given PC serial number, information about the corresponding product and customer is automatically extracted and displayed. Thus, the PC serial number has become the customer's entry 'ticket' to the service centre, and every customer has only one contact person within CompuNet.

The benefits are that time-consuming searches for delivery notes and invoices are eliminated. Cutomers benefit from a real-time guarantee application within contracted time windows which simplifies their guarantee procedures and reduces their overall IT management costs. For CompuNet, the BPR effort has simplified significantly its core activities. Various guarantee-related transactions within the company, as well as with suppliers and customers, are eliminated, thereby reducing CompuNet's maintenance costs by 66–75 per cent.

Reshaping internal service management processes

With the introduction of the Life Cycle Guarantee and the resulting process simplifications, CompuNet's service business has dramatically increased. Offering service as a standardized 'product' is difficult. The main challenge is to maintain a cost-efficient customer-oriented approach to service management that encompasses physically-dispersed support personnel.

CompuNet developed a service management concept, called CallAs (Call Administration System), that integrates SAP and Lotus Notes. When a customer calls CompuNet's decentralized service department to report a PC problem, they only need to provide the serial number of the broken machine. This data item allows CompuNet's service staff to access the customer information immediately and to take the necessary service action. It is also possible to find out directly when an engineer with the necessary know-how will be available, so that the customer can be informed about the date and time of the repair. The schedule of support staff is managed and the necessary spare parts allocated.

CallAS allows CompuNet to monitor pre-determined service levels and to allocate its technical field personnel accordingly. The automation of most steps in the support value chain reduces order processing time and provides continuous on-line information and control of any service activities. To leverage further its new service management application (currently under development) CompuNet aims at increasing the percentage of remote services from today's level of 50 to 80–90 per cent in the near future, a figure which is already common in the US.

Conclusion

CompuNet's outstanding positioning in the PC and network integration market and its shift from sales to service orientation is built on two successful BPR-results:

1 The new packaging of products offered (e.g., the Life Cycle Guarantee).

2 The efficient and creative management of internal and external logistics based on the development and implementation of several state-of-the-art IT applications.

CompuNet, IT provides options for new service offerings and a more efficient handling of service-related business processes.

IT-based BPR in the financial sector: the example of Gerling3

Gerling is a family-owned, multinational insurance company encompassing primary insurance income of about DM7. 1 billion and the world's eighth-largest reinsurance company with a reinsurance income of about DM6.8 billion in 1993. Gerling's organizational structure in Germany consists of four hierarchical levels:

1 Corporate headquarters based in Cologne.
2 Twelve regional centres located throughout Germany.
3 Two to fifteen local branches per regional centre (giving to a total of 180 branches) each employing ten to twenty staff members.
4 Mobile field-service staff.

Across the different levels, Gerling communicates mainly within 'vertical communication clusters', for example, the headquarters communicate with a regional centre, which in turn communicates with its branches.

The baseline: corporate network and logical call centre

Gerling has focused its recent IT-based BPR initiative on implementing a 'logical call centre' and the resulting corporate network as the organizational backbone and technical enabler. The core of the system consists of an automatic number identification and the automatic call distribution system (ACD). This helps determine whether the incoming call is the result of a life or property insurance promotion or whether it is to claim a loss. Further, following the receipt of a phone call, it is possible to display relevant contract information on the service agent terminal. Incoming calls are evenly dispatched by an automatic ACD system among a group of service personnel. A system controller can monitor on the screen the capacity usage and the wait line. This feature allows him/her to increase staff during peak times by 'bringing in' non-service personnel or service personnel from other areas (for instance, life and

---

[3] For a more detailed discussion, see Loebbecke, C., Jelassi, T. (1996 and 1997b).

property insurance). The incoming calls are then automatically re-routed to them without re-dialing.

Benefits and constraints

The initial motivation for the corporate network was to reduce telephone costs. Phone calls within the geographically-spread group become just 'in-house' calls. 'Least cost routing' led to additional savings since calls to external parties are operated through the closest telephone exchange. Productivity increased through a company-wide central exchange that serves all branch offices. Economies of scale and cost advantages for all branch offices were achieved through the efficient use of net capacity and centralized appropriately dimensioned servers. More importantly, the network allows drastic shrinking of both time and distance and thus enables a better flow of information along logical dimensions among employees and between the company and its customers. Gerling has improved its service availability and quality, and achieved great synergy among employees. A centralized claim department at corporate headquarters allows customers to contact the company through a single phone number, 24 hours a day, seven days a week. Furthermore, to cope with the large number of incoming customer calls resulting from a natural disaster (like icy rain or hail), the service centre receiving the calls can re-direct them so they get evenly distributed among all call centres. The new processes also allow remote access and use of scarce expertise in solving specific customer problems. Experts can be consulted rapidly from other geographical areas in order to resolve a customer problem. Finally, the 'logical' central office registers every customer complaint and thus monitors the company's image and its perceived service quality.

From a management perspective, implementing the organizational changes has been slow. According to Gerling's Dirk Nouvortne, 'we know how to do the hard side of things, but still need to learn how to go about the soft matters. To reap the full benefits from new technologies, we've got to be prepared and willing to reorganize the structures. We need to work harder on changing the mindset of our employees. It is primarily a people issue and that's why the process is political and slow.'

Plans for continuous improvement

In the near future, Gerling aims to allow every staff member to identify him/herself at any phone within the company by inserting a 'personal phone card'. Thus, they would have all their calls directed to them and be able to make phone calls 'on their card'. The latter functionality is required for caller identification, billing, and security protocols. Furthermore, Gerling plans to extend the current voice-based corporate network by remote image-processing capabilities in order to share, on a real-time basis, documents such as electronic files containing 30 year-old correspondence (a normal feature for life insurance) among all employees, and to allow remote access of image-data-bases related to technical, transportation or art insurance categories. Another route for continuous BPR will be mobile communication technology for data applications. Almost permanent availability of sales personnel will enhance service quality and reduce the processing time of insurance applications. Each employee will have a single 'communication number' regardless of where they are located or which telecommunication infrastructure is used.

The next generation of customer-oriented business processes at Gerling will be based on digital television. While the telephone as a communication medium is a first step towards a dialogue with customers, reverse communication will be more fruitful with digital TV. Finally, Gerling's management believes that a move from passive to active call centres will strengthen further company's sales. For example, selected customers will be automatically called – the calls initialized by the active call centre – when new products that suit their specific needs become available. 'Active after-sale service' will result in automatically calling a client a number of weeks after they have signed a new insurance contract

Conclusion

For Gerling, the introduction of a logical call centre and the accompanying new business processes are a reinvention of the way of doing business. The company perceives it as a revolution that has already brought important improvements, mostly in customer-related areas. The corporate network makes knowledge and information readily available and integrates them into the company's structure. This allows employees to focus on customer needs and expectations, a key dimension of any sustainable competitive advantage.

IT-based BPR in the manufacturing sector: the example of KHD[4]

KHD (Kloeckner-Humbold-Deutz) is a leading engine manufacturer.[5] Its strength is based mainly on technological innovation and technical expertise.

---

[4] For a more detailed discussion, see Loebbecke, C. (1996).

[5] The development in 1876 of the four-stroke engine by Nikolaus August Otto (who was also the founder of KHD) was the starting point for world-wide motorization.

The company's sales volume puts it third in the world as an independent (i.e., non-captive) engine manufacturer. Their water-cooled diesel engines represent a completely new production line.

KHD has concentrated its recent IT-based BPR initiative on internal and external logistic processes in its new engine production facility which is considered one of the most modern in the world. The company aims to standardize its production programme, ensuring a maximum percentage of common parts, and to gain from synergy effects in world-wide procurement. It wants to intensify collaboration between development and manufacturing, materials management as well as control and logistics. All sectors are involved throughout the process from the initial product idea to the finished goods/service, including the determination of target costs.

The baseline: a new engine factory with an outsourced distribution centre

In addition to the advantages of large-scale serial production (low cost and short delivery times), the business processes in the new factory – combining stand assembly and progressive assembly – increase speed and flexibility. Limiting the production to only four key components, manufactured in-house, enables KHD to cope with the complexity of the production process (lean production).

In the progressive assembly, robots are used for difficult or monotonous processes that require high levels of precision, such as tightening screws, measuring or controlling, and they also offer high process security. Using experience and intuition, employees ensure speed, flexibility and quality.

In the stand assembly where engines are manually customized, automation is very low. Each engine has its own container with all the parts needed to complete it. To compensate for the different assembly times of the approximately 4000 engines, a buffer zone for 170 engines (i.e., equivalent to 50 per cent of production volume) was added before the test floor.

There are no timed assembly lines. Employees work in small teams which control a certain process and largely organize their own workflow. All the data required for certain tasks is displayed on monitors and the necessary material is ordered on-line via electronic data interchange (EDI). Data throughput is almost fully automated. Employees control the production quality so as to deliver only 'perfect' material to customers – who are often the next group in the production process just a few metres away. Maintenance staff are also integrated into the teams. Team-members' wages differ depending on the quality and quantity achieved by each.

KHD has opted to outsource components' purchase and distribution. 'Stute', the forwarding agent, built a distribution-centre 12 km from the factory specially designed for KHD's diesel engines. Every 20 minutes a truck shuttles back and forth between the centre and the factory, and each day approximately 2000 boxes and numerous engines are moved. The centre is electronically connected to KHD and manages the stocking of purchased parts and self-made components as well as the shuttle to the factory. It is also responsible for collecting finished engines, storing them, and then distribution to customers.

Continuous material flow at the core of new logistic processes

Assembly components are delivered just-in-time by 'Stute' with special roll-on/roll-off shuttle trucks: the trucks dock directly to the loading-ramps of the distribution centre or the factory. A transportation line on the truck moves the goods on or off the loading ramps. The whole loading and unloading process takes just five minutes. Data exists only in electronic form, delivered components are identified by bar-code scanners and automatically transported to the progressive assembly. The scanners also transmit components' information to the assembly host system where it is first checked and then forwarded to the material handling system. A transportation-order is generated and transmitted via infra-red light to an automatically-guided vehicle (AGV). The AGVs move through the factory taking boxes to the assembly and buffer areas.

The material flow within the production processes is completely automated, the average material turnover in the factory is four hours. Without hidden material buffers, material flow is constrained by the small store capacity. From entering to leaving the factory the actual material processing time is approximately 50 per cent.

The new internal logistic processes are based on five key elements:

- All necessary material for an engine is available before production.
- The maximum realization time between a material order (from external stock at the distribution centre) and the beginning of assembly is 3 hours.
- The material stored in the containers next to the assembly lines is included in the material stock.
- The inventory is managed by stock- and assembly-quantities.
- The material buffers next to the assembly lines cover a maximum of 4 hour.

The smooth functioning of the logistics substantially contributes to price-sensitive, rapid, and customer-oriented production. However, the tight inter-dependence between the processes increases the risk of interruptions, caused either by man or machine. In particular, the interfaces between logistics and the other production processes require a strong degree of co-operation and co-ordination. The completely automated material flow in the factory demands a detailed planning of containers (including their size, weight and label) during process planning. The short production lead times require a precise delivery of purchased goods (in terms of time and quantity). Hence, each component is marked using short codes so it can be easily handled in the factory.

There are few other businesses which have automated their material flow so thoroughly and with so much impact. KHD's new approach to logistics follows market/customer needs. The development of new engines requires production processes tailored to logistics and the mangement of variants becomes crucial. A compromise between conflicting objectives – mainly customer needs and competitive pricing – is needed at all stages

Conclusion

KHD has shown remarkable creativity in its BPR efforts. It integrates a vast amount of logistical know-how in combination with state-of-the-art IT. The high degree of customization offered by the stand assembly provides the company with a sustainable competitive edge since most competitors only offer 'off-the-shelf' engines.

While EDI-based business processes are not yet widely applied within the production chain of machines with diesel engines, KHD demonstrates the potential of EDI-based business processes within a company or even within a production facility. This potential also occurs if adjustments at the company's boundary is to be achieved 'manually', engine by engine.

Critical assessment of IT-based BPR-initiatives

Critical success factors, used to evaluate the success of redesign initiatives, usually comprise: customer satisfaction; net profit and return on capital; expertise in credit and risk management; staff satisfaction; and asset valuation. In a business case, evaluation of the redesign programme's progress largely uses financial measures; net profit, return on sales, and return on capital.

In terms of production processes, cycle times, stock levels, and work in progress usually fall, and the quality of finished goods improves. However, often the expected financial results do not appear because senior managers lack the ambition for organizational change (Hammer and Champy, 1993). Further, many companies fail to comprehend the degree of change required, not only in business processes, but also in managerial behaviour and organizational structure. Gains in individual processes fail to translate into improvements in the performance of the organization as a whole. Also, redesign often addresses non-critical business activities. Only when the value proposition has been set – a statement of the distinctive value the organization proposes to deliver to customers (McKinsey) – can the core business processes be defined accurately. Short run financial pressures, often accompanied by a lack of allocated resources (Moad, 1993) mitigate against the longer term returns of redesign; profit and earnings per share take precedence over market share and competitive positioning. Successful redesign implies consideration of jobs, structure, values, beliefs, and management and measurement systems. Unless all these features are considered together, the necessary change cannot be achieved throughout the organization.

Hence, measuring the success of BPR initiatives has proved problematic. Indeed, whether organizations who say they are undertaking BPR are actually doing so is a matter of subjective assessment (Visick, Powell and Avison 1999). However, if BPR is a long term phenomenon, the results of which may take ten years to become apparent, the results of rather recent initiatives are too early to evaluate.

Outlook

IT-based BPR has been theoretically examined and widely endorsed by the research community, consulting firms, and many organizations in various business sectors, sizes, geographical locations, and strategic visions. However, the theoretically sound approach to IT-based BPR still raises major problems in the real world. 'Knowing how to do it' and 'actually doing it' are still worlds apart. While information and communication technologies for new business processes have been available at least since the early 1990s, practice shows that restructuring organizations who attempt to implement innovative information systems and employment schemes have set themselves a challenging task. The redesign of organizations and complete economies is an on-going effort that often takes significantly longer than planned or expected.

Nevertheless, IT-based BPR initiatives are in progress in most sectors, though sometimes under a different name. In the long run, there seems little doubt that IT will lead the industrial society into an information society. On the way, it will profitably reshape internal business processes and inter-company processes.

References

Bashein B., Markus M. L. and Riley P. (1993) *Business Process Reengineering: Roles for IT and IS Professionals*, Working Paper, Claremont Graduate School.

Benjamin, R. L., Levinson E. (1993). A Framework for Managing IT-Enabled Change, *Sloan Management Review*, Summer, pp. 23–33.

Bjorn-Andersen, N. and Chatfield, A. (1996). Driving organizational transformation through the use of inter-organizational systems (IOS), *EDI–IOS (Electronic Data Interchange – Interorganizational Systems) Conference*,

Electronic Commerce for Trade Efficiency and Effectiveness, Bled, Slovenia, June, pp. 520–38.

Bui, T. (1995). *Business Process Re-Engineering*, Working Paper, Hong Kong University of Science and Technology.

Cash, J., McFarlan, W., McKenney, J. L. and Applegate, L. (1992). *Corporate Information Systems*, 3rd Edition, Irwin.

Davenport, T. H. and Short, J. E. (1990). The New Industrial Engineering: Information Technology and Business Process Redesign, *Sloan Management Review*, **31**(4), pp. 11–27.

Hammer, M. (1990). Re-engineering work: don't automate, obliterate, *Harvard Business Review*, July–August, pp. 104–12.

Hammer, M. and Champy, J. (1993). *Re-engineering the corporation: a manifesto for business revolution*, Nicolas, London.

Loebbecke, C. (1996). Innovative IT-based Logistics – KHD's 'Vision 2000' engine factory, *EDI–IOS (Electronic Data Interchange – Interorganizational Systems) Conference, Electronic Commerce for Trade Efficiency and Effectiveness*, Bled, Slovenia, June, pp. 123–41.

Loebbecke, C. and Jelassi, T. (1994). Business Value of Information Technology: The CompuNet Case, in: T. Jelassi (ed) *Strategic Management of Information Technology: Some European Case Studies*, Prentice-Hall, pp. 123–46.

Loebbecke, C. and Jelassi, T. (1996). Building the 'virtual' organization at Gerling, in: *Proceedings of the Fourth European Conference of Information Systems* (ECIS), Lisbon, Portugal, July, pp. 1245–57.

Loebbecke, C. and Jelassi, T. (1997a). Business Process Redesign at CompuNet – Standardizing Top-Quality Service Through Information Technology, *Journal of Strategic Information Systems* (forthcoming).

Loebbecke, C. and Jelassi, T. (1997b). Concepts and technologies for virtual organizing: the Gerling journey, *European Management Journal*, **15**(2) (forthcoming).

Moad J. (1993). Does Re-engineering really work?, *Datamation*, **39**(15), pp. 22–8.

Oesterle, H. (1996). Business Engineering: Transition to the Networked Enterprise, *Electronic Markets*, **6**(2), 1996, pp. 14–16.

Venkatraman N. (1991). The IT-induced Business Reconfiguration, in: M. Scott-Morton (ed.) *The Corporation of the 1990s*, Oxford University Press, New York, pp. 122–158.

Venkatraman N. (1994). IT-enabled Business Transformation: from Automation to Business Scope Redefinition, *Sloan Management Review*, Winter, pp. 73–87.

Visick, E., Powell, P. and Avison, D. (1999). Strategic Aspects of Business Process Re-Engineering UK Experiences, in: D. Anketall (ed.), *Managing Change in Living Systems*, Institute of Management Consultants IT SIG.

Part Three
Managing the IS Resource

Philip Powell

This part is concerned with managing information systems. Information systems are difficult to manage both as projects and as a function. While planning can assist in reducing the chances of project failure, management of the IS function entails all the problems of managing a fast changing service organization. These problems are not helped by the poor perception of the IS function in many organizations and senior management's inability to understand its role. Key to improving this is learning lessons from one's own and other organizations.

The chapter by Greenwood and Grimshaw focuses on the role of implementation. Too often implementing – getting the new systems into the organization and making sure they are used effectively – is ignored by developers. Developers concentrate on the system and not its impacts, and the users who are often only tangentially involved in producing the systems and have unrealistic expectations, both good and bad, of what the outcome may be. An implementation driven strategy, as advocated here, is one way forward. The chapter also highlights some of the additional differences that arise in smaller firms. Resource constraints especially of specialist personnel can endanger small firms' efforts. Getting outside assistance, independent from the developers, can provide a valuable new perspective on problems.

The chapter by Philips, Howells and Targett records how a UK utility undertook the development of an information systems strategy. It stresses the interdependence of strategy development, delivery and control. Despite years of discussion about the need for businesses to align what they do with IS with their corporate strategy, few seem to try and even fewer achieve it. Alignment, quite easy to do on paper, often is missing in real life as the strategy changes, it is often not communicated to those trying to build the systems, and there is a lack of appreciation about what IT might do for (and to) the business.

Managing an information systems function proves to be as difficult as getting the IT right in the first place. As businesses become more dependent on their data and on their systems so the need to ensure continuity of service becomes paramount. Disaster recovery has often been the poor relation of other, more glamorous, aspects of IT. Yet, there are many salutary lessons out there which should inspire senior executives to give it more attention. The chapter by Grant and Levy shows how one major retail bank, critically dependent on its systems, undertook the task on ensuring that business continuity planning was driven by corporate strategic requirements. It illustrates how success in the development of disaster recovery systems is critically dependent on management across a large number of other stakeholders in the business.

Alston and Martin report on a failure. Despite the many well-known failures (London Ambulance, London Stock Exchange to name but two), there are not that many detailed analyses of failure. Failure (especially that of others) is a great learning tool. The chapter uses one of the most comprehensive and detailed models of IS success and failure, the 3D Model, to try to understand what went wrong and why. In short, this system lacked need and support but, by undertaking a pilot, the firm involved managed to avoid a much more expensive failure. However, too often, IS projects seem to take on a life of their own and even though most participants are unsure, uncommitted or even opposed, they continue until a big crash. Prototyping will help to avoid this.

11 Driving IS strategy at an SME

David E. Greenwood and David J. Grimshaw
Cranfield School of Management, Cranfield University

Introduction

Implementation is often seen as less glamorous than strategy – the literature is overflowing with papers on information systems strategy yet few mention implementation. This chapter argues that to overcome many of the barriers to implementation (Wilson, 1989) there is a case for using implementation as a driver of strategy. In this way, implementation considerations such as top management support, user participation, etc. are built in to the process of information systems strategy at the beginning.

The published literature surrounding the adoption of information systems strategy within small- to medium-sized companies is limited but what there is has focused strongly on the drivers, which influence investment. There is some debate as to the extent that theories concerning larger companies can be applied or adapted (Doukidis, Lybereas and Galliers, 1996). Much of the work has then attempted to characterize the key drivers influencing the sources of advice, planning and investment decisions which smaller companies employ when taking decisions about information systems.

The methodology applied to a sizeable amount of the published literature focuses on the statistical analysis of questionnaires returned by a variety of small- to medium-sized sample companies. This analysis has been presented in terms to support, or otherwise, the hypotheses promoted. Thong, Yap and Raman (1996) typify this work having considered the significance of top management support, consultant effectiveness and vendor support on user satisfaction, organizational impact and overall information system effectiveness following implementation of information systems in small businesses.

This chapter is based on a case study of Bayford Thrust, a small family owned energy business focused on downstream oil, lubricant and fuel card businesses. The company expressed a desire to review their use of information technology and wished specifically to develop an IS/IT strategy, which was related to the newly articulated business strategy. Having little expertise in this area the company approached Cranfield School of Management for assistance. The chapter explores the relationship of the emergent strategy to information systems implementation.

Company background

Bayford Thrust has supplied energy products since the 1920s and has grown through product diversification and business acquisition to a company today employing just over 100 people. The business continues under the control of second and third generation of family members with a regionally focused asset, distribution and customer base. Until recently information systems investment was very low and was focused on a key operational sales, order processing and accounting system. Ultimate responsibility for IT rests with the Finance Director, with day-to-day running of systems being left to two, part-time, data processing staff. Modest investment in information technology was sanctioned in early 1997 with a network of personal computers, personal pro- ductivity tools, and e-mail installed for twenty-five users at head office. Alongside this investment have come requests throughout the business for new developments including enhanced sales and marketing tools, mobile com- puting and wider communication links.

Until 1996, the company did not have a published business strategy. However, following publication there has been significant efforts aimed at increasing business level accountability, the reengineering of business processes and the personal development of the management team. All these culminated in demands for increased IS resources and to help manage and respond to these demands, an appointment was made in June 1997 under the Teaching Company Programme. This provided for a two-year appointment of an 'associate' responsible for IT development within the business and an aca- demic advisor at Cranfield School of Management.

The appointment was made just in time for the roll out of the PC network to be completed. Early work of the associate involved the establishment of an e- mail policy and, typical of many businesses, attention soon turned to Year 2000 compliance of the company's systems. From an audit completed shortly after- wards, it became apparent that the key sales and order processing system was not compliant and neither was the supporting accounting software. Work aimed at identifying a replacement system was soon identified as a priority and in the framework put in place to achieve this were the beginnings of an implementa- tion approach which would drive the development of an IS Strategy.

The implementation process

At a very early stage the board of directors were keen to see a participative approach adopted in which all the management team were involved. The level of expertise those individual managers possessed varied significantly, as did their exposure to the current sales and order processing system. To bring together this experience a steering group was established and the academic advisor appointed as chair. Such an appointment might be seen as appointing 'an external agent of change'. Anecdotal evidence suggested that Bayford Thrust managers had a greater propensity historically to seek advice from outside the business from vendors, consultants and so on rather than within the business. So the approach aligned well with cultural norms. This also fitted in well with the academic's aims of building up knowledge and a rapport with managers, to promote the development of an IS strategy planning process, that could be continued at the end of the Teaching Company Scheme.

In the early months of the steering group, several aspects of soft systems methodology (Checkland and Scholes, 1990) were used to help define and communicate the project structure and aims. It was also used to help define the nature of the intervention looking from the point of view of both the academic and the associate. At the initial meeting of the steering group, 'rich pictures' were used to communicate the breadth of interacting system requirements, which had already been suggested within the business. Having provided some insight into the 'big picture' using this tool it was then possible to focus users' minds on the sort of issues which would need to be considered when selecting software, not least, in this case, a need for 'open systems architecture'.

It was clear that the desire for management participation, partially at least, was driven by a desire from the board to bring about cultural change within the business. Management team training, a desire to promote empowerment and an increased orientation towards target setting and accountability, was supporting this. The project could therefore be seen both as a trial of 'empowered' participative management quite apart from the need to select a suitable product. For this approach to succeed it could be argued that any recommendation of the steering group would need to be accepted by the board.

Registering users' opinions would be an important part of the steering group process. Following the first meeting a 'wish list' of new functional requirements from the sales and order processing system was drawn up which was then brought together as an overall document for prospective suppliers. Initially eight potential suppliers were identified as potential matches for the wish list. Following discussions with these suppliers, a short matrix was produced describing the basic attributes of the products, which was then supplied to the steering group. After a second steering group meeting, these were whittled down by the group to four by excluding two bespoke suppliers, one where Year 2000 compliance could not be convincingly demonstrated and a fourth supplier where progress towards a 'Windows' environment was some way off. The remaining four suppliers consisted of the existing supplier with an updated product and three other 'industry specific' organizations.

The next task of the steering group was to agree a viable evaluation strategy where the products available could be put to the test in a business setting. What was clear from the steering group was that the evaluation of four suppliers' products was considered to be too many. Taking evaluation of the existing supplier's proposed replacement system as a given, it was generally felt that the remaining three suppliers would have to be reduced somehow. The solution was to hold a 'beauty contest' of potential suppliers to which the steering group was to be invited to attend. This resulted in invitations being issued to the remaining three companies who were asked, presenting one after each other, to compete for the opportunity to have their system evaluated.

Some of the potential benefits and pitfalls of holding such a 'beauty contest' were identified beforehand and their affects assessed. The main concern was that suppliers would attempt to 'blind' non-technical users with science instead of providing a balanced picture of the product itself. To address this, a detailed list of twenty-nine questions was drawn up by the steering group and submitted to each of the suppliers prior to the presentation. Written responses were sought and received which were then circulated to each member of the steering group two days before they were due to review the suppliers. In addition, on the day of the presentations, scoring sheets were given to the steering group members for completion immediately after the presentations had finished. The sheets required users to score twelve aspects of supplier performance as well as a straight 'yes' or 'no' to the question 'I would like this system to be evaluated at Bayford Thrust'. In the final analysis, two scoring measures were available which also acted as a low-level cross validation with each other.

The overall result of the analysis was a virtual dead heat between two of the suppliers. The points scored by each of the suppliers measured as a percentage were within 3 per cent of each other (79.68 per cent versus 77.56 per cent) whilst the whole steering group indicated a wish to evaluate the latter system and all but one indicated a wish to evaluate the former. In the final analysis, the wisdom of the steering group taking decisions on the basis of presentations could well be challenged but in this case, the requirement was to take a decision to evaluate and not to buy. In other words there was scope to rectify a mistake made later. The results of the analysis were then presented back to the steering group who accepted them. They were then formally presented to the board of directors alongside an enlarged matrix, which summarized the questionnaire responses that the suppliers had earlier provided. The board then endorsed the recommendations concerning the evaluation made by the steering group.

Figure 11.1 summarizes the key features of the emergent strategy and is a generalized version of the diagram used to present recommendations to the board.

Having embarked on the evaluation of three products, several issues arose. These were, first the suitability of the steering group to perform detailed evaluations, second the efficacy of the evaluations themselves and third an assessment of the systems in line with the declared aim of securing a system with 'open systems architecture'. This was required to achieve an ease of integration with other products and achieve low costs of ownership.

The first issue was resolved very easily as the majority of the steering group itself recognized that whilst they would have some familiarity with the system in use within their department, they would not be the best qualified of users to put it to the test. As a result, a group of experienced 'user coordinators' were appointed who were given the task of evaluating the system. The second point concerning the efficacy of the evaluations themselves was also important, particularly when focusing on the question of 'task technology fit'. A balance needed to be maintained between exposing users to as many processing options as possible whilst keeping the time required to accomplish key tasks down to an absolute minimum. As a result, the associate was trained to simulate a variety of processing environments and a higher level evaluation was

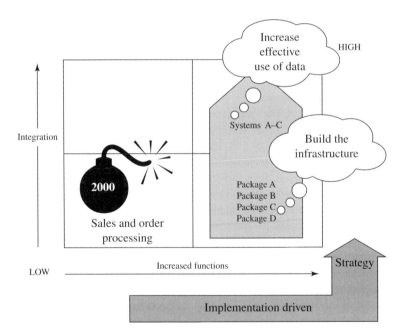

Figure 11.1 *Key features of the emergent strategy*

organized at steering group member level to determine the actual processes that should be used. The result was that the user coordinators were required to assess only a few pre-selected processing methods whilst structured feedback was obtained both at user and steering group level. Finally, the 'architecture' issue was tackled by requesting sample quotes from all of the three selected suppliers for various separate items such as for example 'on vehicle' computing. This clearly highlighted the ease by which the system could be adapted for possible competitive advantage in the future. The evaluation phase continues but it is intended that that there will be a formal analysis of the evaluation 'feedback' and a further meeting of the steering group. At that meeting it is intended that the options to select a preferred supplier then or, alternatively, to invite all three suppliers back for a final presentation and selection decision will be considered.

Some reflections on the implementation process

The application of soft systems analysis, investigating roles, norms and values throughout the intervention proved particularly valuable. This relates very closely to the roles identified by Thong, Yap and Raman (1996) in terms of top management support and external expertise although in this case, it was complemented by the roles of the steering group and user coordinators. At a broader level there was also opportunity to focus on type of forces which might have a bearing on an IS strategy adopted in the future. These are discussed in relation to the different stakeholders in the process: suppliers; the board of directors; the steering group; the academic 'external consultant'; and the user coordinators and data processing department.

As may already be apparent, all these participants worked in an organizational framework that might be regarded as far simpler than that found in many large businesses. During the intervention at Bayford Thrust, the roles and constituent members of the various groups came under a degree of analysis as links were identified between organizational structure and the intended successful implementation of an information systems strategy in the future. Making a comparison with other organizations it is clear that these factors were generally relevant to many smaller concerns. Chau (1995) found, in a survey of fifty-six small businesses, that user satisfaction and the use of information systems increased when formal systems analysis, design and implementation procedures, internal technical personnel and/or hired consultants and extensive vendor services were employed. Montazemi (1988) examined the relationship between organizational characteristics and end-user satisfaction in small businesses and concluded that the number of IS professionals, the level of user involvement, the intensity of information requirement analysis, the proportion of interactive information systems and the degree of decentralization were factors important to end-user satisfaction. Finally, the main findings of Yap, Soh and Raman (1992) were that a combination of information systems experience and knowledge of small business was essential to information system success in small business. In particular, the significant factors were consultant effectiveness, vendor support, information systems experience, sufficiency of financial resources, chief executive support and user participation. Elements of many of these forces can be seen in the intervention at Bayford Thrust and these are discussed as they apply to the different groups involved.

Suppliers

Analysis from a supplier point of view proved particularly beneficial and provided insight into past management of information systems. As was apparent from the events, Bayford Thrust was typical of organizations identified as being highly dependent on vendors in the selection of information systems (Cragg and King 1993). The literature also indicates the importance of consultants, which in this case can be seen as the role of the academic chairman of the steering group. As Thong, Yap and Raman (1994) point out however, for small businesses that want to implement basic operational systems, a vendor can provide the same level of consultancy as the specialist consultant. The processes described above undoubtedly harnessed this to a significant extent. The means by which the vendors were engaged for the evaluations is also of interest, Heintz (1981) identifed three approaches:

1 the reliance on vendor advice;
2 to start with a simple information system and take one step at a time;
3 to prepare a formal 'request for' proposal.

Whilst Heintz (1981) recommended the third approach, it is clear in this case that this engagement of suppliers to provide an evaluation system had elements of all three approaches.

Reflecting on the organizational aspects of a future information systems strategy, most significant was recognition that in the past Bayford Thrust had adopted a 'free market' approach to managing information (Parsons, 1983). Overall, this resulted in most departments initiating and funnelling through new projects for quotation by the existing supplier without restriction. Investigations showed that this proved a past source of conflict between the existing supplier and Bayford Thrust as a result of a low level of quotation uptake, and moreover, confusion as to who was managing the IT functions from the supplier's point of view. It was evident that this had damaged channels of communication to some extent and with a company dependent on a relationship with a key vendor in the future, these were issues that needed to be addressed.

Attewell's (1992) theory of technology diffusion to explain the adoption of business computing by organizations also had considerable resonance with the events described. The knowledge barrier, in this case the lack of internal information system expertise, was clearly reduced by the role of the vendors whose products were all focused on the specialist part of the energy market in which Bayford Thrust was engaged. However, a concern, to be reflected in the final choice of supplier and inevitably an influence on future strategy, was each company's anticipated commitment to this particular market segment in the future. As a result, particular attention was placed on the size of suppliers' customer bases as well as financial indicators to indicate their future viability. It was also important to identify the position of the product in the development lifecycle. Using these measures there arose in this particular case a question mark over one of the suppliers' future commitment to their product and the evaluation process provided an opportunity to assess how real this was.

The board of directors

A number of published articles cite the roles of senior executives and the chief executive officer as important determinants in the success of information system implementation. Mintzberg (1979) has described the highly centralized structures of many small businesses where chief executive officers are making most of the decisions. What is interesting in the case of Bayford Thrust is that in the interests of participative management, much of the responsibility for the evaluation of sales and order processing systems was delegated to the steering group. The board were, however, responsible for the adoption of the Teaching Company Programme within the business and through this have encouraged and supported the work aimed at developing a future information system strategy. It was also clear from the outset that the steering group was to produce a recommendation and not the final decision.

The decision to appoint a steering group could be compared with the autocratic approach adopted by some smaller business. As De Geus (1988) states:

'the level of thinking that goes on in most management groups is considered below the individual manager's capacities. Autocratic institutions will learn faster or not at all – the ability of one or a few leaders being a risky institutional bet.'

Doukidis, Lybereas and Galliers (1996) observed that:

'the organizational culture of such enterprises provides for a very flexible and effective organization. The dependence on one person, however, puts success at risk, in contrast to the collective processes where the chances of a wrong decision are deteriorated (in expense of other elements).'

Throughout the intervention, it was the determination of the board to infuse strategic direction throughout the business. Miller (1983) typified descriptions of the past very accurately describing strategy making in some small businesses as intuitive rather than analytical. The style of management performed by people who had an entrepreneurial 'feel' for their business was now observed to have been supplemented with a long-term strategic direction.

The steering group

McKeen and Guimaraes (1985) suggest that steering committees favour large projects, projects with little vertical integration, lower level projects (clerical to supervisory level), projects with formal proposals complete with cost benefit analysis, and projects which can demonstrate both tangible and intangible benefits for the organization. At Bayford Thrust the use of the group was focused on only one clearly defined project which linked the sales and order process horizontally through the organization.

Chau (1995) listed the following areas where, within other small businesses surveyed, owners and managers had very different views on the importance of factors related to their selection decision:

- The owners took more of a strategic view on software selection than managers did.
- Owners considered the factors related to the technical side of the software package much more important than those related to the non-technical side. The managers took the opposite view.
- Owners considered the price and popularity of the software package the least important factors but managers considered them some of the most important.
- The owners took significantly more serious consideration of the vendors than did the managers, particularly with their past business references and any past experience with them.
- The owners rated opinions given by in-house information experts as most important followed by external consultants and potential vendors. The managers however gave equal importance to their advice.
- The two groups diverged in their view on the importance of opinions from subordinates and outside personal acquaintances. The owners rated subordinates' opinions higher.
- Overall the owners put more emphasis on factors of a technical nature

whilst the managers weighed factors of a non-technical nature more heavily.

The above factors and the potential pitfalls at board level highlight the potential difficulties of subordinating responsibility at board level or steering group level without making one accountable to the other. The process did allow for this and the final decision will require a full exchange of views between both board and user group before a decision to adopt a particular sales and order processing system is taken.

The academic external consultant

The benefits of an academic consultant holding the chairman's role were shown clearly. Effectively fulfilling a consultancy role within the steering group, the academic was used both as a source of impartial advice, to draw steering group decisions together and to act as a link between the board and users in order to set direction and facilitate an exchange of ideas. Newpeck and Hallbauer (1981) believed that an outside consultant is imperative to making the best decisions regarding the acquisition and use of information systems. Yap, Soh and Raman (1992) re-enforced this, suggesting that information system effectiveness is positively correlated with consultant effectiveness although Thong, Yap and Raman (1994) highlighted that there is a risk that small businesses tend to overestimate the impact of external IS experts whilst underestimating the importance of their own involvement. This, as Gable (1989) points out, proves a need for pro-active top management involvement in information system implementation even when a consultant is engaged.

Reflecting on the intervention at Bayford Thrust it was clear that the academic, working with the internal teaching company associate had managed to maintain a balance between these competing forces. This was achieved by delegating day-to-day responsibility for detailed supplier liaison and user evaluation to the teaching company associate whilst maintaining the chair of the steering group and reporting back to the board at approximately fortnightly intervals.

User coordinators and the data processing department

Experienced coordinators were appointed who were familiar with the job at hand. During the evaluation it proved necessary to structure the programs they assessed very carefully. There was a concern that with too many options to evaluate, day-to-day processes might mistakenly have been thought to take too long with resulting negative feedback. Goodhue (1995) who identified that user evaluations were found to be directly influenced by system, task and individual characteristics confirmed this observation. He suggested that the value of technology did appear to depend on the tasks of a user, the user viewing their systems as tools, which assisted or hindered them in their tasks.

Alongside the evaluation performed by the data processing department it also became clear that whilst a highly competent job was being done maintaining data integrity and day-to-day processing, the role was misunderstood through the rest of the business. The efficiency of the department passing requests for new amendments to the existing system discussed earlier, for example, showed an efficient department but not one that was responsible for the strategic management of IS within the business. Unfortunately, some people within the business had mistakenly labelled the department with this role. Thus, in conclusion, it was clear that future IS planning would not only have to embrace frameworks for evaluation but also frameworks for organization.

Conclusions

The key challenge at Bayford Thrust, in common with many such small businesses, was to put in place an information systems strategy process, which could have a reasonable expectation of continuance once the teaching company scheme was complete. Discovering a Year 2000 timebomb in a key operational system was initially a setback. However, by setting in place an implementation programme to overcome this issue, there is now the basis of a process that can deliver an information system strategy. This implementation driven strategy is somewhat novel and further work is no doubt needed to refine the approach.

There will be many aspirations to be realized when the new sales and order processing system is implemented. The need to set out a framework for IS investment is, therefore, an important 'next step' which needs to start as soon as the evaluations are completed. This framework also needs to analyse the roles, which are required to support existing and future information system investment from an organizational point of view.

The intervention has shown that many of the issues and forces confronting small- and medium-sized businesses are also confronting Bayford Thrust. The evidence also shows that the culture has evolved significantly from a relatively reluctant user of information systems to one now aiming to develop a strategic framework for information system management and investment. It is clear that steering groups, the board of directors, academic support and organizational issues all have a part to play in this framework which has successfully been driven by the initial need to update a 'key operational' sales and order processing system.

References

Attewell, P. (1992). Technology diffusion and organizational learning: The case of business computing. *Organization Science*, **3**(1), pp. 1–19.

Chau, P. Y. K. (1995). Factors used in the selection of packaged software in small businesses: Views of owners and managers. *Information and Management*, **29**, pp. 71–78.

Checkland, P. and Scholes, J. (1990). *Soft Systems Methodology in Action*. John Wiley & Sons, Chichester.

Cragg, P. B., and King, M. (1993). Small firm computing motivators and inhibitors. *MIS Quarterly*, **17**(1), pp. 47–60.

De Geus, A. P. (1988). Planning as learning. *Harvard Business Review*, **66**(2), March–April, 70–74.

Doukidis, G. I., Lybereas, P. and Galliers, R. D. (1996). Information systems planning in small business: A stages of growth analysis. *Journal of Systems and Software*, **33**, pp. 189–201.

Gable, G. G. (1989). Consultant Engagement for First Time Computerization, *Proceedings of the International Conference on Organizations and Information Systems*, Bled, Yugoslavia, Sept 13–15.

Goodhue, D. L. (1995). Understanding user evaluations of information systems. *Management Science*, **41**(12), pp. 1827–1843.

Heintz, T. J. (1981). On acquiring computer services for a small business. *Small Business Management*, **19**(3), pp. 1–7.

McKeen, J. D. and Guimaraes, T. (1985). Selecting MIS projects by steering committee. *Communications of the ACM*, **28**(12), pp. 1344–1352.

Miller, D. (1983). The correlates of entrepreneurship in three types of firms. *Management Science*, **29**(7), pp. 770–791.

Mintzberg, H. (1979). *The Structure of Organizations*. Prentice-Hall, London.

Montazemi, A. R. (1988). Determinants of success for computer usage in small business. *MIS Quarterly*, **12**(1), pp. 51–61.

Newpeck, F. F. and Hallbaur, R. C. (1981). Some advice for small business considering computer acquisition. *Small Business Management*, **19**(3), pp. 17–23.

Parsons, G. L. (1983). Fitting information systems technology to the corporate needs: The linking strategy. *Harvard Business School, Teaching Note* 9-183-176.

Thong, J. Y. L., Yap, C., and Raman, K. S. (1994). Engagement of external expertise in information systems implementation. *Journal of Management Information Systems*, **11**(2), pp. 209–231.

Thong, J. Y. L., Yap, C., and Raman, K. S. (1996). Top management support, external expertise and information systems – implementation in small business. *Information Systems Research* **7**(2), pp. 248–267.

Wilson, T. D. (1989). The implementation of information systems strategies in UK companies: Aims and barriers to success. *International Journal of Information Management*, **9**, pp. 45–258.

Yap, C. S., Soh, C. P. P. and Raman, K. S. (1992). Information systems success factors in small business. *Omega,* **20**

12 Managing the IS function in a major utility

Martin Phillips, Matt Howells and David Targett
School of Management, University of Bath

Introduction

Originally the scope of this chapter was to examine lessons learned during the development of an IS (information systems) strategy for a UK utility's distribution business and to propose how to take that creative process forward into the other businesses of the company. However, the analysis revealed a number of critical interdependencies that led us to extend the scope of the chapter to those issues that would facilitate not only the production of the strategy itself but also its successful implementation.

IS strategy development has been addressed by a number of authors. We focused on four key strands. Porter's seminal work (1980) on the 'five forces' is still relevant for high level business analysis; Johnson and Scholes (1997) develop a useful set of theories and tools based around their analysis, choice, implementation model; Mintzberg (1979) remains relevant for analysis, more so for internal dynamics, although his most recent conversion to 'emergent' strategy would seem to add little to the IS world where there has to exist a certain amount of determinism in order to actually plan and build systems; the CCTA (Computer and Communication Technology Agency – formerly a part of the government and now an agency advising government departments on the use of IT) have provided a good deal of practical advice aimed at the IS practitioner.

There is little doubt that IS are a 'moving target'. The shelf life of technology specific literature and articles is therefore often far shorter than would normally be experienced for other subjects. However, where the theory addresses generically the impacts and considerations of IS on business, this is less the case. Where the literature included checklists, or specific activities or

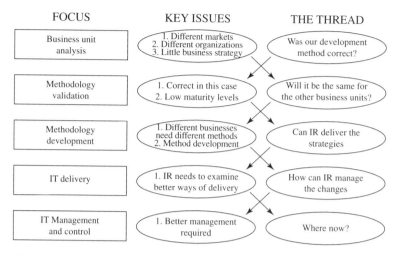

IR = Information resources i.e. : NEGB's IT department

Figure 12.1 *The scope of the research*

outputs, we were able to use them to identify gaps. Business and IS alignment appears to be the 'Holy Grail' of IS strategy development This is a difficult issue and has always been problematic, even at the levels of producing a user requirement that the users and the IT (information technology) providers can agree upon.

Figure 12.1 shows the scope and structure of the chapter. We start with a business analysis of the utility's business units. The second section looks at the IS planning method used in one unit, distribution, and critically assesses its effectiveness. We next consider what sort of methodology might be needed for other business units. The fourth section deals with how the IR (information resources) function needs to be structured in order to deliver IS strategies for the utility. Finally, we consider how IR should be managed and controlled by the organization. For the remainder of the chapter the utility will be referred to as 'NEGB'.

Analysis of NEGB business and context

Porter (five forces model) and Mintzburg (organizational configurations) provide the primary models used in this analysis (Porter, 1980 and Mintzberg, 1979). Table 12.1 shows the main businesses of NEGB and their principle objectives. With particular reference to the role of IT, Table 12.2 summarizes NEGB's businesses in terms of Mintzberg's organizational configuration.

Table 12.1 *NEGB business*

	Summary	*Implication for IR*
Distribution	Stable business Stable internal structure Regulated monopoly No threat of entry (except possible takeover) Generates majority profit Efficiency driven Clear business	Support of distribution is business as usual for IR however: Focus increasingly on cost and ROI drives need for better estimates and performance More predictable delivery times needed Decrease in operating costs very important
Franchise Non-Franchise	In transition from regulated to deregulated and open to competition Mature internal structure but will change	Currently like distribution Will become more like non-franchise and gas businesses
Other utility business	Traditional market now deregulated Immature internal structure Cost of customers switching suppliers is low Tight margins Requires volume for profit New business Immature internal structure Cost of customers switching suppliers is low Tight margins Requires volume for profit Growing quickly Big problems with current systems due to growth/product selection	Significant challenges relating to: – uncertain business direction (retentive Vs growth) – robustness of systems – flexibility of legacy systems – volume/speed of change – changing structure of business Significant changes relating to: – growth of business – scalability of systems – suitability of systems – volume/speed of change – unstable business processes – IR has not had significant input to technology choice

Essentially the present time is a period of change the like of which has not been seen in the utility industry for at least fifty years. The opening of the markets to competition has required a complete restructuring of the industry and the change is not yet complete. It is for this reason that IR strategy is very important at this time.

Table 12.2 *NEGB vis à vis Mintzberg*

Configuration	NEGB business
Simple structure	**Gas**
	Non-franchise
Machine bureaucracy	**Franchise**
	Distribution
Professional bureaucracy	
Divisionalized	
Adhocracy	
Missionary	**Non-franchise**

Planning methodology validation

IS strategy development in NEGB's distribution business

This section explores the IS Strategy development method adopted by the strategy development team (SDT) for the distribution business of NEGB. There are a plethora of IS strategy and business strategy development models, methods/methodologies, frameworks, tools and techniques. While Doyle (1991) asserts correctly that this presents its own problems we believe also that it presents opportunities. The most significant of these are:

- The ability to validate the chosen development method against existing models.
- The ability to consider more thoroughly and thoughtfully a future course of action and the tools that should support it
- The breadth of issues addressed in the models – while this in itself creates problems of focus, it also allows the issues that are likely to be important in the development process to surface.

The principle applied in this analysis has been to research models thoroughly and then to cross refer between models and NEGB current practice for verification.

The level of maturity of strategic planning in general, and IS strategic planning in particular, throughout NEGB was found to be key. The highest level results of an IS strategy review conducted in 1995 by a major consultancy,

Table 12.3 *Consultancy findings*

Problem area	Problem area addressed?
There is no published IT Strategy articulating overall systems architecture, skills requirements, IT investments and processes	✗
The desire to satisfy the user has led to the development of multiple diverse technical solutions which are difficult to integrate and costly to operate	✗
The existence of two departments, IT and communications is unproductive and inhibiting	✓✓
There is a lack of focus on 1998 and its requirements	✓✓
The IT department is locked into major developments which are consuming management time – no time is devoted to assess direction and focus	✗
IT investments for the next 5 years are underestimated	✓
There are polarized, inconsistent views of the IT department	✗

which made an assessment on a number of issues relating to IS maturity, are summarized in Table 12.3. The table denotes whether the problem area has been positively addressed. A cross denotes no progress, one tick denotes partial progress and two ticks indicate progress has been made.

Initially, it appears little progress has been made and it is therefore imperative to use other models to support this. This is a key element of the model espoused by Ward and Griffiths (1996). Ward's eclectic approach uses a set of models to provide pointers to strategies for IS resourcing, structure and management that are demonstrably linked to business strategy. We concur that it is essential to assess the maturity of IS strategy planning, including the attitudes towards the IT department, in order to define a pragmatic strategy development process and in turn an implementable IS strategy. For example, it seems almost self evident that attempting a strategy development process which requires very high levels of management commitment, high user inputs and potential high risks, simply will not work where there is limited interest or high scepticism regarding IT and the IR department.

The first frame of reference (and perhaps the bluntest) helps orientation and is provided by Earl (1989). Earl tracks the evolution of the IT function itself from the DP era to the IT era. If the two eras are taken to be the furthest points on a continuum, the closest positioning of NEGB is posited. This is demonstrated in Table 12.4.

While the results above may appear inconclusive in placing NEGB in absolute terms using these definitions, it is instructive that some of the more

Table 12.4 *IT Focus (adapted from Earl, 1989)*

Distinctor	DP Era	IT Era	NEGB (closest)
Financial attitude to IT	A cost	An investment	DP Era
Business role of IT	Mostly support	Often critical	IT Era
Applications orientation of IT	Tactical	Strategic	DP Era
Economic context for IT	Neutral	Welcoming	DP Era
MIS thinking on IT	Traditional	New	DP Era
Stakeholders concerned with IT	Few	Many	IT Era
Technologies involved with IT	Computing	Multiple	IT Era
Business management management posture IT	Delegate/abrogate	Leadership involvement	DP Era

important distinctors (for example business management posture) show NEGB closer to the DP era. This drives out a significant issue – that the IT department itself possesses some maturity in that the applications it develops and supports are both pervasive and often critical. Despite this, the posture adopted by business management is not yet mature (nor aligned to the IT era). The conclusion to be drawn from this analysis is therefore that attitudes towards the IR department and planning are not yet mature.

Other models use slightly different techniques and allow a more sophisticated judgement to be developed. The model produced by the MIT90s work is still relevant (Venkatraman, 1991). While this model specifically states that it is not a maturity model, it maps the outcomes that IT can enable and defines them as evolutionary or revolutionary. Figure 12.2 reproduces the model. Our judgement of NEGB's location is the shaded area.

The (paraphrased) definitions used by the MIT team are:

1 Level 1 – Localised exploitation. Exploitation of IT within the business functions. Deployment of IT so that it enhances business efficiency of operations.
2 Level 2 – Internal integration. IT capabilities are exploited in all the possible activities within the business process, to achieve greater effectiveness. The deployment of the IT platform therefore serves to integrate the organization's business process.

As shown in Figure 12.2 the development of the IS strategy so far indicates

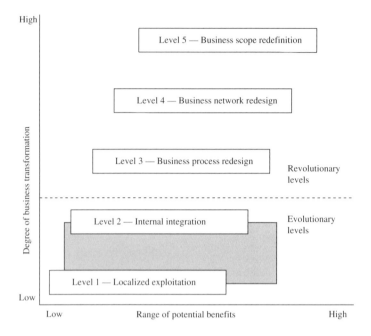

Figure 12.2 *IT induced business reconfiguration (source: Venkatraman, 1991)*

that NEGB's distribution business sits somewhere between Level 1 and Level 2. While there are elements of an integrated technical platform (a common communications network and evidence of an emerging technical policy to ensure inter-operability) integration is neither complete nor satisfactory.

The audit stages described later and completed as part of the IS strategy development identified the following key issues which militate against effective internal integration:

- Systems audit. There are a range of systems, a number developed by individual business areas, without reference to the IT department. A particular problem is the use of different databases. Examples of databases used in system development, excluding the mainframe, showed Lotus 123 (used to create databases), Lotus Approach, Microsoft Access, and FoxPro. The corporate standard is now Oracle!
- Technology audit. Hardware, software tools and operating systems have proliferated due to the lack of an effective policy. This is not because the IT department is unaware of the problem or have not drafted a policy – it has simply lacked 'teeth'.
- Data audit. Significant evidence of duplication of data, double entry, duplicate updating requirements, etc. Data submitted from the field workforce is

updated in a number of systems at different times, causing potential differences and inaccuracies. The review (creation, review, updating, deletion) showed almost no common data infrastructure in use.

The conclusion is that the outcome enabled by the IS strategy (and therefore the primary objective of the strategy) must exceed local exploitation and must achieve at least internal integration to deliver significant added value and justify the planning effort. It will probably fall short of business process redesign on a large scale (due to level of maturity).

The principle reason for NEGB's decision to focus on achieving internal integration, rather than Level 3 process redesign is simple. It is not believed that a high risk approach is necessary for three reasons:

1 The distribution business is a stable business where the barriers for entry are very high and the use of IT is likely to be defensive (efficiency and effectiveness based).
2 The potential pay off for a high risk approach does not appear to be commensurate with the risk level.
3 There does not seem to be a significant possibility of harnessing sufficient business management involvement to mitigate risks acceptably.

NEGB's IS strategy process

We now focus on addressing business strategy issues where they interface directly with the IS strategy planning processes. Figure 12.3 depicts the process originally planned for NEGB. We will attempt to validate the rationale and, as an example, the chosen activities undertaken in Step 1.

A summary of Steps 1–5 (Figure 12.3 is taken from the original strategy process scoping paper) produced prior to commencement of the IS strategy development is shown below:

1 Create and maintain an up-to-date view on the technology, systems and data currently in use within the business.
2 Observe potential shortfalls and problems with the current situation and create a list of opportunities.
3 Opportunities are refined alongside identified stakeholders, working toward the vision, within the business model.
4 Costs and benefits for each opportunity are established.
5 Business cases including an NPV programme and project outline are presented to the executive for review and approval.

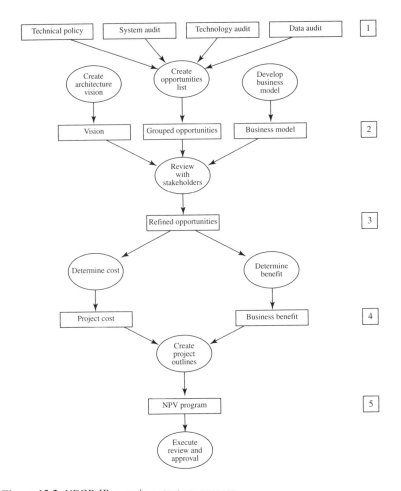

Figure 12.3 *NEGB IR overview strategy process*

As an example, a summary of the outcomes and issues arising from Step 1 of the IS strategy process is shown in Figure 12.4.

Validation of NEGB's IS strategy process

Earl (1989) defined IS strategy development in three stages. The model he uses, although having a sound intellectual base, is also practical for validating a strategy development process in that it defines when each of the main stages is likely to be undertaken as well as defining the methodology and teams required. The model is shown in Figure 12.5.

Infrastructure audit (technology, data, hardware)

- Many small systems
  - Non-integrated
  - Different data sets
  - Currency issues
  - Overlap data
- Systems not used consistently
- Some systems hard/impossible to maintain
- Bespoke systems require IR to maintain skills requirement
- Vulnerable – rely on one individual
- Systems are not designed for end-to-end process
  - No drill down
  - Cannot go across systems (relationally)
  - No flow
- Crown (Work management, assess management, customer service system)
  - Too big, non-modular
  - Poor implementation
  - Many data-sets that don't belong
    - Connectivity
    - Costing
- Poor/No documentation
- No overall live information strategy or framework in which to make changes/enhancements
- Reactive changes out of context and therefore perpetuate the problem

Figure 12.4 *Summary – high level Stage 1 finding and issues*

A key check is therefore to validate when Earl believes each stage should be undertaken. Earl states:

> While this [the bottom up leg] may not seem strategic, most organizations when they begin or renew their attempts to plan IS strategically need to understand and evaluate their current IS investment. (Earl, 1989)

The level of business planning referred to earlier in this section and the level of IS maturity displayed indicates that it is the bottom up stage that is the most appropriate to NEGB and its distribution business at present. In particular, two reasons given by Earl and paraphrased here are key in the NEGB environment. First, it is necessary to demonstrate the quality and coverage of IS and gain credibility. Second, it is necessary to inform top business management about the current position of IS and to gain understanding about the capabilities currently available.

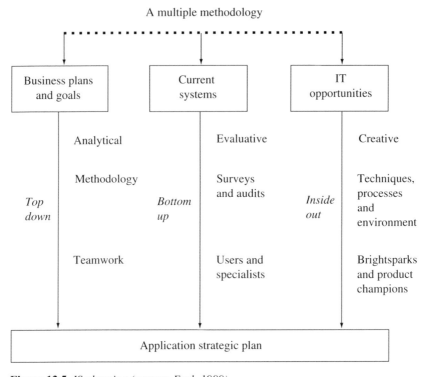

A multiple methodology

Figure 12.5 *IS planning (source: Earl, 1989)*

A crucial point made by Earl is that systems which deliver competitive advantage or which are otherwise considered strategic in nature are often evolutionary rather than revolutionary in nature. Thus, the opportunities presented by the bottom up, or evaluative, approach has three distinct advantages for the distribution business at this stage. It is lower risk than other strategy process stages; it is pragmatic and fits the current state of maturity in NEGB and its distribution business at present; although designed to deliver efficiency and effectiveness benefits, it could deliver strategic benefits.

The outputs from Stage 1 are also validated by the CCTA methodology (1989) which states that the systems audit should allow the technological and business implications of the existing systems to be understood.

A more sophisticated validation which also offers some direction comes from the MIT90s research. The model produced uses a simplistic but useful articulation of the likely systems planning characteristics. Table 12.5 is an extract of the MIT90s team model (there are clear consistencies between this model and the Galliers model referred to later in this section at Figure 12.6).

Table 12.5 goes further than validation – it points intuitively to where the

Table 12.5 *Systems planning characteristics (from Scott Morton, 1991)*

Distinctive characteristics	Independent	Reactive
Description	Design of IT infrastructure is independent of the strategic	Design of IT infrastructure is derived from strategic context
Leading indicators	Relatively low level of the IS function	Increasing stature
Systems	IT planning is operational and IS independent of strategic planning	IS/IT planning is derived from business plans

strategy development process *should* be focused. Although the Step 1 activities appear to be pragmatic and have delivered outputs broadly in alignment with the current maturity level of NEGB and its distribution business – it should clearly not be the extent of the IS strategy objectives.

In assessing aspirations for NEGB and the IS strategy, Robson (1997) makes the following point:

> It is possible to conduct a strategy planning exercise as a 'kick start' one off project in order to raise the awareness of the potential impact of IS and to, hopefully, get senior management commitment to implementing the results of the strategy planning exercise.

We concur, although we would view this as more than a one-off exercise. We see gaining senior management commitment as a key success factor for the entire project.

The conclusion from using the alternative analyses delivered by the models is that they validate the Step 1 methodology of the IS development method and activities and that they are aligned to the maturity of NEGB as it currently stands. They also demonstrate that, in the current circumstances, this should not be the extent of the objectives of the strategy and that further activities are required which should explicitly aim to gain senior management support. A gap in our outputs exists and must be addressed. The information we have on system costs efficiencies is insufficient as is the high level business impact of systems.

Figure 12.6 indicates that if efficiency only is the outcome required, a bottom up analysis may be sufficient. However, this would be a very limited objective, given that, as described earlier, NEGB does have some factors which enable internal integration. The MIT90s model states clearly that the achievement of internal integration allows the achievement of effectiveness benefits. This indicates that a strategy aiming only to deliver efficiency would not:

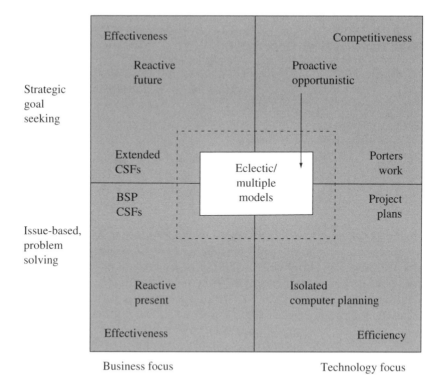

Figure 12.6 *IS planning (source: Galliers, 1991)*

- Be ambitious given the technology base already existing;
  justify the planning effort;
- act as a 'kick start' to embedding IS strategy planning in NEGB.
- allow NEGB to migrate towards better alignment.
- improve the standing of the IR department.

Our judgment is that, in adopting an approach whereby the IR function has worked primarily from documentation, we are weak in agreeing business direction and priorities, successfully decomposing business objectives, and generating and harnessing senior management drive.

Planning methodology development

IS strategy development in other business units

The department has a traditional IT focus on supporting the business rather than helping change it.'(Consultancy report)

The previous section assessed the IS strategy method adopted for the distribution business. The objective of this section is to increase the chances of success of the IS strategies for the other business units in NEGB. It reflects our belief that if the IS strategy is to be completed effectively and successfully in NEGB, the differences between the business units must be recognized and addressed.

Earlier we examined each business unit within the context of:

1 the stability of its market;
2 the internal structure it exhibits;
3 the business unit's objectives and what was pragmatically achievable given the maturity of business and IS planning within NEGB.

The analysis of the business units clearly demonstrates that the business units are very different, as are the businesses themselves.

We believe a common mistake made in large federal organizations is the adoption of a single method for IS strategy development for all business units. This occurs for a number of reasons:

1 The available skills are those within the IT department. They will naturally use those methods, tools/techniques with which they are familiar or feel comfortable.
2 The use of consultants. Globalization of markets has caused large consultancies to adopt single (supposedly) all embracing methods.
3 Success of IS strategy. Success of an IS strategy development model within one business unit will inevitably imply this should be used in another.
4 Lack of appreciation of the complexities of IS strategy development.

In the previous section it emerged that the appetite for IS strategy planning is low in NEGB and this was to a large extent why the chosen IS development method was selected for the distribution business. It is clear, however, that the maturity and stability of the distribution business allowed us to accept and work within this constraint. Where a business is not operating in a stable environment with a stable internal structure, this constraint may not be acceptable.

Galliers (1991) states that there are four key reasons for failure in IS strategy of which one is '... a failure to secure commitment to and involvement in IS strategy planning on the part of senior and middle business management'. A key element of the development method is therefore to secure commitment for the IS strategy planning process. The caveat we would add to this is '... where this involvement early on is an imperative, or where it will impact the result of the strategy adversely if it is not obtained'.

While much of the management literature discusses the need for management involvement, there is little to indicate at what stage this becomes an issue,

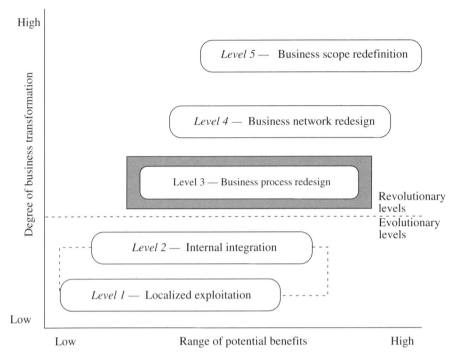

Figure 12.7 *Positioning NEGB businesses*

the extent to which it is needed – and why. The implication is that involvement is required from the outset and that it should be at the direction setting level.

Although clearly desirable, we question whether it is always a requirement, and whether it is always achievable. In the previous section we have shown that the bottom up elements were completed largely by the IR department. Similarly, the first activities within the top down analysis were also initiated by IR, using the available planning documentation. This allowed us to produce a number of IT enabled opportunities arising from the move from localized exploitation to internal integration, shown in Figure 12.7. The dotted rectangle shows the distribution business, while the shaded area shows the transition and deregulated businesses.

The validation of the process adopted for the distribution business showed that to complete the Step 2, top down process, a senior management workshop was required to discuss and build on the opportunities and obtain business management 'buy in'. However, this would involve the business management some way into the process with initial opportunities already developed. We no longer have a 'blank canvas'. Although this gap was usefully pointed out by the analysis, it is doubtful that we would have managed to gain senior management input from the outset. Their 'buy in' is more likely to be obtained because we have developed efficiency and effectiveness opportunities (which is the main business management focus).

The involvement, then, clearly depends on a number of issues:

1 How radical are/could the proposals be?
2 How certain can the development team be of the objectives and critical success factors (CSFs) of the business they are examining and that these will remain relatively constant?
3 How certain can the development team be of the appropriateness (stability) of the current processes in the business to those required to underpin the objectives and CSFs?
4 How certain are the IT issues of flexibility and scaleability?

The opportunities developed by IR for the distribution business on the basis of CSFs and data sets (and their location) were underpinned by a high level of business certainty. The processes of the distribution business are very unlikely to change radically, therefore the information flows are likely to be stable. The focus and objectives of the strategy were to deliver efficiency and effectiveness because the need for competitive advantage, in an industry where the barriers to entry are, amongst others, capital costs of approaching £1 billion, is low. Therefore the information itself is unlikely to change radically. IS projects are unlikely to be very high risk.

In the period preceding the deregulation of the supply business, there was a heavy and understandable emphasis on the applications that would be delivered to the business particularly on billing systems. This equates to the Type 1 systems described by Rowe, Mason, Dickel, Mann, Mockler (1994). They define Type 1 systems as those which allow the organization to transact business. There was however little or no emphasis on Type 2 systems, which are defined as those which guide business decision making. The supply business now requires these systems to compete but does not yet have them. This is a clear example of a top down/bottom up approach where there was no inside out, creative opportunity spotting prior to deregulation.

There will be choices to make regarding the IS strategy development method to use, dependent upon the business under examination. From our previous analysis the principles behind making the choices would seem to be:

1 The IS strategy development method will consist of a number of steps, within which there are activities, some requiring the use of specific tools. The involvement required from business management and the stage at which this is required should be explicit.
2 The number of different methods used within NEGB will be kept to a minimum to promote understanding and consistency.

3 The development method chosen should be driven by:
  a the external market within which the business operates;
  b the levels of internal stability;
  c the likely aspirations of the strategy given the above (although this will
    not always be known).
4 All development methods should be scoped and agreed with the IR manager
  and the director of the business unit before commencement of the full
  study.
5 The scoping study will define the classification of the business and type of
  IS strategy to be adopted.

Delivering strategic IT

The previous section identified the need for the IR department to move the
organization away from its current delivery focus. This change will allow the
IR department to enable, rather than constrain, the development of true 'inside
out' IS strategies for the remaining business units in NEGB. As discussed this
did not seriously affect the development of the distribution business IS strategy so far. However, a delivery-only focus will not allow the IR department to
develop the understanding and relationships with the business units that are
needed to develop truly competitive strategy.

   This section deals with the next issue – how to organize and structure in
order to deliver the re-oriented IR – one that is able to develop and deliver the
IS strategies we recommend for the remaining business units. Clearly, while
doing so, IR cannot lose sight of its current drivers, efficiency and cost effectiveness. In a cash-constrained environment, IR must examine *and* leverage all
opportunities to both modernize its approach and reduce or contain its costs.
This section therefore:

1 Provides a high level examination of the structures and organization that IR
  uses to deliver its products to its customers.
2 Examines the role and location of IR within NEGB.
3 Describes how IR is evolving as the company moves toward the next deregulation.

IR development since 1995

It is useful to examine the development of the IT and telecommunications
functions since their merger into a new department – IR. This merger was
directly as a result of a finding in the report commissioned in 1995 following
its take-over by a US utility:

The existence of two departments, IT and communications is unproductive and inhibiting.

The drivers and results of the merger are interesting. The objectives of the merger were to:

1 obtain economies of scale;
2 remove the duplication of tasks (and therefore effort);
3 allow for de-layering of middle management;
4 bring all costs together to better understand and control spend.

The resultant structure is shown in Figure 12.8.

The initial results fell short of the objectives. Broadly, the IT department had a very large applications development function and a small networks function. The reverse was true of the telecommunications department and merging them therefore simply created a 'super' department. Duplication of tasks within the applications development and networks functions was removed, however the economies gained were not significant. The benefits gained were at the expense of more complex processes being created. We concluded that the objectives of the merger were not strategic. Even so, they were not fully achieved and organization and structure were not optimized. The new structure, Figure 12.9, therefore attempted to address this.

The recommendation in the consultancy report that the IR manager should be selected carefully seems to be a truism but was important. The manager appointed was not drawn from either of the technical departments but came from the distribution business. His background did however include previous experience of the IT and Telecoms industry. This is the first appointment in NEGB of a 'hybrid' IR manager (Earl, 1989).

The IR manager, using the insight gained being a customer of IR services introduced two groups to provide a much clearer customer focus. The groups are:

1 Customer business – Small groups (one per business unit) that exist to bridge the gap between technology and NEGB's businesses.
2 Commercial – Service managers that act broadly as account managers and maintain relationships with the primary users.

Both are roles that have proved to be critical to the improvement in image and credibility of IR in the company. However, it is important to note that these are roles that focus more on the relationship with the customers of IR rather than providing a strategic focus for IR itself. Thus, there has been no real home in the organization for strategic analysis or thinking. This is aligned with the conclusion that IR has been largely at the delivery stage of development.

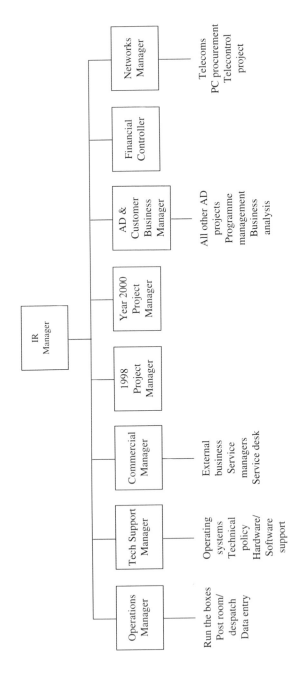

Figure 12.8 *Merged structure (Mark I)*

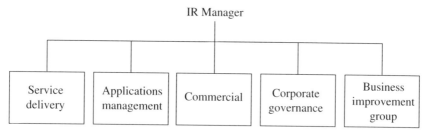

Figure 12.9 *Merged structure (Mark II)*

Strategic delivery issues

Earl (1989) has suggested four dimensions under which a technology-strategy connection can be made, these are shown in Figure 12.10.

We have already considered how to develop an IS strategy that supports the business strategy (top down and bottom up), and how strategic opportunities may be created (inside out). This section considers both delivery mechanisms and organizational capability, the remaining factors identified by Earl.

The remainder of this section is based upon a structure given to this topic by Robson (1997) who proposes that IM can be considered employing three specific themes:

1 Role – What IS will do?
2 Location – Where IS will be?
3 Organization – How IS will be arranged?

1	IT can support business strategy.
2	IT can create strategic options. For example applications can spearhead quite revolutionary approaches to either the market place or internal operations.
3	IT delivery mechanisms may have to be conceptualized and planned strategically, IT architecture then becomes a strategic concern.
4	Organizational capability in IT and IS may intervene for better or worse in applying or delivering IT for strategic advantage. Thus management of information resources becomes a strategic matter.

Figure 12.10 *The technology/strategy connection (adapted from Earl, 1989)*

Table 12.6 *Five models of IS structures (from Sullivan-Trainor, 1989)*

Model	Description
Service	This formalizes the interaction between IS and its user community into a service obligation. This model is very appealing to organizations who feel they are still catching up on IS management issues
Partnership	This breaks down the functional lines of the service model in order to develop close alignment between IS and its business user community
Vendor	Any version where IS seeks to market itself and sell its service to its user community. Organizations that are concerned about value to the business from IS are attached to this model
Expansion	A model that has IS creating a flexible architecture that will support common systems to accommodate a user community's growing set of IS issues. This model is attractive to large and growing organizations
Strategic advantage	Where the identification between IS and its user community is so close that competitive products are jointly developed

The role of IS

As already discussed IR needs to change its role in NEGB to improve its alignment. This change can be characterized as the need to extend its role from one of provider of business support to include one of enabler of organizational transformation. To assist in driving out the true implications of this change we have used the five models for IS structures proposed by Sullivan-Trainor (1989) to map the current situation and to indicate a more appropriate future role (Table 12.6)

We have analysed the current IR role and Table 12.7 shows how this maps onto the five models. It is significant that the current situation has features of

Table 12.7 *NEGB and the five models*

Model	Fit to current IR	Fit to future IR role
Service	✗	✓✓
Partnership	✓	✓✓
Vendor	✓✓	✓✓
Expansion	✓	✓✓
Strategic advantage	✗	✓✓

more than one of the models and that there is no dominant one. We believe that this is because the role has evolved over the years and that it has not been considered an important facilitator to delivery. Flexibility has been confused with drift – the concern being that the role should be 'whatever the customer wants', rather than designed to bring about a planned outcome.

Our conclusions from this are, first, that the charging mechanism should be exploited further to demonstrate IR is delivering value for money (VFM) services, for example benchmarking. Second, service level agreements should be negotiated and put into place to support the above conclusion.

A further dimension is added in relation to the new structure of IR. In this structure it is clear that the different functions have different perspectives. For example service management is principally concerned with delivering today's installed service and therefore can be best managed with an emphasis on reliability and cost effectiveness. Applications development, however, is project based and therefore is more concerned with business alignment and value for money, with developments treated as investments. This suggests further conclusions that the appropriate elements of each of the models should be brought out to design an appropriate role for IR and that performance measures for the new organization should be developed and they must be contingent with the purpose and role of the individual functions.

The location of IS

The second dimension to be examined in this section is location – where is IR sited within NEGB. Three possibilities are shown in Table 12.8.

IR is currently spread across the geographic area of the company, and has several centres within the company where its staff are located. In terms of management nothing has been devolved, indeed where devolved groups have grown they have quickly been re-centralized.

The situation is now that, although the departments are split internally by function, they each have a single manager, budget and set of goals, set by the

Table 12.8 *IS location*

Loaction	*Description*
Re-centralized	One single-access function: IS provides one single service, with single-access provision
Decentralized	Lots of single-access functions: IS being a number of single-site, single-access centres, a collection of 'mini' DP departments
Devolved	Geographically and managerially dispersed: IS is a web of lateral linkages plus a significant degree of end user control over: (i) Processing (ii) Application systems development and environment

centre. We consider IR to be (re-) centralized in terms of the types shown in Table 12.8. Therefore, although the functions are geographically dispersed, the *control* is (and in fact the current thrust of the finance director's thinking is to have the full IS/IT budget fully centralized).

Robson suggests that:

> the way to decide upon an appropriate location for elements of IS is to test them against the IS strategy that defines the goals for IS. (Robson, 1997)

IR currently has no defined strategy, therefore our conclusions include the fact that IR should not change its location until the IR strategy has been developed. If the IR department is to remain centralized until there is an imperative (possibly driven out by the IR strategy) to change, it is important to consider whether the operation of IR is maximizing the benefits and minimizing the disadvantages of the current arrangement.

Robson has analysed the benefits and disbenefits of centralized IR department. These are summarized in Table 12.9 alongside our analysis of how IR is performing against each one. This allows us to identify those areas where the benefits of centralization are not being fully leveraged.

Table 12.9 reveals a number of situations that are causing IR problems in terms of efficiency and user perception, whether these are known or not. These areas represent opportunities for the IR department to harvest some quick wins. It is ironic that the 'distance' created by the centralized location is probably shielding IR from understanding what it is actually doing badly.

The efficiency approach to systems development is not being achieved for three principle reasons:

1 Projects are set up in dispersed locations in an attempt to align with customers, and are therefore 'out of sight' of the centre.
2 Large projects tend to have a manager responsible directly to the IR manager rather then through applications development.
3 Each project is considered to be in some way significantly different and as such redefines many of the procedures that should be standard, e.g. documentation, change control, configuration management.

Potential for incompatibilities in systems has been encouraged by the systems development problem, a lack of implemented technical policy and a lack of a process for decommissioning old technology. Cross-department systems are not well supported because several departments have unique IR services and technologies that cannot now, or ever, be integrated. There is no individual recommendation associated with this but rather it re-enforces the requirements revealed by the analysis above.

It is therefore recommended that:

Table 12.9 *Benefits/disbenefits of centralization/de-centralization*

Benefit of centralization	IR realization
Greater control over the operation of the IS resources including systems production, database integrity and security	✓✓
Providing an efficiency approach to systems development that allows the centralized resource to build expertise in productivity methods	✗
Reduced duplication of effort, resources and expertise means that economies of scale can be reaped; also organizational cost savings	✓
The centralized resource should have the capacity to handle large and complex projects	✓
By centralizing the IS resource there is less potential for incompatibilities in systems and, more importantly, data since standardization is part of a centralized IS provision	✗
The larger more varied IS function will find it easier to recruit and manage specialist staff, particularly in times of shortage	✓
The central provision of an IS service supports the cross-department systems associated with business process redesign	✗
Disbenefits of centralization	*IR avoiding*
The IS function is divorced from the 'coal face' of the business and by being removed from the real business arena it can be equally divorced from the concerns and priorities of it. Since it is often difficult for the isolated, fortress based IS staff to relate to the real work of the business hostilities may emerge	✗
Little scope for personal attention to any individual group. The span of responsibility of the IS function makes it a mass market provider rather than a personal service one and this can easily lead to true business priorities being ignored	✓✓
Diseconomies of scale. Since the service is away from the action it has to adopt a range of general policies for its behaviour that in specific instances may be inappropriate	✗
Access, particularly at peak times may be slowed. In general the more centralized the service the more difficult capacity planning. Larger number of users result in larger peaks/troughs in demand	✓
The communication costs can be very high since the distances between the host and client can be very great	✓

1 The developments should be brought together under one manager (done in the re-organization) and standardization enforced.
2 The technical policies recently developed should be adhered to rigorously if incompatibilities are to be reduced.
3 The business analysts should look to help produce business cases that support the decommissioning of old technologies.

Re-centralization can create super-centres. A super-centre is a utility that serves an entire organization, and a good utility is about high volume, low costs and quality service. IR has some features of the super-centre although the issue of physical location has not been explicitly addressed. Other utilities have taken advantage of the super-centre to allow it to serve more than one company.

Organizing IS – opportunities for outsourcing IR functions

For clarity it is important to understand precisely what is meant by outsourcing. Gilbert (1993) has defined it as follows:

> Outsourcing is the process by which a corporation, a governmental agency or another business entity sub-contracts to a third party – the 'outsourcer' the performance of certain services or the operation of certain equipment required for its internal operations. (Gilbert, 1993)

The underlying reasoning is exposed by Quinn (1982):

> Each activity within a firm's value chain and within its traditional staff groups must be considered a service which can just as easily be purchased externally.

Quinn's point seems to be that we should not just assume that because an activity must be done by a firm that it must be done internally. A conscious decision should be taken rather than a default. We believe that IR may well be undertaking too many tasks itself which requires development and maintenance of a very wide range of skills in-house. This appears possibly to be an expensive and ineffective way of operating. Mintzburg, in discussing bureaucracies, has concluded that:

> The obsession with control helps to explain the frequent proliferation of support staff in these organizations. Many of the staff services could be purchased from outside suppliers. (Mintzberg, 1979)

In addition to our opinion, supported by Mintzburg, outsourcing is considered here for three further reasons.

1 IR has not significantly outsourced any of its operation – against the trend in the industry; whilst this is not necessarily wrong it warrants examination.
2 Sourcing is so important that it should be considered explicitly and approached in a manner that is not 'the way we have always done it'.
3 The current location of IR (re-centralized) should facilitate outsourcing more than any other so the time may now be right to move in this direction.

Having discussed *why* outsourcing should be considered the remainder of the consideration of it will be *what* are the likely candidates for outsourcing, and what form it may take. The literature tells us that not all of the functions of IR are appropriate for outsourcing. In fact there are some that should most certainly be kept in-house. This part of the chapter explores the functions of IR to identify the most likely candidates both for outsourcing and for retention as activities undertaken by IR and develops the rationale for making the decisions.

Candidates

There are a number of outsourcing models available in the literature and a useful one has been selected for consideration here. This is the services snake produced by the CCTA (Figure 12.11). It is a generic model that shows that the easier and more appropriate outsourcing activities tend to be those at the bottom of the snake. The more strategic services that tend to be at the top of the snake are kept in-house as these are the high value 'demanded' services.

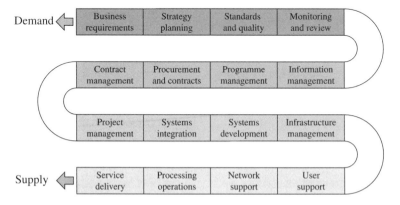

Figure 12.11 *Outsourcing options (CCTA)*

Motivation

In any consideration of outsourcing options it is imperative to understand the motivation behind it. The IR manager at NEGB explained that, in his opinion, there were two principle motivations in the case of IR. The first was that there could be a big cost saving. The second was that buying in the billing service from someone with a proven capability was a way of reducing risk but not necessarily cost.

Willcocks and Choi (1994) have focused on the motivation behind outsourcing deals and have devised a continuum along which the arrangement can be located as shown in Figure 12.12. They have asserted that as companies outsource more of their important functions over time, then the relationships become strategic alliances rather than merely 'contracted out'.

For NEGB outsourcing arrangements could fall at either end of the continuum. The straightforward outsourcing of computing power could be done using the 'contract' approach, in that service required can be clearly defined and monitored. The billing service is so critical to the operation of NEGB that any outsourcing should be considered 'strategic' in nature and a very different relationship formed. Billing processes and procedures are by no means static and so a strong relationship will be required to ensure that both parties 'work together' to ensure that deadlines (business imperative or statutory) are met by robust and accurate billing procedures.

IT management and control

In their publication *Managing and Controlling the IS Strategy* (CCTA, 1989) the CCTA draw a useful distinction between the *targeting* of IS to meet business needs and the *management and control* of IS. The targeting of IS is achieved through the use of strategic planning for IS. The management and control effectively provides the framework within which the IS strategy planning takes place. The following issues, explored in previous sections of this chapter are key to the analysis in this section:

1 The organization of the IR department is changing, from delivery (Phase 1) to re-orientation (Phase 2) and may change again.
2 The level of interaction between the IR department and the businesses does not fit the aspirations expressed in this chapter by the IT manager.

Contract/transaction focus   *Trust/partnership focus*

Contract out 'mind set'   Strategic alliance 'mind set'

Figure 12.12 *Outsourcing continuum (source: Willcocks and Choi, 1994)*

3 There is no history of IS strategy planning in NEGB, either business or IS and the appetite for, and appreciation of, it in the business is low.

Three dimensions of 'management and control' are explored in this section: steering arrangements; locating key IR tasks within the IR department; and the role of the IR manager.

Steering arrangements

Rockart and Treacy (1982) state that one of the four priorities of an IT director is to address strategic planning, top management responsibility and steering committees, both inside and outside the IT department. This section explores a key issue which is crucial to the development of IS/IT within NEGB – the steering arrangements for IS/IT strategy development and the IR department. The management literature available concurs with Rockart's statement, indicating that this is an area which organizations frequently do not address. The work of Ward and Griffiths (1996) concludes that the selection and agenda of steering committees is vital and must match the circumstances of the organization and that, frequently:

1 the wrong people attend and the right do not attend;
2 they have the wrong terms of reference;
3 they discuss the wrong things;
4 they meet too frequently, or infrequently;
5 they make too many or not enough decisions;
6 they do not understand the real issues;
7 they are too remote from reality.

An analogous situation is that of an IT project. While the project feasibility and definition documents will plan the deployment (targeting) of the IT, a coherent and appropriate steering structure (the project boards and coordinators) are required to effectively steer the investment. It is very often the appropriateness and quality of this steering and coordination that dictates the success or failure of the project, rather than the original definition. This applies equally at the strategic level although the issues, aspirations, rationale and implementation are more complex.

We have paraphrased below the definitions of the key issues, with the extent to which NEGB achieve them. One tick denotes partial compliance and two ticks denotes full compliance in Table 12.10.

The key business imperatives that we have shown need to be supported (as a minimum) by the steering committees in NEGB are that they:

Table 12.10 *Key steering tasks (Robson 1997)*

Key task	NEGB achieves
Direction setting. An IS strategy must be developed and maintained that determines the organizations use and management of IS	✓
Co-ordination. Reusability and standards	✓
Support. Provision of infrastructure and assistance in problem solving	✓✓

1 fully support the process of IS Strategic planning, which is the main focus of this chapter;
2 forge and nurture a much closer understanding and working relationship between the IR department and the business;
3 focus on the right issues at the appropriate levels;
4 facilitate the transition of the IR department from Phase 1 (delivery) to Phase 2 (re-orientation). The location of NEGB IR is summarized (shaded) in Table 12.11 (from Earl, 1989).

Using the analyses above the areas where NEGB is deficient become clearer and the following key conclusions can be drawn:

1 There is insufficient emphasis on IS strategy planning at the steering committees. Further business clarity (a CSF from Earl's model) is needed.
2 The steering committees are delivery focused. While fitting with the current (Phase 1 – delivery) IR status, it does not fit with the desired (Phase 2 – re orientation) status.
3 While consideration is being given to the IR department strategy, the following applies:

Table 12.11 *NEGB IR aspirations (adapted from Earl, 1989)*

Phase	Delivery 1	Re-orientation 2	Re-organization 3
IT Executive	External IT recruit	**Inside business recruit**	Same person
Management focus	**Within IT**	Into the business	The interfaces
Primary concern	**Credibility**	Strategy	Partnership
IT Executive Leadership	**Reactive**	Proactive	Interactive

a it is not being extensively discussed within the committee;

b the key CSF, of a clear mission or objectives does not exist.

4 The key strength to be leveraged is the background of the IT manager.

Locating key IR tasks in the planned IR organization

The management tasks which this section has identified are not currently fully discharged by the IR department need to be placed correctly. This will enable successful migration to re orientation (Phase 2) and the benefits from a central IR department to be achieved. We have located these activities where we believe they will best be discharged and explained our rationale. We use the five generic IS management tasks (Figure 12.13) described by Robson (1997).

Once the generic tasks and the management structure are defined, the placing of the existing tasks and those that are not currently discharged is surprisingly straightforward.

1 *Establishing infrastructure systems.* This is clearly the core business of the service delivery function which will take responsibility for networks, operations and service support. The skills of the staff in this area are also clearly aligned to the infrastructure tasks. There is also little scope to increase the

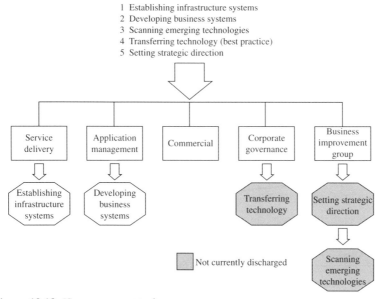

Figure 12.13 *IS management tasks*

responsibilities of the department significantly given the functions it already
fulfils.

2 *Developing business systems.* The core business of the applications development function again clearly maps to the development of business systems. The technology skills allied with the project management skills
(which are being drawn in from the millennium and 1998 projects) also map
well with the development of business systems.

3 *Scanning emerging technologies.* This activity is not currently carried out to
any significant degree by the IR department. There are two possible locations:

a led by the applications and service delivery functions – because they
understand the technologies);

b led by the business improvement group (BIG) – because they will understand better the business opportunities and potential uses for new technologies).

We believe that it is the business focus (provided by the BIG) that is most
important. We would suggest that considerable liaison between the three
groups should exist if full opportunities are to be identified and harnessed.

4 *Transferring technology.* This covers not just technology, but the way it can
be applied to processes. It is mostly concerned with corporate learning and
the spread of best practice. We believe this sits best with the corporate governance function although again there is a need for close liaison with the
function with responsibility for setting strategic direction.

5 *Setting strategic direction.* The business improvement group is newly
formed. We would recommend that the strategic direction is coordinated
from this function for three key reasons:

a the business analysts will be part of BIG. It is imperative that these analysts (who have the closest business contacts and are often drawn from
the businesses themselves) are closely involved with contributing to IS
strategy development and opportunity spotting;

b the BIG will manage the transition from delivery (Phase 1) through to re
orientation (Phase 2) and will assess the scope and requirement for a
move to Phase 3 (re-organization);

c enlightened leadership and advocacy will be required.

The role of the IR manager

We state earlier in this section that we believe that the skills of the IR manager
should be leveraged in order to effect the changes required in the development
of IS/IT in NEGB and the IR department itself. We provide a brief validation
of this assessment in the skills required by the IR manager from the management literature in order to validate this assessment. The shaded areas in Table
12.12 represent the attributes of the current IR manager.

Table 12.12 *Characteristics of IT managers (adapted from Earl 1989)*

The DP manager	The IT director
A technical manager	**A functional manager**
Technical and management skills	**Plus business and organizational skill**
Planning and control focus	Strategic and political posture
Clear role and relationships	**Mixed role and relationship**
Senior position	**Board or near Board**
A DP career	**IT or general manager**
Hands on internal style	**Hands off internal style**

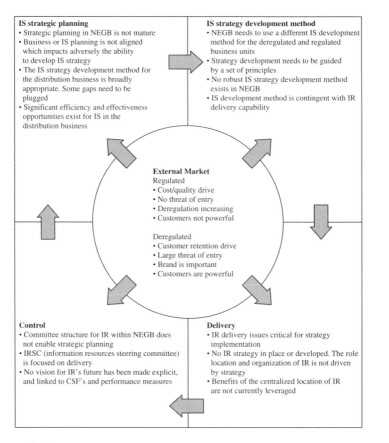

IS strategic planning
- Strategic planning in NEGB is not mature
- Business or IS planning is not aligned which impacts adversely the ability to develop IS strategy
- The IS strategy development method for the distribution business is broadly appropriate. Some gaps need to be plugged
- Significant efficiency and effectiveness opportunities exist for IS in the distribution business

IS strategy development method
- NEGB needs to use a different IS development method for the deregulated and regulated business units
- Strategy development needs to be guided by a set of principles
- No robust IS strategy development method exists in NEGB
- IS development method is contingent with IR delivery capability

External Market
Regulated
- Cost/quality drive
- No threat of entry
- Deregulation increasing
- Customers not powerful

Deregulated
- Customer retention drive
- Large threat of entry
- Brand is important
- Customers are powerful

Control
- Committee structure for IR within NEGB does not enable strategic planning
- IRSC (information resources steering committee) is focused on delivery
- No vision for IR's future has been made explicit, and linked to CSF's and performance measures

Delivery
- IR delivery issues critical for strategy implementation
- No IR strategy in place or developed. The role location and organization of IR is not driven by strategy
- Benefits of the centralized location of IR are not currently leveraged

Figure 12.14 *Key findings*

IS strategy and planning	**IS strategy development method**
● Strategy development procedures °and products should be formalized within NEGB ● Closer and more productive two-way relationship between users and IR ● To complete distribution business IS strategy we need: 　● improved costing information for existing systems and a rigorous (validated) CSF analysis 　● focus should be on improvements to data and systems integration	● Regulated business requires top-down efficiency-biased strategy development method ● Deregulated business requires inside out competitiveness-biased strategy development method ● The guiding principles developed in section seven should be implemented ● The end-to-end IS strategy development method in section seven should be adopted for the deregulated and franchise business
Control	**Delivery**
● ToR of all IR fora should be critically reviewed to accommodate strategy ● The IRSC should focus only on strategic issues	● IR should develop and implement a strategy ● Appropriate SLAs should be developed, agreed and implemented for each of NEGB's businesses ● Meaningful performance measures should be developed ● Strategic outsourcing opportunities should be explored ● Benefits of IT standardization in NEGB should be leveraged immediately

Figure 12.15 *Headline recommendations*

Table 12.12 suggests that the background, skills and position (near the board) are all key elements which point to the IT manager enjoying a clear opportunity to effect the changes we advocate in this and other sections of the chapter. The credibility (the IT manager was formally a CEO of a business unit within NEGB) and the mandate for change also exist. Earl et al. (1989) show that 30 per cent of IT managers have general backgrounds and are brought in to 'turn round' the IT department into a strategic capability. The current IR manager has been charged with effecting significant improvements in IR, although not explicitly in the area of leveraging its strategic capability.

Conclusion

The main findings and recommendations of this study are shown in Figures 12.14 and 12.15. They have been presented in this way to indicate the interdependence of the strategy development and the delivery and control of its implementation within IR. Thus, the overall summary indicates that unless the department is organized, structured and controlled in a suitable manner any strategy, however elegant and aligned it may be, is certain to fail.

References

CCTA (1989). *Managing and Controlling the IS strategy*. The Stationery Office.

Doyle, J. R. (1991). Problems with Strategic Management Frameworks. *European Journal of IS* (IS) Volume 1.

Earl, M. J. (1989). *Management Strategies for IS*. Prentice-Hall.

Galliers, R. D. (1991). Strategic IS: myths, realities and guidelines for successful implementation. *EJIS*. **1**(1), pp. 55–64.

Gilbert (1993). *Journal of IT*.

Johnson, G. and Scholes, K. (1997). *Exploring Corporate Strategy*. Prentice-Hall.

Mintzberg (1979). *The structuring of organisations*. Prentice- Hall.

Porter, M. F. (1980). *Competitive strategy, techniques for analysing industries and competitors*. Free Press.

Quinn (1980). *Strategies for change – logical incrementalism*. Irwin.

Robson, W. (1997). *Strategic Management and Information Systems*. Pitman.

Rockart, J. F. and Treacy, M. E. (1982). The CEO goes on line. Harvard Business Review, January–February.

Rowe, Mason, Dickel, Mann, Mockler (1994). *Strategic Management, a methodological approach*. Addison-Wesley.

Scott Morton, M. S. (1991). *The Corporation of the 1990s*. Oxford University Press.

Sullivan-Trainor (1989). Challenging the fixtures in the house that IS built. *Computerworld*, 24 July.

Venkatraman N. (1991). The IT-induced Business Reconfiguration, in: M. Scott-Morton (ed.) *The Corporation of the 1990s*, Oxford University Press, New York, pp. 122–158.

Ward, J. and Griffiths, P. M. (1996). *Strategic Planning for IS*. John Wiley.

Willcocks and Choi (1994). *Management research papers*, Templeton College, Oxford.

13 Ensuring the disaster recovery planning process delivers business continuity – the experience of a major UK retail bank

Carl Grant and Margi Levy
Warwick Business School, University of Warwick

Introduction

Business continuity planning and IT contingency is taken very seriously by the major UK retail bank (The Bank) discussed in this chapter. The Bank has put in place a set of policies, standards and processes across its business units to ensure that they can survive a major disaster and that it complies with the financial services industry regulations. This chapter shows that business continuity planning needs to be driven by corporate strategic business requirements. Indeed, the final success of a disaster recovery policy is critically dependent upon good management across multiple stakeholder groups.

Background to The Bank

The Bank is, essentially, a set of financial services businesses based in the UK but operating globally. The businesses are broadly defined by customer base and services, and this is reflected in the organization structure. The business is split between two divisions:

1 Bank UK (B-UK) serving personal customers in the UK and some overseas,

small businesses and medium/large corporate customers offering 'high street' banking services.

2 Bank Markets (B-WM) serving some personal customers, but more generally medium to large corporate customers requiring specialized banking services.

B-UK is structured into six businesses:

1 Retail Banking Services (primarily personal and small businesses customers);
2 Corporate (medium to large corporate customers);
3 Card Services (plastic card services for personal customers and retailers);
4 Life and Investments (specializing in life and pensions);
5 Insurance (products for the personal and business sectors);
6 Mortgage Services.

IT Operational Services is the primary supplier of day-to-day operational IT services to all B-UK businesses. In addition, each of the businesses has their own IT development resources.

The importance of disaster recovery planning

Mistakes are a critical part of every service. Hard as they try, even the best service companies can't prevent the occasional late flight, burned steak, or missed delivery. The fact is in services often performed in the customer's presence errors are inevitable. (Hart, Heskett and Sasser, 1990)

Banks are service organizations and the operations of service organizations are being transformed by the use of IT (Lovelock, 1992) so the likelihood of IT failure impacting some part of service delivery will increase. The impact of 'not insuring' against service failures and particularly 'IT disasters' may be measured in several ways including actual financial losses, corporate litigation, replacement costs, reputation damage, loss of competitive edge and loss of consumer confidence in the organization or its products (Menkus, 1994). There are a number of well-documented information systems failures which give insight into potential issues of concern:

● AT&T telephone exchange failure, September 1991, causing the cancellation of 500 flights due to the disruption caused to air traffic control.
● French Computer wholesaler, Omnilogic, had offices and computer equipment destroyed in a fire in June 1994.

- Disk failure in an IBM System38 at the British Linen Bank, Edinburgh – system unavailable for twenty hours at critical year end processing time.
- Mainframe processor 'crash' at The Bank of Scotland caused 400 branches to be halted for more than five hours.

One reason for the importance of regulation of the financial services sector's IS is because of concerns of the impact of these disasters on the wider economy. For example, it is speculated that the collapse of one of the UK's four major clearing banks would result in a crisis for the UK economy.

Disaster recovery practice at The Bank

At The Bank, contingency planning and implementation for IS has been undertaken for some years and has resulted in a large IT infra-structure to support it. Over the last ten to fifteen years the reliance upon IT to enable The Bank to carry out its business has grown considerably. However, The Bank has now recognized that this planning is insufficient and that an integrated, end-to-end business continuity planning process needs to be put in place. This has resulted from high profile events such as the bombs in Bishopsgate, Docklands and Manchester, all of which affected The Bank's operations and required the integrated recovery of business premises, IT, paper documents and other resources to support a full business operation the next working day.

This change in policy creates new levels of complexity. Some is due to the technical solutions required to support the requirements, some to the management processes and the implementation of these. The perceived benefit to The Bank is that in building a new management process that fits the organization and its technology, the bank can be confident it will be able to survive even with the catastrophic loss of one its data centres.

Perspectives on business continuity

To appreciate the issues in the context of The Bank, it is necessary to consider a number of perspectives such as:

- The Bank's business unit perspective;
- the internal service provider (The Bank's IT operational services) perspective;
- the regulators' perspective (external – represented by such organizations as the Bank of England – and internal – represented by The Bank's own internal auditors).

Other stakeholder perspectives such as customers, staff, The Bank's board and shareholders could also be considered. However, their views will, in the main, be represented by the three primal groupings.

The business unit perspective

From the business unit perspective, disaster recovery planning for data centres possibly creates more problems than the value it delivers. Whilst it is recognized that disaster recovery planning is good business practice, it is an activity that usually results in considerable demands on resources, usually in the form of extra costs.

The Bank, like all financial services businesses, is under pressure from customers and senior management to reduce costs. In addition, the businesses are attempting to improve service quality, and to be increasingly innovative, particularly in the use of technology, to meet new customer requirements and improve competitiveness. These pressures mean that managers find it difficult to justify expenditure on activities that cannot prove their immediate benefit. However, the business decision criteria are not simply financial; stringent industry regulatory requirements create additional pressures and complications in the decision process.

Internal service provider perspective

For the internal service provider, disaster recovery planning is a key process for ensuring that the needs of its customers (the business units) and the needs of The Bank are met. The current Bank processes, and the supporting policies and standards have been developed from the industry, and business perspectives, but have excluded the internal service provider perspective.

In an environment such as The Bank, where multiple autonomous customers share the same technical infrastructure, there are many issues and problems. These include competing priorities, differing requirements, different funding commitments, technical constraints and perceived ownership. All these are in the context of cost and competition pressures faced by the business units.

The regulators' perspective

The regulators are faced with ensuring that the industries and organizations 'represent good and safe propositions to the stakeholders in those industries and organizations' whilst at the same time ensuring that those same industries and organizations flourish and grow. The case of disaster recovery planning represents a dilemma for regulators who see the need to protect the various interests and to safeguard the businesses. However, they also face pressure from the same organizations and businesses not to impose overly restrictive policies which potentially hinder development of the sector. In the UK, the primary set of regulations are seen to be open to interpretation, allowing organizations to decide their own agendas, leaving internal regulators 'without teeth'. It is, however, likely that the regulators will soon be forced to adopt more specific and stringent regulations in relation to IT disaster recovery.

The different stakeholders and their conflicting requirements mean there are many pulls on the disaster recovery planning process, and the policies and standards supporting the process. The Bank's 'system' can be set in the context of the wider issues outlined in Figure 13.1.

Business continuity planning

Business continuity planning extends the idea of computer disaster recovery to address the whole business' ability to respond to a disaster affecting its

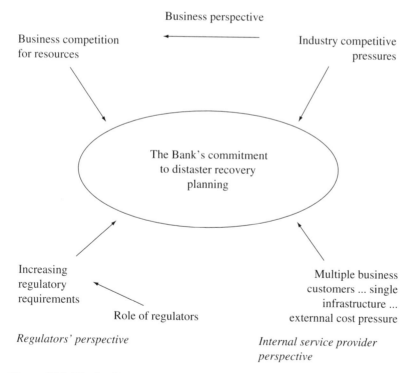

Figure 13.1 *The Bank's disaster recovery planning in context*

normal day-to-day business. While loss of the computer system would seriously impede the organization, the need to broaden planning to include all business critical services and resources is recognized. The existence of an IT disaster recovery plan alone may not be sufficient to assure corporate survival. The objectives of business continuity planning can range from the minimal maintaining business operations in survival mode to enabling 'business as usual – business services'. (Corby, 1992). Business continuity planning has two main planks. First, ensuring technical continuity and, second, ensuring the appropriate management processes are in place to enable business continuity. This is demonstrated through the following model (Figure 13.2) used at The Bank.

Galliers (1992) suggests the following management themes may need to be addressed if any project is to be successful:

● management commitment;

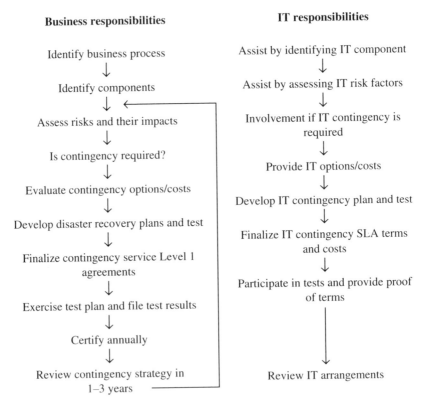

Figure 13.2 *Responsibilities for business continuity planning*

- good leadership/process champion;
- integration with business strategy;
- quantification of benefits;
- user/process education.

These issues need to be considered as an integral part of the development of the business continuity solution.

Towards a business continuity plan for The Bank

The issues which The Bank needs to address to develop a business continuity plan can be summarized as below.

Complete and fully integrated business planning

The disaster recovery process should be undertaken as a part of the main business planning process. Complete business planning should account for all aspects of the business including disaster recovery. This will require a change in The Bank, where disaster recovery is currently planned for separately.

Many of The Bank's IT services are provided from the Data Centre across the telecommunications network to many different end points in the business network. However, planning is generally carried out separately for different technical areas i.e., data centre contingency planning, network communications contingency planning and business unit contingency planning. Coordination policies will need to be put in place to ensure consistency of planning and provision across the group.

Disaster recovery management commitment, leadership and control

The evaluation of risk and implementation plans is currently left to individual business units. Central coordination for disaster recovery planning within The Bank will provide a means for comparing the various policies and ensuring consistency. The advantage of this will be that service providers can provide an agreed level of service across the whole bank. This will have the effect of reducing costs due to economies of scale.

The possible scenarios giving rise to the invocation of a contingency plan are many, as are the precise implications of a disaster. As a result, the planning for such scenarios must incorporate significant flexibility. However, flexibility comes with a price, and this requires explicit direction in risk management to understand the potential value of planning.

Once disaster recovery is recognized as a part of business planning, managers are more likely to be motivated to include it higher in their list of priorities. This will lead to more resources being made available to ensure that training and education are carried out.

Application of disaster recovery policies and standards

Implementation of disaster recovery policies and standards requires full management commitment. This will ensure that the quality of the policies and processes are assessed regularly alongside other management issues. Benefits and risks associated with a disaster recovery policy can be quantified and measured, enabling managers to determine the level of resource that needs to be made available to ensure the highest quality provision.

IT and disaster recovery ownership

The policies of The Bank state that the ownership of, and responsibilities for, the implementation of IT within a business unit lie with the unit which may use other providers (e.g., IT operational services) to execute those responsibilities. However, the acceptance and implementation of these policies is not universal across the bank, with some units finding it difficult to skill these requirements and the internal IT providers in some cases unwilling, or unable, to give up their traditional role in The Bank.

IT disaster recovery implementation and control

The Bank's technical infrastructure is configured as a set of shared technical components. Individual workloads across these components are balanced and tuned for optimum performance given the constraint of variable workloads. However, the workload priorities within, and across, business units, is not universally understood nor agreed at group level. This is further complicated by the levels of interconnectedness between IS supporting the various workloads. This issue of priorities becomes important in the contingency scenario where resources may be constrained.

Once in place, contingency plans must be kept current with changes in the day-to-day operational systems to ensure that the business requirements can be met. Changes in technical infrastructure must also be reflected in the contingency plans to ensure that the contingency infrastructure can support the agreed IS requirements. With approximately 2000 technical changes per month, this represents a challenge in maintaining the required integrity in the contingency plans, where the change controls may not be adequate to meet the need at both an evaluation level and an implementation level.

The accepted way of ensuring that contingency plans for IS are valid, and will achieve the objective when required, is to carry out tests. This usually takes the form of invoking a test plan and building the contingent environment. However, in The Bank's current IS contingency strategy, some constraints exist which preclude full testing and live invocation of the solution. Not least is that the invocation of the contingency solution would result in a lesser service being delivered to customers. Additionally, as UK banking moves towards twenty-four hours a day operations, the opportunity to test becomes more difficult. Current modelling techniques are inadequate in proving contingency solutions and testing is also expensive. The current complexity of The Bank's data centre environment, the multiplicity of recovery strategies and inadequate past change controls make validation of the IT disaster recover plans difficult.

Placing the issues in context

As discussed, the issue sets identified sit within much wider organizational and industry contexts (Figure 13.3).

Large and established organizations, such as The Bank, are having to re-think how they organize and reengineer to ensure they are best placed to face competitive pressures. This requires clear and close integration of the organi-

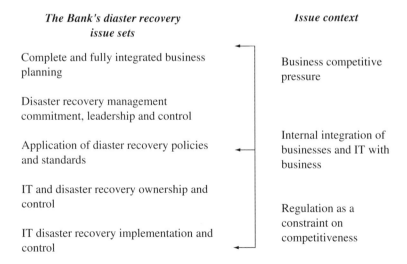

Figure 13.3 *The Bank's disaster recovery issues in context*

zation's various businesses and business delivery infrastructure, including its use of IT.

The UK financial services industry is a classic example of one which had to deal with massive deregulation in order to remain competitive, but after a number of high profile regulatory 'incidents' (e.g. BCCI in 1991 and Barings in 1994) is now facing a period of further regulatory change.

Potential impact of issues

This section examines the potential impact of the issues on the 'success' of The Bank (i.e. failure of the disaster recovery planning process to achieve its objectives). The impact is considered from the perspective of an absolute failure of The Bank's data centre disaster recovery plan (i.e. bank failure). It is also considered from the perspective of a failure of the recovery plan to achieve recovery as required by service levels but not to the degree of 'Bank failure' and therefore its impact in terms of The Bank's business performance measurement system. The latter discussion is at a generic level.

The Bank's business performance measurement system for each of its businesses, including IT operational services, has been built on the principles of the Balanced Business Scorecard (Kaplan and Norton, 1992). The Balanced Business Scorecard recognizes that successful organizations develop strategies and goals in four different aspects of the business. The model shows that these different aspects interact and influence the achievement of each other. The Balanced Business Scorecard provides a means for businesses to judge the effect of a strategy in one area on all the others. The Bank's scorecard takes the four perspectives – customer; financial; internal/quality; innovation and learning/HR – and each business develops a set of measures appropriate to their business. Examples of some of the measures in each category are shown in Figure 13.4.

On the Scorecard there are no direct measures of data centre disaster recovery capability. Thus, the analysis is aimed at a generic level i.e. how major disasters affect these types of measures.

Customer

From the customer perspective it is likely that prolonged recovery times will impact customer confidence and customer satisfaction. A less tangible impact is that on bringing products to market. The Bank's mainframe recovery strategy is based upon 'rebuilding' production systems from the failed data centre primarily in the development capacity. Currently, in

Customer	Financial
Customer satisfaction surveys Time to market	Profit Income Costs
Service level achievement Change success Problem management	Staff skills match Staff satisfaction Management competence
Internal	*Human resources*

Figure 13.4 *Example measures within The Bank's Balanced Business Scorecard*

certain scenarios, the 'development data', e.g. programs, would be completely lost. In other scenarios, if the disaster invocation were to last for any substantial length of time then the development facility would be unavailable unless alternative provisions were made. This could have serious impact on The Bank's ability to deliver new products to customers, or to deliver enhanced systems to meet new regulatory requirements. An additional problem is looming with the projected redevelopment required to meet Year 2000 compliance.

Financial

The potential financial implications to The Bank of poor disaster recovery planning and plans include reduced incomes, increased costs, and hence reduced profits.

Internal

Many of the current internal measures reflect business requirements in order to provide services to customers. Whilst failure to meet some of these measures would not directly impact The Bank, there would be implications for other parts of the Scorecard; for example, a missed measure might indicate dissatisfied customers and hence a reduction in profit.

Human resources

The impact of a disaster on staff and staff morale is interesting. The specific impacts are likely to be dependent upon the particular circumstances of the recovery and probably the internal relationships. For example, if no staff are harmed, but the recovery is not as efficient as expected and a 'blame culture' prevails, it is possible that staff morale could significantly drop. It is likely that the incident will create uncertainty throughout the organization not only during the recovery process but also post-incident as the recovery issues are explored.

Systems for effective business continuity planning

As described, the issues associated with business continuity planning can be described in terms of five issue sets, or four sub-systems (issue sets 3 and 4 being combined as both are part of a technical solution) within the single system of business continuity planning.

1 The business planning system;
2 The leadership and control system;
3 The policy and standards application system;
4 The solution control system.

A set of performance criteria are identified for each of the sub-systems. These measures are defined in terms of efficacy (does the means work?), efficiency (are minimum resources used?), and effectiveness (are longer term aims served?) The systems are defined as below.

The business planning system

A Business-owned system with the purpose of delivering budgeted IT risk management programmes within the overall business plan and through the business planning activities, which ensure that an individual business unit has a balanced portfolio of IT investment requirements within its overall 'afford-ability' targets.

Efficacy (E_1) Do plans contain a service delivery risk assessment for both new and continuing customer services?

Efficiency (E_2) Are plans produced within required timescales and with minimum resources?

Effectiveness (E_3) Are external and internal auditors satisfied with The Bank's service delivery risk management?

The leadership and control system

A business unit owned system aiming to transform scheduled activity into actual monitored work and solutions so that the individual sponsors or business units can be confident of delivering service continuously to their customers in the event of an IS failure.

Efficacy (E_1) How many of the risk management solutions scheduled are implemented?

Efficiency (E_2) Is The Bank's time to market for services significantly different from its competitors?

Effectiveness (E_3) Are The Bank's service costs or service losses significantly greater or less than industry competitors?

The policy and standards application system

A business unit managed system aimed at improving the understanding of business unit managers and project teams of the service continuity need to their business goals, through the encouraged adoption and application of bank policy, standards and methodologies.

Efficacy (E_1) Do key Bank personnel have the required risk management policy standards knowledge and methodology practice?

Efficiency (E_2) Is the knowledge training achieved at significant cost excess against other types of training?

Effectiveness (E_3) Does the overall appreciation of the value of service continuity increase within The Bank's businesses?

The solution control system

A business unit and supplier owned process aimed at ensuring that the IT Contingency plans are managed and validated through knowledge and appropriate controls and testing activities so that the business units can be confident that should the need to implement arise their solutions are valid and proven.

> Efficacy (E_1) Does The Bank achieve a greater success in validating their IT contingency solutions from both the service delivery and regulator perspectives?
>
> Efficiency (E_2) Do The Bank's IT operational services provide a competitive IT contingency service when benchmarked against competitor organizations?
>
> Effectiveness (E_3) Do The Bank's IT operational services achieve the required service level agreements with its customers?

Building a programme for change

Tichy (1983) proposes an approach to build a change programme based around an overall alignment of technical, political and cultural systems. Further, he suggests there are 'levers' within organizations and across the systems, which can be pulled to effect the required and desired changes. However, the key factor is that the activities in the change programme need to be aligned.

The *technical* system is described as those resources – technical, financial and social – that need to be arranged to produce some desired output. The *political* system is concerned with the allocation of power and resources and is reflected in such issues as compensation programmes, career decisions, budget decisions, and the internal power structure. The *cultural* system is concerned with the values, objectives, beliefs and interpretations shared by organizational members. The Tichy approach builds upon the categorizations to suggest that each of the individual systems are intricately interwoven. He uses the metaphor of a rope to underline this and to demonstrate that should one of the strands (or system) become unravelled then the overall change programme is weakened.

The 'levers' proposed are:

1 Mission and strategy;
2 Tasks;
3 Prescribed networks;
4 People;
5 Processes;
6 Emergent networks.

In large organizations such as The Bank, where complexity abounds, it is difficult from a distance to distinguish the individual strands. Each of the business units has its own culture, politics and ways of doing things. Tichy suggests that each of the strands needs to be understood and dealt with. Within the individual Bank business units, and across the business units, it is important that the three strands do not work at cross-purposes, otherwise the programme will quickly become unravelled. There are changes required to the technical (business planning system and solution control system), the cultural (policy and standards system) and the political (leadership and control system).

The idealized programme for change

The programme for change is proposed in terms of the Tichy model and the 'levers' required to effect change. In Table 13.1 the proposed changes are discussed in terms of idealized changes. Later, the changes will be evaluated in terms of benefits or impacts, in order to attempt prioritization.

Benefits management approach

There is much evidence of the lack of actual success, or lack of satisfaction, with project results generally, and 'IT related' projects particularly, whether it be an IT outsourcing project (Lacity and Hirschheim, 1993) not delivering the expected cost or efficiency gains, or a business process reengineering project (Carr and Johansson, 1995), or a general IT investments (Kearney, 1990). Many issues relating to this are, according to Willcocks and Lester (1993) due to the lack of, or inappropriate, project evaluation, measurement and monitoring.

An 'idealized' programme of change was proposed, above, in terms of the technical, political and cultural sub-systems within the organization. However, this programme does not represent what is best for the organization in terms of affordability, or contribution to, strategic goals or corporate measures of success. Based on the above a formal method of project evaluation and prioritization is required.

Many methods have been put forward to enable the evaluation and prioritization of project elements. Some are based on a straight financial assessment (Cougar, 1987) through to a more strategic and rounded analysis of the benefits based around softer issues as well as the financial measures. (Tichy, 1983). Whilst these methodologies address primarily the project evaluation process, Earl (1990) suggests that the evaluation process needs to be combined with the project management process to the extent that the focus during implementation should be managing the benefits, not just the project.

As previously highlighted, The Bank's business performance is assessed in terms of its Balanced Business Scorecard. This same mechanism is used to

Table 13.1

	Technical System	*Political System*	*Cultural System*
Mission and strategy	Integration of risk management into the full business planning cycle	Ensure risk manager included in mission/strategy formulation	
Tasks	Introduction of external IT contingency bench-marking activities	Re-introduction and reinforcement of bank-wide business continuity governance role	Build service continuity evaluations into regular service reviews
Prescribed networks	Introduction of service continuity risk management role into project management organization	Establish service continuity role as main board member within each business	Make service continuity information available through the whole organization, driven from the customer perspective
People	Hire service continuity/risk professionals	Build service continuity targets into both business and IT managers performance contracts	Build training programme for The Bank promoting service continuity values
Processes	Development of automated knowledge base, fully integrated into change control system. Formal agenda item on individual business units board agendas to facilitate and promote information flow.	Make rewards partially dependent upon test results for operational acceptance tests and contingency tests for project teams	Introduce service continuity training into induction training programme and IT analyst training
Emergent networks	Ensure continuity information and service design and strategy information available to all project teams and technical specialists	Reinforcement of service continuity values through education and awareness programme	Reinforcement of service continuity values through education and awareness programme

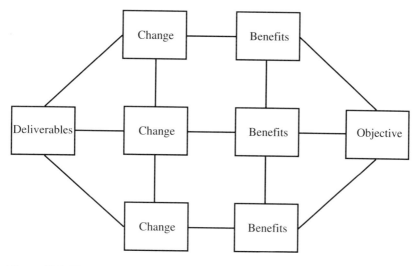

Figure 13.5 *The Bank's benefit management methodology*

assess the 'business case' for change. A methodology has been developed within The Bank which combines an evaluation process for change pro-grammes (non-IT and IT based) in terms of the impacts on the Business Scorecard, which is then combined with The Bank's project management approach. The initial evaluation process is applied to the proposed 'idealized' programme of change to determine the desirable (and feasible) set of changes. This is known as the benefits management methodology (Figure 13.5).

The mapping exercise contains four stages:

1 listing the deliverables;
2 identifying expecting changes;
3 identifying the resultant benefits;
4 relating the benefits to the Balanced Business Scorecard objectives.

As the exercise is likely to generate many expected changes and many expected benefits the simple rule of thumb is to use the most significant six or seven at most.

This approach is applied to the six areas which have been identified as nec-essary for the business continuity programme to be successful.

The potential costs and benefits of change programmes

The potential change activities as identified can be grouped as follows in order to assess the potential benefits and costs of the programme.

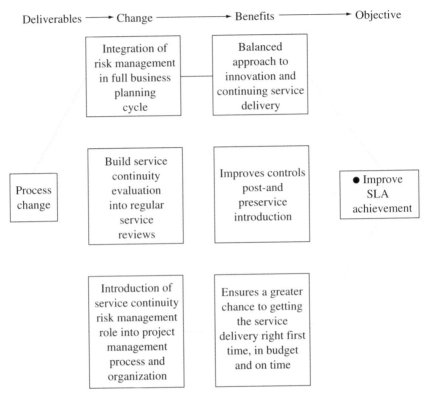

Figure 13.6 *Process change*

Process change

- Integration of risk management in full business planning cycles.
- Build business continuity evaluations into regular service reviews.
- Introduction of business continuity risk management role into project management process and organization.

Structural change

- Reintroduction and reinforcement of bank wide business continuity governance role.
- Ensure risk manager included in mission/strategy formulation.
- Establish business continuity' role as main board member within each business.
- Formal agenda item on individual business units board agendas to facilitate and promote information flow.

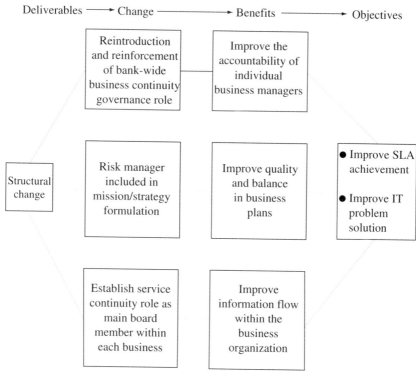

Figure 13.7 *Structural activities*

Training and development

- Hiring of business continuity/risk management professionals.
- Build training programme for The Bank promoting business continuity values.
- Introduce business continuity training into induction training programme and IT analyst training.

Education and awareness

- Introduction of external IT contingency benchmarking activities, and building of risk impact database.
- Make business continuity information available through the whole organization, driven from the customer perspective.
- Reinforcement of business continuity value through education and awareness programme.

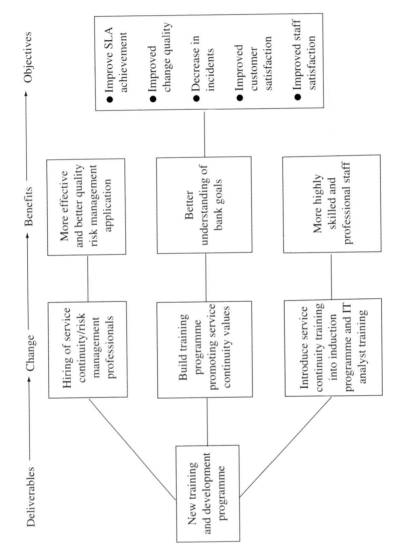

Figure 13.8 *Training and development*

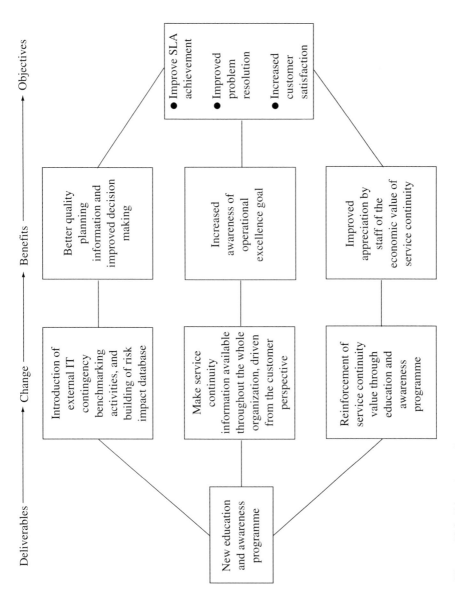

Figure 13.9 *Education and awareness*

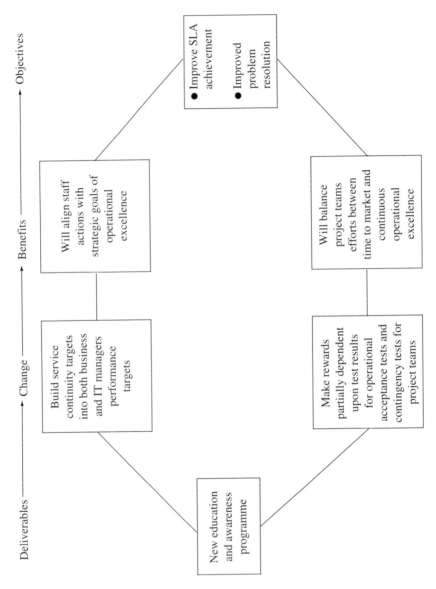

Figure 13.10 *Performance management*

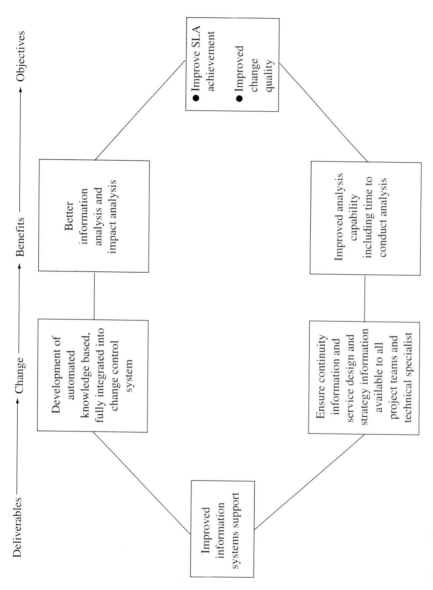

Figure 13.11 *Information systems support*

Performance management

- Build business continuity targets into both business and IT managers performance contracts.
- Make rewards partially dependent upon test results for operational acceptance tests and contingency tests for project teams.

Information systems support

- Development of automated knowledge base, fully integrated into change control system.
- Ensure continuity information and service design and strategy information available to all project teams and technical specialists.

The benefits can be seen to tie in with the goals identified in The Bank's Business Scorecard. The changes and benefits are practical and their achievement can be measured, thus ensuring that the business continuity plan is monitored effectively.

Conclusions

The Bank, like its competitors, considers it takes the subject of business continuity planning and IT contingency planning very seriously. It has put in place a set of policies, standards and processes across all its business units to ensure that its businesses can survive a major disaster and that it complies with the necessary financial services' industry regulations.

It is shown here that business continuity planning requires more than the introduction of the policies and standards. There is a need to consider business continuity planning as a part of the whole business planning system. Alongside this it has been shown that there is a need for considerable input from senior management to the implementation of business continuity planning. Implementation will also only be successful if users and managers are aware of the reasons for the programme. Information technologists also need to understand that the technical solutions should fit with the business requirements.

The approach The Bank has taken to introduce this change is through the use of the benefits methodology which enables the changes required and the concomitant benefits to be identified which support particular business objectives. This provides the rationale for acceptance of the strategy and implementation of business continuity planning throughout The Bank.

References

Carr, D. K. and Johansson, H. J. (1995). Best Practices in Re-engineering. McGraw Hill, pp. 22–23.

Corby, M. J. (1992). *Managing Disaster Recovery Testing*, Datapro Reports on Information Security, McGraw Hill, March.

Cougar, J. D. (1987). Techniques for estimating system benefits. In *Information Analysis Selected Readings* (Robert Galliers, ed), Addison-Wesley.

Earl, M. J. (1990). *Putting IT in its Place: A Polemic for the Nineties*. Oxford Institute of Information Management.

Galliers, R. (1991). Strategic Information Systems Planning: Concepts, Methods and Critical Success Factors, University of Warwick.

Hart, C., Heskett, J. and Sasser, E. (1990). The profitable art of service recovery. *Harvard Business Review*, **4**, July–August.

Kaplan, R. S. and Norton, D. P. (1992). The balanced scorecard – measures that drive performance. *Harvard Business Review*, January–February.

Kearney, A. T. (1990). *Breaking the Barriers: IT Effectiveness in Great Britain and Ireland*. CIMA.

Lacity, M. and Hirschheim, R. (1993). *Information Systems Outsourcing – Myths Metaphors and Realities*. John Wiley & Sons.

Lovelock, C. H. (1992). *Are Services Really Different?* Prentice-Hall.

Menkus, B. (1994). The new importance of 'business continuity' in processing disaster recovery planning. *Computer and Security*, **13**, pp.115–118.

Tichy, N. M. (1983). *Managing Strategic Change*. John Wiley & Sons.

Willcocks, L. and Lester, S. (1993). *Evaluating Information Technology Investments: Research Findings and Re-appraisal*

14 Electronic requisitioning at an electricity generator – a case study of IS failure

Rupert Alston and Andrew Martin
Warwick Business School

Introduction

The main purpose of the project was to investigate apparent resistance to a pilot implementation of an electronic order requisitioning (ER) system initiated by the procurement department of a UK electricity generator. The project concerns a large mainframe-based financial accounting package which had been significantly customized. Analysis by procurement and IT departments showed that the package was not being used to its full potential for order requisitioning. The pilot study was initiated at the company HQ in order to assess the potential of ER (Pye, Bates and Heath, 1986) and it was felt by management that the ER pilot 'has not proved as successful as had been hoped'.

Manual and computer-based requisitioning systems

In the manual system, the person needing to make an order requisition, the *originator*, fills in an 'R1' form, passing it to his or her *authorizer* who countersigns it. The order is then sent via internal mail to the finance department where a management accountant checks that a budget exists and corrects any cost code errors. The R1 is then sent to procurement where it is entered onto the computer, and the buyer can print the order electronically (Figure 14.1). This figure shows six different places where a requisition can become delayed.

Under the computer-based electronic requisitioning the difference is simply that the originator types the requisition directly into the system. The system

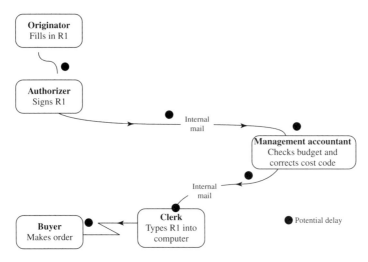

Figure 14.1 *The paper process*

will not accept invalid cost codes. The requisition information can then be sent electronically to the authorizer who can call up the requisition information and authorize the requisition in a few keystrokes. The requisition is then transmitted electronically to the buyer. At any point in this process the progress of the requisition can be traced using the system.

Methodology

Since the problem seemed to revolve significantly around the social situation and interactions between different departments it was considered that a 'soft' approach was required when selecting a methodology, as suggested by Le-Saint (1991). It was important first to investigate and define the problem as part of the project. Soft systems methodology (SSM) was a candidate methodology, since it is 'a process of tackling real-world problems in all their richness' (Checkland and Scholes, 1990, p. 5). However the final stages of SSM involve taking action, and this was not within the scope of the investigation. A 'looser' methodology was developed that suited the less specific nature of the problem. According to Mitchell (1993), 'the way to [solve the 'real' problem] is to have sufficient understanding of the system under study'. The investigation used the modelling tools of SSM to structure the 'messiness' of the problem and in this way to gain an understanding of the company processes.

In broad terms the investigation consisted of first 'divergence,' collecting as broad a spectrum of information as possible. Then, investigations focused on the suspected root causes which are analysed in more depth, allowing the pro-

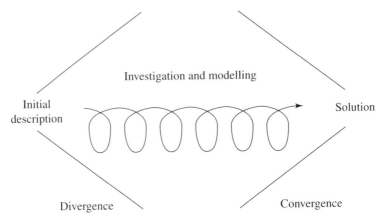

Figure 14.2 *Methodology*

ject to 'converge' iteratively towards understanding and potential solutions (Figure 14.2).

Given that the nature of resistance is potentially a contentious issue within organizations and that cultural factors often play a part, it was decided, from the start, that the main method of data collection would be through interview, where a better idea of the political issues involved in the processes would be more likely to be conveyed. At a later stage, quantitative data would be collected in order to support or otherwise the inherently subjective information gleaned through the interviews.

Business context

The company ('A') is an electricity generator, running several power stations around the UK. Competition is on the basis of price and there is excess capacity in the market. These factors lead to strong downward pressure on costs and staffing levels. The waves of Figure 14.3 indicate the turbulence of the market: generators sell their electricity via contracts and into the *pool* which can provide an unstable market with large spot price changes on a day-by-day basis. Those generators which are not equipped to cope in a hot competitive environment will struggle to survive.

Literature search – project success and failure and the 3D model

A search of the relevant literature was undertaken to identify which factors

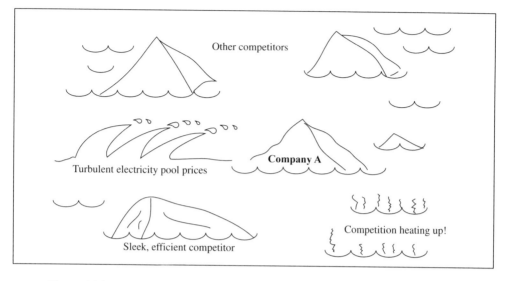

Figure 14.3 *Representation of Company A's environment*

were historically the worst culprits for causing resistance to information system implementation. A summary table of the results is shown in Table 14.1.

It should be noted that most of the cited papers deal with the full implementation of large information systems, whereas the Company A situation reflects a *pilot study* for the adoption of an existing computerized system into their manual process. However, since the users of ER would be new to the system and that the ER process itself was new, the potential failure factors are just as relevant to this case. The literature indicates that information systems 'fail' more often due to managerial problems than to technical difficulties.

The 3D model

Ballantine et al.'s (1996) '3D model of information systems success' was consulted in particular detail for this investigation. The 3D model, shown in Figure 14.4, breaks the IS introduction process down into different levels, and allows different methods and measures of success evaluation to be used at each level.

The 3D model identifies three separate stages to successful IS introduction:

1 *Development* of the technical system.
2 *Deployment* of the system to the user.

Table 14.1 *Project failure factors*

Possible failure factor	Reference
1 Bad technically developed system	Grimshaw and Kemp (1989), Eason (1989)
2 Physical access to terminals	Healy (1987)
3 Inadequate training/system misunderstood	Grimshaw and Kemp (1989), Grimshaw (1988), Healy (1987)
4 No user 'ownership'	Ballantine et al. (1996), Grimshaw and Kemp (1989), Healy (1987)
5 Resistance to change in working practices	Healy (1987)
6 No user motivation/not responsible for results of action	Grindley (1991)
7 Poor implementation	Grimshaw and Kemp (1989)
8 Poor choice of pilot project group	Eason (1989), Pye, Bates and Heath (1986)
9 Lack of Budget-Holder Support/Mgt support	Pinto and Slevin (1987), Strassman (1984)
10 No top executive commitment/no sponsor	Ballantine et al. (1996), Hammer (1990), Edwards (1989), Grimshaw and Kemp (1989), Pinto and Slevin (1987)

3 *Delivery* of the business benefits of that system.

At each of these levels *influencing factors* are identified 'which collectively determine the quality of the information system within their respective levels,' (Ballantine et al., 1996, p. 10). Thus, according to the model, the technology, user involvement and the quality of the data used all have an influence on the quality of the information system being developed. Between the different levels, the 3D model identifies *filters* which can slow or block progress from one level to the next. The filters 'contain influences which inhibit or encourage the adoption of the system at the next higher level,' (Ballantine et al., 1996, p10).

Ballantine et al. describe the 3D model primarily as a 'conceptual awareness model' (p. 13), designed to draw attention to the dynamism and complexity of introducing an information system. However, they state that 'the model can also be used for planning and evaluating IS success'. The 3D model was therefore used as a framework for evaluation of the ER pilot, alongside the project failure factors literature.

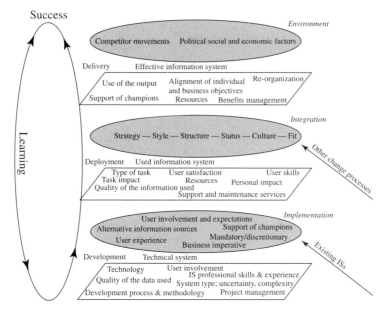

Figure 14.4 *The 3D model*

Initial positioning of ER within the 3D model

At Company A, the information system had already been *developed* and ER is beginning to be *deployed* to the users in the form of the pilot. The 3D model therefore clearly points in the case of ER to the first filter and the deployment level as the main focus of attention. However, it still remains worthwhile to evaluate the *fruits* of the development stage, in that, as Ballantine et al. point out, while the influencing factors in this first level help to dictate the quality of the system, 'it could still be that a low quality technical system is still successfully deployed,' (p. 12). For this reason an evaluation of the quality of system development was attempted using this model.

Development

The reputation of the software developer and the use of their systems by many other large firms would suggest also that the quality of data used, system type and technology were all indicating a high quality technical system. The introduction of a pilot showed that users were being involved prior to a full implementation at the deployment level.

Development–deployment filter

The filter to the deployment level posed many more questions. Again, the use of a pilot suggested that user involvement was occurring, although nothing was known about their expectations. Moreover, it was suggested at an early stage that, 'there was a fundamental question of competence' with those in the business units at Company A with respect to use of information technology. This suggested that user skills and experience would be a filter blockage to deployment. Furthermore, it would seem that a mere *requisitioning* system had little value adding business imperative, and the continued existence of the paper system indicated ER's use was discretionary rather than mandatory.

Deployment

Given that a number of people were already using the system for requisitioning purposes in the pilot, it was also viable to evaluate the influencing factors suggested in the deployment level of the 3D model. Little was known initially about any of these factors, but they provided a list of areas to investigate in the 'divergence' stages of the project.

In this way the 3D model provided a powerful structure and checklist for the early stages of the investigation. Enquiry and analysis could then establish which factors were, indeed, inhibiting the ER pilot.

A critical analysis of the pilot implementation

Structured interviews with representative stakeholders were held, and informed the following analysis, which follows the structure of Table 14.1 and the implementation filter of the 3D model.

The developed system – user-friendliness

The system itself appears to be reliable and useful, however the presentation of the information and the difficulty of using it are definite stumbling blocks to the introduction of ER. Every single interviewee volunteered the information that the system was not user-friendly, although those familiar with its use said that once learnt it was a powerful system to be able to utilize. The format of the information supplied is not obvious to the inexperienced user and navigation between screens requires knowledge of the correct codes. Further, some of the keystrokes are inconsistent on different screens. However, only two screens were required for electronic requisitioning, and the amount of information to be input was small.

Authorizers in particular complained that the system was too difficult to use or to learn or that electronic authorization is too time consuming compared with a simple signature. Further, authorization is the simplest task of ER, requiring a minimum of keystrokes once the system has been accessed. Due to their seniority and their key position within the ER process, these authorizer complaints are serious from the point of view of resistance to ER.

Physical access

The fact that some engineering requisition originators currently sometimes fax their R1 forms from site into the office suggests that physical access to terminals was a potential problem (as suggested by Healy, 1987), although it was a minor one.

Training

The training was carried out by procurement staff – the duration of which was approximately one hour – and involved being led through the two appropriate system screens. Originators were then offered follow-up support when they next wanted to make a requisition. The training itself was thorough, however there was no documentation to accompany the sessions. A half-finished 'Electronic Requisitioning Handbook' was located, which had been put together as an explanatory document by the finance department and turned into a step-by-step guide to using ER by procurement. It had not been made available to the pilot participants as it had not been completed. Difficulties arise where many of the requisitions, or originators, only fill in a few R1s per year.

Ownership

The clerks trained to use the system did appear to have gained some 'ownership' of the ER process. This ownership had been facilitated by singling them out for training and the continued support and use of ER. Budget holders, however, seemed uncommitted to ER.

Actors, politics and resistance to change to working practices

Authorizers

Authorizers were complaining about ER because they saw it as a transferral of procurement's clerical work to them without any extra clerical help being made available to them. An advantage to authorizers is that the system immediately has up-to-date budgetary information, however this advantage was not being perceived or exploited.

Finance

Under ER the finance R1 checkers would no longer have to carry out this task. It was therefore seen as a possibility that under the company's cost-cutting environment these people would be unwilling to lose this function for fear of making themselves dispensable. Yet, it was found that finance would in fact be pleased not to have to carry out the disruptive work of checking people's R1s. However, they believed that training would be required in 'proper' detailed budgeting and in the use of the system for checking budgets before cost code awareness would filter down through headquarters. This would be a far more complex training requirement than simply teaching originators to use the requisition and authorization screens on the system.

Originators

Such a move would force the originators to learn their account codes and cost codes, and emerges as a possible hidden agenda for ER. Many interviewees explained that the cost codes themselves were complicated and very problematic for requisitioners. One buyer admitted that on the R1 form the cost code section was 'often' left blank; another method was to 'fill in the R1 and then wander around until you find someone who understands the cost code'.

Procurement

When the manual R1 reaches procurement it gets allocated to a buyer, then sent to a clerk who types it in, and finally it arrives on the buyer's desk with the paper duplicate, where it is actioned. Under ER the electronic R1 information arrives on the team leader's screen and is allocated electronically. Electronic allocation did not appear to be a popular proposition, perhaps because of the extra transparency it would give. Elsewhere in procurement, complaints were voiced that sorting out the different types of requisition was difficult when several arrived in the 'mailbox' at once. On investigation, however, it was found that the current method is to take each requisition in turn regardless of type in any case, therefore ER would be no different. The inference is that the buyers in procurement were at best ambivalent to ER.

It was found that the R1 was still being raised by originators, then given to the clerk for entering onto the system. The original intention was that the actual originator should input the information directly into the system. It appeared that nominated pilot members were unaware of the intended process rather than being deliberately opposed to training originators, although there was some resistance when the correct process was suggested to them. The use of a clerk not only eliminates the saving of duplicate work proposed by ER, but also makes that clerk central to the procurement process within that department. To some this is seen as an advantage in that there is a 'key point of responsibility' within the process, but conversely this is a disadvantage from the point of view of workforce flexibility, since the clerk has made him or herself less dispensable.

Motivation

None of the actors mentioned so far has reason to be motivated to commit to ER. This is shown by Figure 14.5, a 'rich picture' of the paper versus ER processes.

Implementation (see Figure 14.4)

Users were involved through training but not through education into the total vision for ER. There was no clear management champion who wanted the implementation to succeed. The system was not made compulsory, mainly because there was no clear business need for ER, and the old system was a readily available alternative. Some users were experienced in the ER process

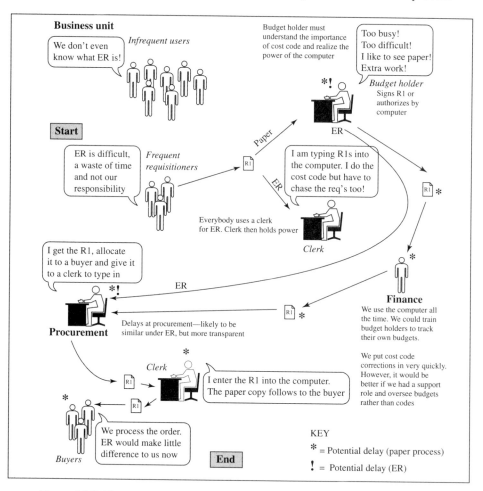

Figure 14.5 *The requisition process*

and the technology and coped well, but new users were less comfortable with the changed practices.

Choice of pilot group

Sixteen people from four business units were nominated for training in the use of the system for requisitioning. Two originators who had been given training were unable to participate as they were never given the system access and this was not followed up. Two other business units involved in the pilot had used ER previously while stationed at another headquarters site; they tended to use one 'the system officer' to place requisitions electronically, as had been the process at that site. This left only two 'originators' and two authorisers from one business unit undertaking to use ER and the appropriate the system screens for the first time. In all cases it was clerical staff who were nominated for training, rather than the actual requisition originators.

Management support and project sponsor

The financial accounting manager was also the formal system sponsor. However, his interest in the system stretched only so far as his own function. The management accounting manager confirmed that he would not be upset for the management accountants no longer to have to check R1s. However he took a wider view of the role of finance and procurement departments and, whilst acknowledging that the company had to modernize and processes had to change, remained unconvinced that electronic requisitioning was the correct action to be taking in this respect. His feeling was that a more fundamental review of the complete ordering process would yield the most promising results. This issue is taken up in the discussion of the VISA system below.

The nearest person to an actual project sponsor was the procurement manager, who as chair of the Steering Committee, endorsed the business case for ER and had the authority to progress the pilot and provide motivation to complete the various tasks (Edwards, 1989, pp. 3–4). She was pushing the business case for the introduction of ER and was overseeing the pilot, encouraging those on the committee to progress with the review and handbook. When interviewed, however, the procurement manager admitted the ER pilot had stalled somewhat, partly due to the infrequency of the Steering Committee meetings, and partly because the work of another review task force (see VISA below) was delaying the endorsement of the business case for ER, albeit informally. Furthermore, the advantages seen by this manager were solely those to procurement – the elimination of the back end clerical work – which explained why there was no pressure to train originators rather than clerks at the front end.

In order to map the overall management imperative for the introduction of ER, an influence diagram was constructed and is shown in Figure 14.6. The figure shows that at the management level the overall keenness to introduce ER is not great and that this is particularly weak on the finance side.

Identifying the potential costs and benefits of electronic requisitioning

Streamlined process

Under ER a clerk is no longer required to enter the written requisition information into the system. The finance checks by the management accountants

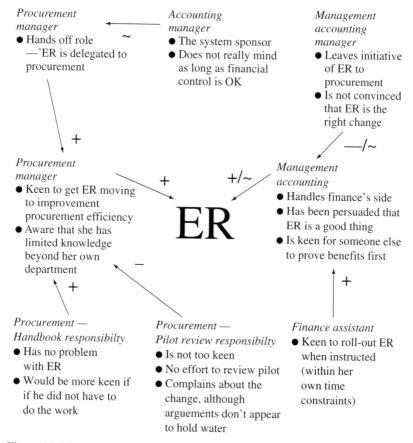

Figure 14.6 *Management influence on the ER pilot*

are also by-passed. In terms of tasks saved, this amounts to approximately six minutes per requisition.

Improvement in turnaround time

Currently an order requisition can take three or four days to reach the buyer. Under ER, the electronic information can be on the buyer's screen within minutes. This eliminates the need for requisitioners to physically and personally 'walk through' an urgent requisition from authorizer to procurement, which takes more than thirty minutes. Evidence from the management accountants suggests that upwards of 20 per cent of requisitions are currently 'walked through' in this way. ER could potentially save 650 hours of non-value-added work per year at headquarters in this way, and another 650 hours from reduced finance and procurement clerical work.

Improved reliability

Under the current system there are seven different places where the R1 might become 'lost,' and there is no easy way of ascertaining its whereabouts. Location of the electronic requisition information can be checked quickly and easily through the system. Although this improvement is difficult to cost, it is a substantial improvement in reliability and efficiency.

Budgetary control

ER can improve the quality of financial control at headquarters. First, the amount requisitioned is immediately entered onto the system which will improve the quality of information to budget holders on how much has been spent. Second, the inability to type in invalid cost codes will have the effect of making people at the front end more aware of budgetary structures and spending. Currently, because there has never been any reprimand for writing an incorrect cost code, most R1s have errors on arrival in finance.

Costs

The main tangible costs are training costs, since the system is already owned. This reinforces the suggestion that a key motivation for ER was management's desire to gain benefit from their large investment sunk into the system.

Analysis of Company A headquarters structure and culture

Since the firm has historically been a public sector organization, but is attempting to come to terms with competitive forces, tensions and insecurity are already present within the company. As Scase and Goffee (1989, p. 58) point out, old style public sector firms tend to be 'especially constrained by formalized procedures' because of the nature of their public accountability. There is evidence of this in the bureaucratic procedures in the company, not least ER. According to Scase and Goffee, 'in such contexts, the introduction of more task-oriented styles of management [the modern format] can cause considerable confusion and resistance'.

Another example of a public sector 'adherence to routines and procedures' rather than goal oriented management, is the manner in which promotion has taken place in the past at Company A. Two separate departments described how people were promoted to management positions on the strength of technical merit and length of service rather than management ability. Many departments now have a 'huge raft of people' at middle management level. Such a situation not only potentially weakens the quality of management decisions at this level, but it also acts as a block to high-quality employees rising through the ranks. Jackall (1988, p5) describes the internal politics that come into play in such situations, stating that 'Bureaucratic work ... creates subtle measures of prestige and an elaborate status hierarchy within an organisation'.

Management influence between the departments at the company works through director level interventions. While this is not unusual for a traditionally structured organization, the effect of this is that finance and procurement, although keen to overhaul their processes, without senior support are forced to rely primarily on informal influence to bring about the changes to processes which affect other business units.

These different influences to the culture at headquarters are all subsumed in the more overt atmosphere which the continuous cost saving initiatives generate. With continuous downwards pressure on costs and little possibility for product differentiation ('our electricity is exactly the same as everybody else's electricity'), it is necessary constantly to be paring back central costs and thus jobs. The subsequent insecurity has the effect of freezing up the ability of the firm to bring about change. The cognitive map in Figure 14.7 shows powerfully how the cost-cutting culture leads to this 'freezing up'. Scase and Goffee explain the cause behind the situation:

> The subsequent breakdown in operating practices [from resistance to changes] can lead senior managers to actually reassert traditional bureaucratic values and to tighten their controls over operating procedures. (Scase and Goffee, 1989, p. 58.)

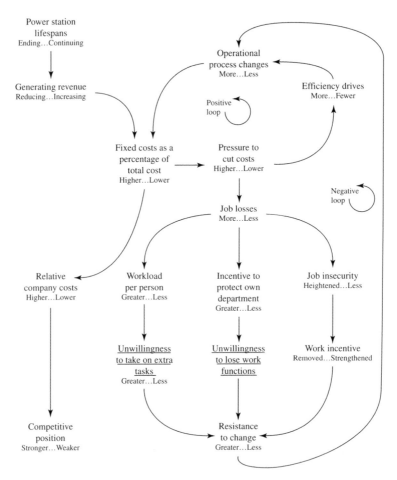

Figure 14.7 *Cognitive map explaining resistance to change at Company A*

The map shows the negative spiral of disincentive that fights against the pressure for change (the positive loop near the top of the map). The disincentive comes from job insecurity. However, what is interesting is the manner in which the map shows this to be happening. On the one hand job losses increase the workload on the individual which makes them resistant to taking on more work. On the other hand, threatened job cuts give managers the incentive to protect their own departments, and thus they are unwilling to lose functions that their people carry out for fear of laying their department open to the cost-cutting axe. The result, born from the same cause – a down-sizing environment – is two opposing reactions (underlined), and through this change becomes very much more difficult to force through. The situation is that employees are 'paid slightly too much money for slightly too little work'.

Comparative study at another generating site

A comparison of headquarters with one of the company's active power stations was made. The station site implemented ER seven years ago and have been using it ever since. The visit showed that having the originators enter information into the system was possible, but also highlighted the significant resources that would be required to train everybody. Budget holders confirmed that if they were keen to implement ER, then originators would follow. One budget holder's assertion that 'my engineers don't have a problem with ER' illustrated this: they had little choice. It seems that in a live power station culture, budget holders would be able to influence the process because the management structure is much tighter. The relatively small workforce together with the functional structure brings about a single powerful point of reference, the station manager, in stark contrast to the headquarter's bureaucracy.

Root cause analysis

The analysis described above identified some key factors at work in the Company A situation. In order to combine and narrow down the long list of possible causes of resistance to ER and to separate causes from symptoms, a root cause analysis was conducted. This took the form of an Ishikawa or fishbone diagram and is shown in Figure 14.8.

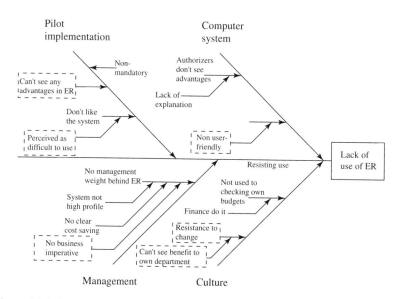

Figure 14.8 *Root cause analysis*

It can be seen that the two root causes of resistance to ER, particularly at the front end, are the perceived difficulty of learning to use the system and that its users do not see the benefits of ER. It is a hurdle that users are unwilling to cross, especially because there is neither a 'carrot' nor a 'stick' to encourage them to use the system. Lack of awareness of the vision also leads to the 'incorrect' process of using a clerk, which reduces the benefits of ER.

Previous analysis has already established that the support of the champion and the weak business imperative contribute to a 'blocked' implementation filter. The business case for ER could be displayed more clearly if a positive cost-benefit analysis could be put together. The identifiable cost savings identified were quite small, in the region of £20,000 if all of the savings are realized. Overall the cost-benefit analysis indeed does not seem convincing without a full commitment to implementation and use.

The broader picture – process streamlining versus redesign

A further task force was reviewing the requisitioning process as a whole and in contrast to the ER pilot was noting the success of Company A's alternative requisition process for low-value items, called VISA. VISA requires no authorization, finance checks or action by a buyer; the originator can use designated suppliers and bill to a dedicated VISA account. A comparison with the ER process (Figure 14.9) shows why the VISA system was more successful. ER produces improvements by removing one task (the finance check) from the requisitioning process and from improving the speed and reliability of the process. VISA removes all but one stage from this chain (the originator). The potential savings are therefore even greater, and the system is user-friendly and familiar. The clear disadvantage of VISA to management is that the expenditure is less tightly controlled, and that better value might sometimes be achieved through use of the buyer's negotiating power.

Extension of alternative requisitioning processes such as VISA will further reduce the potential savings produced by ER by reducing the number of orders requisitioned electronically. This possibility seemed to be partly behind management's reluctance to back the ER project and it is clear that the result of this review is a precursor to a decision on full ER implementation.

Discussion

A final 'rich picture' was constructed which attempted to draw together all of the influences facing the implementation of ER at Company A (Figure 14.10).

This metaphor is the problem of crossing 'the mountain', which represents the difficulty of learning to use the system. Training and support is represented

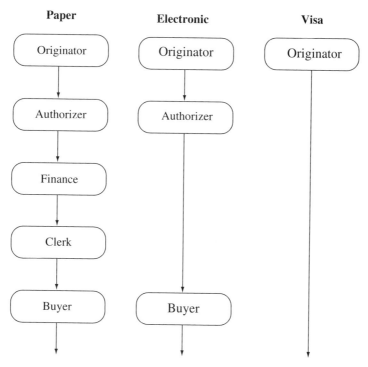

Figure 14.9 *Comparison of alternative systems*

as a walking stick to help climb the mountain, and any incentive that can be given will act as a carrot. On the other side of the mountain, if ER can be successfully introduced there is the sunny atmosphere of people working more flexibly and with increased budgetary awareness. If the benefits of ER are seen purely in straight financial terms, then the plateau on the other side is relatively low; if the intangibles are taken into account, a better view is assured. However, there are a number of factors undermining the expedition. The originator wants to delegate the task to a humble clerk. The budget holder is not convinced that the venture is necessary, and fears that he or she might be required to make the crossing too. Those directing ER in commercial services are one stage removed from those on the ground, and thus their power to influence the process is not as strong as they might like. They are still considering other solutions to the requisitioning problem, so not all of them are convinced that there isn't a better way across. Finally, enthusiasm is damped down by the dank atmosphere of the Company A competitive environment and the marshy terrain that resists change.

Table 14.1 on page 220 summarizes the findings against the original list of failure factors. Various practical possibilities for alleviating the situation were

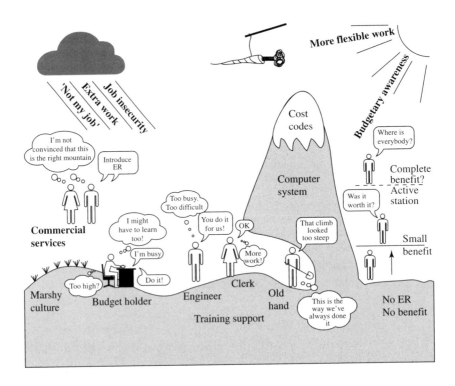

Figure 14.10 *The 'mountain'*

recommended to management, but these are beyond the scope of this chapter. However, it can be seen that there are strategic considerations with respect to positioning for the future which might outweigh the lack of short-term justification for the further use of electronic requisitioning.

Evaluation of the 3D model

The 3D model gives a powerful insight into the analysis of a failed system by breaking down the development stage into a number of factors. Its particular strength is that it codifies the different stages to introducing an information system and also that it is general enough to be applied in many contexts. The idea of 'filters' is helpful, as the model can then explain the incidence of an outstandingly developed technical system that failed to be deployed properly. Within the filters the inhibiting factors listed act as a checklist against which to evaluate the ease of passage of the introduction, and similarly the influences listed at each level, to measure the quality of the IS at each stage. Ballantine et al. (1996) do not claim that these consist of a complete list of factors. Nevertheless a measure of completeness would be desirable; in particular 'user-friendliness' should be in the development level, and 'culture' has been shown to be relevant to the implementation filter as well as the integration level.

The differences between filter factors and level inhibitors is blurred, and the generality becomes a weakness when trying to pin down and apply the model. Ballantine et al's (1996) statement that, 'Some factors may work at more than one level' may be true, but adding, 'Not all factors have to be positive.... There may be interrelationships between factors both within and across levels,' (1996, p. 10) side-steps the detail. For this reason it was found that lists within each level or filter were *only* able to act as a checklist in the Company A context. The stated aim of producing a 'conceptual awareness model' (p. 13) rather than a complex evaluation model shows why the model's limitations are quickly reached when attempting in-depth analysis. In the Company A case the model was useful when being used as a diagnostic tool, but it might be of limited use as a more fundamental approach to evaluation.

Conclusions

The pilot implementation was a clear failure, due to many factors, in particular: the 'unfriendliness' of the system, the lack of business imperative and motivation, lack of management conviction and organizational inertia. The pilot stalled at the implementation stage. It is important to note that this is not a bad result for Company A – indeed it rewards their wisdom for invoking a pilot study before full implementation. However, there are lessons of implementation to be learned. Further, the need to review the whole business process is seen to be a precursor to computerization of 'current systems'.

'Rich pictures' (their concept if not exact form inspired by soft systems methodology) were found useful to express the understanding of the situation at several points. The 3D model was extremely useful for initial positioning of the situation and generating avenues and issues for investigation, and some improvements to it are suggested. For detailed analysis, other modelling tools such as influence diagrams, cognitive maps, simple data analysis, and Ishikawa (fishbone) diagrams were found to be useful. The cultural analysis provides an invaluable historical and behavioural context. Together such a set of techniques could prove useful in planning other investigations of this nature.

Acknowledgements

We would like to thank Company A for inviting us to carry out this project, and for their ongoing advice and support.

References

Ballantine, J., Bonner, M., Levy, M., Martin, A., Munro, I. and Powell, P.L. (1996). The 3D model of information systems success; the search for the dependent variable continues. *Information Resources Management Journal,* **9**(4) Fall, pp. 5–14.

Checkland, P. and Scholes, J. (1990). *Soft Systems Methodology in Action.* Wiley, Chichester, p. 5.

Eason, K. (1989). *Information Technology and Organisational Change.* Taylor and Francis, London.

Edwards, B. R. (1989). Project sponsors: Their contribution to effective IT implementation (or 'no project sponsor, no project!'). *The Oxford/PA Conference,* Templeton College, Oxford, 25–27 September.

Grimshaw, D. J. and Kemp, B. (1989). Office automation in local government. *Local Government Studies,* March/April, pp. 7–15.

Grimshaw, D. J. (1988). The use of land and property information systems. *International Journal of Geographical Information Systems,* **2**(1), pp. 57–65.

Grindley, K. (1991). *Managing IT at Board Level – The Hidden Agenda.* Pitman.

Hammer, M. (1990). Re-engineering work: Don't automate, obliterate. *Harvard Business Review*, July–August, pp. 104–112.

Healy, M.(1987). Office Systems Implementation: The Critical Success Factors. IBM UK, July.

Jackall, R. (1988). *Moral Mazes – The World of Corporate Managers.* Oxford University Press.

Le-Saint, F. (1991). Performance Evaluation Using SSM. *Management Accounting,* **69**(4), April, pp. 34–6.

Mitchell, G. (1993). *The Practice of Operational Research.* Wiley, Chichester.

Pinto, J. K. and Slevin, D. P. (1987). Critical factors in successful project implementation. *IEEE Transactions on Engineering Management,* **34**(1), February, R12–27.

Pye, R., Bates, J. and Heath, L. (1986). *Profiting from Office Automation: Office Automation Pilots Final Evaluation Results.* KMG Thomson McLintock, DTI, London.

Scase, R. and Goffee, R. (1989). *Reluctant Managers – Their Work and Lifestyles.* Unwin Hyman, Boston.

Part Four
Communications and Information

Philip Powell

This part comprises four chapters grouped around the general theme of communications and information provision. As technology has become cheaper, faster, smaller and ubiquitous, so problems over the mechanics of IT have given way to discussion about how the information (and now knowledge) that organizations have can be stored, shared and used. Instead of information technology being a barrier to people working together, it is now a facilitator. This is especially true in knowledge intensive firms such as consultancies. However, as the first chapter illustrates, developing groupware is just as problematic as for any other type of system.

The first chapter sets the scene on groupware and Lotus Notes. While much is written in the trade press about these tools and some organizations are reported to have reaped great benefits from them, there is little survey work which shows who is using them and for what. Based on an extensive questionnaire, this chapter argues that a lack of awareness about the role and functions of groupware can seriously inhibit success. Again, a business need is paramount. Unless organizations need to share data and knowledge then groupware will have little impact. The issue of alignment comes up here again – groupware needs to be part of the strategy. Finally, a champion is needed who can open doors and push through the technology.

Davies and Powell, in the second chapter, use the 3D model of information systems success to analyse investment in IS infrastructure – in this case an intranet (internet technology used within the firm) designed to let consultants share knowledge across a multinational consulting firm. While many IT projects fail, it is often those labelled as strategic ('we have to have this as it is strategic') or infrastructure ('you can't evaluate this on its own as it is an enabler') which seem to fare worse because they avoid many of the usual appraisal procedures. Davies and Powell argue that this is a mistake and that infrastructure can and should be evaluated. While the intranet project was a technical success, the driving force was the technical managers with the result that there was little buy-in from the business. Cultural differences also inhibited the international aspect of this project.

The third chapter by Ballantine reports on a case of much older technology but one which never quite fulfilled its promise. This case is based in the public sector – a hospital trust. The organization was unable to fund the development of a large scale fully-integrated hospital information system so they built an executive information system (EIS) to extract management information from the existing core operational systems. While the implementation was thought out, there were still problems of information overload and the need to provide more diagnostic information to users. Development of the EIS also brought into play the desirability of decentralizing information systems. Decentralization can be beneficial but it requires that the appropriate support and skills and available in all the sub-units.

This chapter shows how the simple concept of sharing information can be fraught with problems often not to do with the technology but with other, organizational, aspects. However, a planned approach, prototyping and appropriate evaluation can help such initiatives succeed.

The final chapter by Smith et al. deals with a topic which is at the heart of information management. How can an organization derive all potential business benefits from an extensive database? How can the question of whether to upgrade the database be addressed? The chapter examines these issues in the context of the UK Overseas Development Organization.

15 Experiences in using Lotus Notes

Mike Sanocki
David Targett
School of Management, University of Bath

Introduction

Many organizations are 'data rich' but 'information poor'. This is because the data is not easily accessible or in a form that is easily digested to impart real knowledge. This chapter is concerned with the impact on organizations of information technology (IT), in the form of groupware and specifically Lotus Notes, particularly with regard to how those organizations turn data into information and knowledge, how they have implemented software and how it has affected the way they work, their culture and the business itself.

The development of groupware to fulfil the expanded requirements of business to share knowledge about customers, new opportunities, new markets and products goes a long way to fill the gaps left by the usual, transactional based application software which forms the base of organizations' IT processing. But what is groupware? How does it work? Who uses it? How do they use it? What benefits do they get? What impact does it have on the organization? This chapter will attempt to answer some of these questions.

Definitions

Information and knowledge

According to Checkland and Holwell (1998), the term *data* refers to the general mass of available facts. In their example of a furnishing store, all the sales figures are data. When a subset of data is selected for special attention, they coin a new word *capta*. So, the sales of a particular model of kitchen chair are capta. If these capta are put into context and given meaning they become *information*. For example, the capta concerning kitchen chair sales would yield information concerning the readiness of people in different geographical areas and different socio-economic groups to buy the product. This in turn can lead to larger structures of information which they refer to as *knowledge*. For example, information about buyer behaviour for kitchen chairs contributes to the organization's knowledge of the house furnishing market.

In summary, data is a mass of facts; capta are specially selected facts; information is capta in a meaningful context; knowledge comes from relating structures of information to one another.

Workflow management

Laudon and Laudon (1996) describe workflow management as:

> The process of streamlining business procedures so that documents can be moved easily and efficiently from one location to another.

This is achieved by storing documents electronically and automating processes such as routing the documents to different locations, securing approvals, scheduling and generating reports. Document integrity – protection against loss, destruction or prying eyes – can be handled through data backup and log-in security as with any other application. Two or more people can work on the same document simultaneously allowing quicker completion of work. The 'file ' is always available, cannot be lost and information can be retrieved, i.e. sorted, in whatever way is required by each individual based on the content of the document.

Groupware

Groupware is

> software that recognises the significance of groups in offices by providing functions and services that support the collaborative activities of work groups. (Laudon and Laudon, 1996)

Information, even at one's fingertips, is no longer enough. Groupware offers a way of collecting and storing information in such a way that it can be shared; it becomes the *'corporate memory'* (Turrell, 1995) capable of being accessed around the organization, retrieved and viewed in a variety of ways through templates, search criteria, indexing on text and database inquiry. Groupware offers an organization the ability to create and maintain a corporate history, available and instantly accessible in a vast variety of pre-defined views or customized enquiries. It also allows organizations to re-evaluate what they do and how they do it. In other words it creates knowledge.

Business process reengineering

Business process reengineering is, according to Laudon and Laudon (1996),

> the radical redesign of business processes, combining steps to cut waste and eliminating repetitive, paper-intensive tasks in order to improve cost, quality or service, and to maximise the benefits of information technology.

Workflow management and groupware software are often implemented as a means of reengineering business processes. Or the reengineering of results from the act of implementing the software takes place without a conscious decision to change being made.

Lotus Notes

The most commonly used and, arguably, the best example of groupware is Lotus Notes which was first conceived by Ray Ozzie, an American software designer, in 1979. The first version of Notes was released in 1989 and with Lotus Development's marketing expertise sold many millions of copies.

Notes offers the ability to manage workflow, reengineer business processes, allow users to share information and build up a knowledge database. A further advantage is that this knowledge can easily be 'replicated' from one computer to another and this feature lends itself to the use of remote communication as in the case of personnel who travel but need access to the database.

The nature of the problem

IT, that is the use of computers to process data, has come a long way in the last fifteen years or so. A significant reason for this has been the introduction of the personal computer (PC) which has now established itself as an indispensable part of everyday life as a 'personal productivity tool'. But have the millions of computers purchased by business actually brought any overall

improvement to productivity? According to Bowen (1989) the best information available suggests that it has not.

Part of the problem is that productivity gains in these areas are very difficult to measure especially as some benefits are qualitative, i.e. things are being
done now which were previously impossible – the assertion that the work
being done is not cheaper but of a higher quality.

Brynjolfsson's (1992) discussion of private benefits and missing productivity suggests that negative factors like oil price rises, recessions, a rise in the
number of uneducated workers entering the work force in the USA and just
plain bad management have, perhaps, swamped the benefits of PC investment.
In a later paper (Hitt and Brynjolfsson,1996) he separates the impact of IT into
three areas: productivity, business profitability and consumer surplus. They
find that IT has increased productivity and created substantial value for consumers but that it has not resulted in supranormal business profitability.

A great deal has been written about how businesses need to be able to
change and adapt, to restructure in order to survive and grow in the ever
changing business environment of today. Business process redesign (BPR)
allows IT to play a part in this change process by being a part of organizational
life with the aim of becoming a strategic element and an integral part of everyday survival. It is because of this strategic requirement that tools are being
sought to facilitate the process of BPR. Groupware technologies and particularly Lotus Notes are extremely important in the continuing development of
BPR in an attempt to provide strategic information systems.

Change

But why change? What makes it necessary for organizations to look at how
they operate and want to change? What has brought about this desire or need
to critically assess how an organization is structured? How does change affect
individuals working in the organization? These are some of the questions that
are considered below.

In turn-of-the-century organizational theory and its 'scientific management'
legacy devised by F. W. Taylor, individuals were considered parts of a machine
programmed by others to perform pre-defined tasks. These individuals were
not considered assets of the organization but sources of error in the smooth
running machine. Ideally, organizations were designed to free themselves
from human error or intervention and to run automatically so that management
had to handle only the few unexpected events that might occur. But organizations are not machines, they are communities of people who:

> behave like any other community in that they compete amongst them-
> selves for power and resources, they have different opinions and values,
> conflicts of priorities and of goals. (Handy, 1993)

It is the very differences in people that allow them and the organization itself, if it is to survive, to adapt to the world around it, to change, to develop and to continue 'the never ending search for improvement' (Handy, 1993).

An organization run as a machine does not encourage the innovation necessary for the search for improvement. It is a question of trusting the people, not trusting the system, and the challenge for management is to harness the energy and thrust of individuals so that the organization continues to develop. Handy (1993) suggests that 'without politics we would not change and without change we would wither and die'.

Whether organizations want to change or not they must acknowledge that there is no such thing as standing still. Without continually trying for improvement an organization goes backwards, even if only as the result of its competitors moving forward. Productivity improvements often require innovative changes to how jobs are designed and departments are composed. This has a knock-on effect in that the culture of organizations is changed. Ansoff (1987) concludes that the world is changing faster and is becoming less easy to predict, that organizations are becoming more complex as are the people who inhabit them. Ansoff considers that because of the way problems are solved in Western society there are 'human and organizational inertias which have to be overcome when strategic change becomes necessary'. His suggestion is that if people are involved in change decisions, as is the custom in Japan, they are less likely to be resistant to that change.

Business process redesign

It was in one of the most extensive studies into best management practice that has ever been carried out, the MIT-led 'Management in the 1990s' programme, that the term business process redesign (BPR) was first used. BPR is often called business process reengineering and in this paper we consider the terms to be synonymous. Conducted by the Massachusetts Institute of Technology from 1984 to 1989, the survey involved a far-ranging enquiry into management methods most likely to contribute to the success of the coming decade. One of the findings highlighted the use of information technology to facilitate ways of streamlining processes, as opposed to simply automating existing procedures. Others followed up and elaborated upon these findings, but responsibility for giving reengineering a wider currency as a concept lies with Hammer and Champey (1993). Hammer and Champey define BPR as:

the fundamental rethinking and radical redesign of business processes to achieve dramatic improvement in critical measures of performance such as cost, quality, service and speed. (Hammer and Champey, 1993)

BPR is, according to the Butler Cox Foundation (1993)

> ... a way of transforming the business, which frees it from the restrictions of the traditional approach by cutting across functional divisions. Information systems ... are the fundamental ingredient of redesigned business processes. (Butler Cox Foundation, 1993)

Whatever the definition of BPR it is agreed by serious practitioners that it involves *fundamental* change to business processes, managerial systems, job definitions and organizational structures. BPR takes change on to a new plane where nothing is fixed and everything is questioned.

MIT90s – five levels of IT induced reconfiguration

The 'emerging strategic role' of IT identified by Venkatraman suggests that:

> Astute managers have recognised that IT offers the capability to redefine the boundaries of markets and structural characteristics, alter the fundamental rules and basis of competition, redefine business scope, and provide a new set of competitive weapons. (Venkatraman, 1991)

Venkatraman suggests that the strategic role of IT needs to be redefined as a result of 'the convergence of two concurrent (and perhaps equally powerful) forces – technology push and competitive pull'.

Venkatraman believes that IT can provide new weapons in the pursuit of competitive advantage. Further, it was recognized that IT could significantly enhance productivity at varying levels within the organization, for example at individual level, group level and across organizations, and would provide a basis for changing business processes. The five levels model of IT induced business reconfiguration suggests that these levels are:

- Level 1 – Localized exploitation – localized use of IT-systems restricted to individual functions or isolated activities.
- Level 2 – Internal integration – common IT platforms and integrated systems.
- Level 3 – Business process redesign – IT used as a central lever to redesign business activities.
- Level 4 – Business network redesign – changing the way the business works with its external partners through the use of electronic integration.
- Level 5 – Business scope redefinition – concerned with the *raison d'être* of the business and enlarging it through the use of IT.

Levels 1 and 2 are evolutionary and often happen naturally; Levels 3, 4 and 5 are revolutionary and are achieved as a result of recognition of the need to use IT.

Research method

A thousand named individuals were asked to complete a questionnaire prepared by the authors. This sample was formed by selecting names at random from the list of all people who had purchased at least one copy of Lotus Notes and registered their purchase with the registration card in the package. The selection was made at random by the database administrator at Lotus Development. The questionnaire was divided into five major sections in order to elicit not only data about Notes but also information concerning the types of organizations, their size and so on. Some of the important issues are considered below.

Results

MIT90s level of IT induced reconfiguration

Objectives

- To determine the level of integration achieved as depicted by the MIT90s study into IT induced business reconfiguration.
- To determine what level of integration between Notes applications and existing 'core' business systems, i.e. front office/back office integration, is being achieved by normal Notes users.

We firstly consider the relevance, within the respondent organizations, of Venkatraman's model of how organizations might use IT to change their working methods.

Level 1 – localized use of IT
The results suggest that a minority of organizations pursue a purely localized exploitation of IT in general and expend little effort on it. The situation is different for Lotus Notes. This is illustrated in a question which asked 'are any of your Notes applications and databases integrated with any other line of business or transaction processing applications ...' 52 per cent of respondents answered negatively, suggesting no integration, compared with only 35 per cent who have localized use of IT in general.

Level 2 – internal integration
When looking at Level 2 of the MIT90s model the results of the survey suggest that there is a high degree of internal integration with most effort

expended in this area. This is to be expected, as the more normal benefits of IT of cost and labour reduction are realized as a result of the initial installation of integrated business systems, used corporate-wide and most often sharing a common hardware platform. Notes, however, is not necessarily part of this corporate integration.

Level 3 – IT used as a central lever to redesign business activities
Redesigning business activities, equivalent to Level 3 of the MIT90s model, is a relatively high priority. Solutions based on 'off-the-shelf' packaged solutions play a significant part in this.

Level 4 – business network redesign
Business network redesign requires more than just developing or buying software to satisfy a need or desire to change. Many respondent organizations claim a high degree of effort in redesigning their communication mechanism with external contacts. Notes appears to play a part in providing such mechanisms.

Level 5 – business scope redefinition
Notes appears to play little part at this level of the model.

Some questions were aimed at determining how widespread and successful Notes implementations are. The answers suggest that no matter how widespread the implementation is, i.e. limited to one workgroup/application or multiple applications used organization-wide, the success rate is usually high.

What is surprising, however, is that a large proportion of respondents claim that they have multiple applications used corporate wide but, in view of the relatively low level of integration, these are presumably mainly stand alone.

The most popular Notes applications

Objective

• To determine which applications are most popular within the Notes environment and why.

Business process applications
'The organizational information systems problem is,' according to Maddison and Darnton (1996), 'how best to provide and use information systems and services to support the people and activities within the organization'.

Given the nature of groupware, and Notes in particular (in that it is designed as a database tool to do just this by easily storing and retrieving information which is 'soft', i.e. information which is not structured, indexed or sorted by, for example, customer or part number), it is not surprising that the commonest applications are those that consist of a mass of unstructured text not easily catered for elsewhere in computer systems applications.

The two most popular or common business process applications, both developed mainly in-house, are customer service and marketing information. Of all respondents two thirds claimed to have a customer service system whilst a similar number also claimed that they have a marketing information system. Few respondents purchased the software, suggesting either that it is not easy to find 'off-the-shelf' packages and that it is necessary to buy-in bespoke development of such important, customer facing systems.

The third most popular area is concerned with quality when used to help control and remove the invariable mountain of paperwork required particularly by ISO9000 and the like. Such applications increase control and discipline and yet get the information to where it is required easily and relatively cheaply.

Discussion databases
These are less common than business process applications. The most common are concerned with customer service and often take the form of an aid to communication. E-mail also plays an important part in Notes implementation and is often quoted as being the main reason for using Notes. The concentration on 'softer' non-core, non-transaction processes explains why integration of Notes with the core processes is not as successful is it might be

What is the justification for investing in Lotus Notes?

Objective

- To determine the important reasons, and arguments used, to justify investment in Notes.

The need to share knowledge is amply demonstrated by the popularity of customer related uses to which Notes is put. This is borne out by the fact that improved customer service is the most important reason used for justifying an investment in Notes. This is followed very closely by a desire for improved knowledge sharing (defined as knowing how we do things) and improved effectiveness suggesting that organizations believe that they need to work smarter than they do.

The 'normal' justification for IT investment such as cost savings identified as a result of a cost-benefit analysis has been dismissed in this survey as being unimportant because the investment is invariably relatively small and the return on investment (ROI) is likely to be very high.

Who makes Notes work and how?

Objectives

● To determine who within organizations are the actual champions who promoted the introduction and implementation of Notes, lead project teams and make Notes work.
● To consider whether implementation is used to reengineer existing processes or whether new developments purely mimic the old ways of doing things.

The decision to invest in Notes is often made outside any IT strategy which might exist but the implementation is no different from any other IT project as it still needs someone to ensure that it is implemented.

The results of the study indicate that IT people, including lowly developers, far from stifling Notes development, act as champions in nearly 40 per cent of organizations. Main board directors, by comparison, are rarely involved as champions. Furthermore, it is the IT department which has to carry out organization-wide Notes training in order to ensure that users can benefit from the software.

The use of multi-disciplined or cross functional project teams to oversee change is not significant in Notes implementation. It is the IT department which has the lions' share of responsibility for Notes projects and, far from being the stumbling block preventing change, is more often the driving force behind it.

Over half of the respondents claim that they mimic existing processes rather than redesign them whilst the remainder actually attempt to change their processes. Unfortunately, the change is in the tools used to perform the function and not necessarily the function itself as demonstrated by the prevalence still to mimic existing processes.

Important triggers and inhibitors

Objective

● To identify the important triggers of success, and the inhibitors preventing success, in implementing Notes.

The questionnaire cited a number of common factors believed to be significant in the successful implementation of any business application system. Those that have a positive or beneficial effect are termed triggers or enablers, whilst those that are obstructive by nature are termed inhibitors.

The need to reduce cost has little bearing on whether Notes is implemented, either successfully or not. Similarly, the cost of the investment in hardware, software and training is not an inhibitor to Notes introduction.

The prime mover for Notes application roll out is the requirement to fulfil a business need, an increasingly common reason cited for IT system investment. This is closely followed by an understanding or vision of the potential of what Notes can do of benefit to the organization.

The availability of strong, powerful 'off the shelf' or shrink wrapped business process applications can aid the acceptance of new technology, particularly where the benefits of using these is abundantly apparent to all involved in their implementation.

The need to change is *not* considered to be a significant trigger in successful Notes implementations possibly because many implementations only mimic old processes. The major inhibitor to successful Notes implementation is seen as a lack of management support. The lack of awareness of what Notes can do and poor understanding of groupware, cited as other major inhibitors, also support the view that the champion is ineffective in getting the message of Notes across. If the champion cannot get the message across to management of an organization by educating them about Notes then he or she must expect them to be unenthusiastic about the concept.

Lack of resource and suitable hardware and software infrastructures are also seen as major inhibitors to implementing Notes successfully. A shortage of people whose presence is fundamental to a new system will obviously affect the outcome of any project.

Resistance to change is often a major inhibitor to Notes deployment according to the respondents to the survey. One might expect this in situations where people have to approach their work in a fundamentally different way. However, although this is cited as an inhibitor, the results of asking for staff reaction to change suggests that they are fairly ambivalent towards it.

Notes and the internet

Objective

● To examine the relationship between Notes and the internet and intranets.

Users of Notes do not believe that it is being replaced by the Internet – Notes is considered very much alive and kicking by users. It is seen as a safe bet by managers in search of groupware because it works. However, the Internet can be used to do many of the things that Notes does. If an organization does not require the functionality available in Notes, but purely an information browsing tool, then an internal web site, or intranet, may suffice.

Some respondents believe that Notes and the internet are competing technologies but, in fact, Notes encourages discussion in a controlled, secure and structured environment whilst the internet tends to be a publishing tool with no central register of documents and relatively crude navigational aids suggesting there is little competition.

In fact the environments in which Notes and the Internet exist are to a very large extent different. The Notes environment is, according to Moira Chin (1995),

> a closed, categorized and indexed reference to organizational information. It allows individuals to work as part of a team with provision for multi-user access to single documents and co-authoring facilities.

She continues that the internet (web) is

> a very different type of environment. Either from work or from home individuals can access the web to find information on any topic that interests them.... What is more difficult is for the user to query the organization for more information. (Chin, 1995)

It is, perhaps, because the benefits of using Notes and the internet are different that the majority of respondents considered that the technologies are complementary although there are moves to give each the ability to make use of the functionality of the other, both adding to the solution of a business problem – how to communicate and share knowledge securely and cheaply.

Business and IT strategy alignment

Objective

● To determine the degree of business and IT alignment within organizations.

Having an IT strategy which supports and is aligned with the strategy of the business would seem, at first glance, to be a fundamental requirement of any organization. Alignment, in this context, is defined as having goals and objectives which lead to the same outcome but it excludes any broader concepts of alignment in terms of structure, processes, people and technology. It is possible for IT strategy to determine and drive business strategy in different directions but some respondents suggest they are not aware that they have a business strategy.

It is unlikely that funds are invested in IT systems without someone knowing the reason for the investment and many do seem to support the supposition that the majority of organizations know where they are going, what their goals and objectives are and, presumably, that they have plans to get there, and yet only half of respondents claim Notes to be part of their strategy when first implemented.

Expectation of cultural change

Objective

- To examine the comparison between the expectations of cultural change and what actually happened.

Schein (1985) defines culture as: 'a pattern of basic assumptions – invented, discovered, or developed by a group as it learns to cope with its problems ....'

Implementation of Notes applications can change the culture of an organization, at least outwardly. Three quarters of respondents expected some cultural change, based on the premise that changing the way that things are done must change the basic assumptions in Schein's definition. However, cultural change actually reported was somewhat less than anticipated which, perhaps, is because of the nature of the applications that were implemented. Notes, by its very nature of facilitating easier communication and the sharing of information and knowledge, must help break down any functional barrier and change the culture of the organization making it more open and free in the process.

Conclusions

Triggers

The idea that a 'silver bullet' exists to make Notes deployment successful is not sustainable given the innumerable factors which contribute to success or failure. However, the survey made it possible to identify factors whose absence will certainly contribute to failure.

The first of these is *vision and understanding of what Notes is.* The lack of awareness of what Notes can do and a poor understanding of groupware is often cited as a major inhibitor of success. Vision is a much quoted word where Notes is concerned but it does require someone with vision in order to get the best from the software. Vision communicates something which helps clarify the direction in which an organization needs to move. Failed projects often have numerous plans but little vision. Lotus Notes offers organizations the opportunity to do things they have never done before, quickly and cheaply. The trick is to match the vision with realistic objectives and actually make it happen.

Second, there must be a requirement to fill *a real business need* in order that a Notes application may stand any chance of being implemented successfully.

The application should have both tangible and intangible business benefits if the organization is to 'buy-in' to the effort, disruption and change which is likely to be required.

Notes applications, in today's competitive environment, fill a real business need for information and knowledge sharing not easily found in core business systems.

The most important individual in any project is the person who has the job, and the power, to get things done – *a champion*. This strong individual needs to be the 'champion' of the project, ably supported by the sponsor if this is a different person, and he or she must ensure that anyone involved with the implementation is fully committed to the objectives.

In order to do this it may be necessary to 'sell' the concept of the project to the organization as a whole, from board level down to the shop floor, paying particular attention to people who are directly affected by any changes which are likely to occur. To gain acceptance of change, the champion might attempt to make *not* changing seem more dangerous than the apparent dangers of moving into the unknown.

This study appears to contradict previous studies which have suggested that IT personnel have been both disruptive and obstructive where the adoption of Notes applications are concerned. It seems that in order for Notes implementation to succeed it is desirable and necessary to have *committed and motivated IT people* involved and often acting as project managers and/or champions of the project.

IT departments should be like spiders sitting at the centre of a web feeling vibrations from all directions and by this knowing what is going on in all corners of that web. IT departments should sense the vibrations in all parts of an organization and act in a coordinating and communicating role in solving business problems.

Effect on culture – the implications

Lotus Notes will have some impact on the form and culture of an organization but it appears from this study that the impact may not be as great as one might initially expect and will depend on circumstances, i.e. whether the processes are reengineered or mimicked, whether there are organizational structure changes as a result of implementation and so on.

Notes offers an opportunity to re-evaluate how things are done now but does not force change, as many organizations have found that by mimicking existing processes it is possible to bring about incremental change, getting people used to the new technology gradually and making future fundamental changes more acceptable to the people likely to be affected.

Less important factors

Some factors are less important in ensuring successful Notes implementation, for example, *the alignment of business and IT strategy*. Strategy is concerned with getting from *here* to *there*, *there* being defined within the strategy. The difficulty often encountered is that *there* constitutes a different place to different people. The aim of aligning business and IT strategy is to ensure that every one has the same *there*.

Implementing Notes appears initially not to be part of *there*, that is the strategy, for a large proportion of organizations. However, these organization, none the less, deploy it successfully to fulfil a business need.

The use of *cross functional or multi-disciplined project teams* appears from this study not to be an essential element in the implementation of Notes provided there is someone to drive the implementation forward.

Notes investment is justified on the basis of improved customer service, improved knowledge sharing and improved effectiveness. Cost savings and the cost of implementation, by comparison, are minor considerations.

Summary

There is no one 'best' way of implementing Lotus Notes and no 'silver bullet' nor panacea which will ensure successful Notes implementation. The 'best' method will depend on the circumstances, the organization and its culture, the people and their attitudes to innovation and change. The whole area of groupware, workflow improvement and the search for the holy grail of white collar productivity is still in its infancy and Notes' part in it will develop and continue to run for many years to come.

Bibliography

Ansoff, H. I. (1987). *Corporate Strategy.* McGraw Hill.

Bowen, W. (1989). *The Puny Payoff from Office Computers, Computers in the Human Context.* Blackwell.

Brynjolfsson, E.(1992). *Productivity of Information Technology – Review and Assessment.* MIT CCS Working Paper No. 130.

Butler Cox Foundation (1993). *The Role of Information Technology in Transforming the Business.* Butler Cox Foundation.

Checkland, P. and Holwell, S. (1998). *Information, Systems and Information Systems.* John Wiley & Son.

Chin, M. (1995). *A Comparative Review of Lotus Notes and the World Wide Web.* Httl://is-2.stern.nyu.

Hammer, M and Champey, J. (1993). *Re-engineering the Corporation: a Manifesto for Business Revolution.* Harper Business.

Handy, C. (1993). *Understanding Organizations.* Penguin.

Hitt, L. M. and Brynjolfsson, E.(1996). Productivity, business profitability and consumer surplus: Three measures of IT value. *MISQ,*, **20**(2), June.

Kanter, R. M. (1988). *The Change Masters: Corporate Entrepreneurs at Work.* Unwin Hyman.

Laudon, K. C. and Laudon, J. P. (1996). *Management Information Systems: Organization and Technology.* Prentice-Hall.

Lloyd, P. and Whitehead, R.(eds.) (1996). *Transforming Organizations through Groupware: Lotus Notes in Action.* Springer.

Maddison, R. and Darnton, G. (1996). *Information Systems in Organisations: Improving Business Processes.* Chapman and Hall.

Schein, E. H. (1985). *Organizational Culture and Leadership – A Dynamic View.* Jossey-Bass, San Fransisco.

Scott Morton, M. S. (ed.) (1991). *The Corporation of the 1990s: Information Technology and Organizational Transformation.* Oxford University Press.

Taylor, F. W. (1947). Scientific Management. Harper and Row.

Turrell, M. (1995). *Deployment and Beyond.* Imaginatik.

Venkatraman, N. (1991) in *The Corporation of the 1990s: Information Technology and Organizational Transformation* (M. S. Scott Morton, ed). Oxford University Press.

16 Appraising investment in IS infrastructure

David Davies and Philip Powell
Warwick Business School, University of Warwick

Introduction

As the balance in advanced economies shifts from manufacturing towards services, so the benefits from projects become less tangible and hence less amenable to traditional cost-benefit analysis. Information systems (IS) projects, in particular, require innovative methods for their evaluation because their success and hence potential for delivering benefits is closely tied to the participation and involvement of users. For example, there is a growing need to support knowledge workers which requires the provision of comprehensive IS infrastructures.

Despite its importance, investment in IS infrastructure is seldom evaluated, and investments are often undertaken as an act of faith (Silk 1990). The lack of evaluation can be attributed to the difficulty in identifying the intangible benefits associated with infrastructure. For instance, when IS delivers tangible (especially financial) benefits e.g. reduction in staffing levels, assessment is reasonably straightforward. Conversely, where benefits are intangible, such as 'improved access to corporate information', quantification is seldom attempted, and hence monitoring is rarely undertaken.

Few organizations undertake a complete appraisal of investment in IS infrastructure from initial feasibility stage through to tracking of benefits in the post-implementation stage. This results in under-performance of IS, as according to Willcocks (1994, p.5) there is a 'strong correlation between IS control and measurement and IS success'.

This chapter investigates the appraisal of investment in infrastructure projects, as they predominantly deliver intangible benefits, and hence receive little attention. It proposes that infrastructure projects be subject to formal evaluation which would increase the likelihood of success. This contention is examined by analysing a case study of investment in support infrastructure – an intranet implementation.

Current investment appraisal practices

Evaluation of an investment in IS can be undertaken pre- and post-implementation and during its development. According to Hamilton and Chervany (1981) there are two main types of evaluation; *summative,* which is used to produce a conclusion, judgement or assessment, and *formative,* which is used to elicit information to guide incremental improvements. The traditional concept of investment appraisal is a form of summative evaluation, used to assess whether or not to proceed with a project. An example of formative evaluation is where users are asked for their feedback, and subsequent releases of the system reflect these opinions.

Other purposes of evaluation include the identification of opportunities to improve delivery of benefits, providing feedback on performance to facilitate system tuning, and supporting the typical project management goals of planning, monitoring, and control. All types of evaluation should feed into the learning process of the organization, whichever method is used.

Pre-implementation evaluation

Traditional investment appraisal methods typically balance the costs of a project against the financial benefits. Drury (1992) surveyed capital budgeting practices as outlined in Table 16.1.

Table 16.1 *Use of investment appraisal methods*

Method	Firms using method %
Payback	90
Accounting rate of return	83
Internal rate of return	83
Net present value	78

Drury shows that most firms use a combination of methods, and concludes that this may indicate either:

1 no single appraisal technique is sufficiently simple for managers to understand yet sufficiently complex to encompass the investment issues, or:

2 the manager selects the technique to best support the project they believe should be accepted.

The first conclusion is supported since, although it is known that internal rate of return (IRR) is flawed in certain cases, and net present value (NPV) is theoretically sound, IRR is more commonly used – probably because it is easier to understand. A further factor that drives the choice of appraisal method concerns the way in which the performance of the manager is measured. Drury illustrates this with an example where a manager measured on return on investment (ROI) chooses the project with the highest average ROI, even though this has a negative NPV and would be the worst choice.

Evaluation during implementation

Avison et al (1995) stated that evaluation during development is rare. Once the feasibility study has been carried out it is unusual for the system development to be diverted, much less stopped, and when it does happen on a major project it is often classed as a scandal (e.g. London Stock Exchange). If evaluation were carried out during development e.g. by monitoring the progressive achievement of benefits, there would be a greater chance of realizing the full benefits.

Post-implementation review

Post-implementation review (PIR) of IS investments is important as it enables the organization to learn from experience, which helps to ensure that future implementations are more effective and efficient in minimizing costs and resources in their development, and maximizing the subsequent realization of benefits.

Lack of evaluation due to the 'difficulty of identifying benefits' can obscure bad investments and hamper subsequent evaluation. Indeed, simply the process of identifying benefits is often of value, as fundamental questions must be asked about the motivation for the investment.

The Butler Cox Foundation (1990) find that post-implementation reviews are not generally carried out as:

- 'It is too difficult' – many systems can be used by several business areas, and benefits that accrue over time in these areas are hard to identify.
- 'It is not necessary' – correct investment appraisal and implementation imply the benefits must accrue and hence there is no need to check for them.
- 'It is too costly'.

- 'It is against our culture' – the IS department (the provider of professional services) do not see their role as checking the delivery of benefits.

Underlying these reasons is the fundamental issue that the manager who made the decision to invest does not normally seek a review in case the outcome is unfavourable. Blackler and Brown (1988) noted that evaluation tends not to be carried out in circumstances where unfavourable results may occur.

Drury (1992) admits that a post-audit review of capital decisions is very difficult, and can obscure the fact that the original investment decision was made under uncertainty. It can also lead to the danger that managers will submit only safe investment proposals and will avoid taking risks, something that is essential for the future of the company.

Use of traditional methods for IS investment appraisal

Strassman (1990) argues that investment in computers has long been evaluated in strictly financial terms; a hangover from when manufacturing dominated the economy and inputs and outputs were easy to identify. Organizations use the same forms for procurement of computers as for fork lift trucks, etc., and also use the same investment appraisal process. Strassman claims that the application of strict cost-benefit analysis to computer projects can result in elaborate, lengthy and tortuous approval procedures. Investment-oriented executives fail to recognize that computerization is an incremental, continuous and evolutionary learning process.

Angell and Smithson (1991, p.191) argue that:

> the difficulties in the formal evaluation of IS originate from the fact that IS are social systems, and the difficulty is of placing a value on information itself. We are concerned with the evaluation of IS as they operate within organisations. The complexity and ambiguity inherent in organisations when considered as social and political systems implies that the simplistic notions of objective measurement and positivist causality are quite inappropriate.

This points to the use of methods of evaluation which are broader than cost-benefit analysis and which take intangible benefits into account.

Difficulty in defining intangible benefits

Tangible (usually financial) benefits are commonly viewed as the only important benefits, and intangible benefits are often overlooked in formal appraisal methods as they are difficult to define and monitor. However, many examples exist of intangible benefits of great value including customer service, sales effectiveness and staff motivation

Willcocks and Lester (1994) surveying IS investment evaluation practices find that all except two organizations use cost-benefit analysis in their evaluation process, and the next most popular parameters are competitive edge, service to the public, and quality of the product. Sixty-two per cent of organisations use cost-benefit as their first priority, despite the fact that 'the literature shows that the cost-benefit analysis used by organisations is outdated and does not show the true worth of IT' (p. 63).

When so much literature argues against using traditional methods for IS investment appraisal it is illuminating to investigate why they persist. Methods for investment appraisal can be defined in terms of processes and outcomes, but people are involved in their operation, and can be enthusiastic or obstructive depending upon their position in the organization and their interests.

People also have concerns regarding evaluation as summarized by Legge's (1984) crises of evaluation:

- Crisis of utilization – will the evaluation results be used by decision makers?
- Crisis of verification – have the methods used produced valid results?
- Crisis of accreditation – the effect of the underlying values of the evaluator and the evaluator's sponsors.

Walsham (1993, p.179) argues that a formal evaluation exercise can be seen as a ritual which:

> may express symbolic belief in management competence, or the underpinning for an action rationality where choice has been restricted in order to reduce uncertainty. Rituals are an important aspect of human life, but a formal IS evaluation viewed as a ritual can be a device to reinforce structures of domination, and can also be a major hindrance to innovative organisational change.

Walsham put forward interpretative evaluation as a way of involving a wide variety of stakeholders and raising their concerns, issues, and values. A focus on learning and understanding helps to generate involvement and commitment, although consensus is not always achievable by such an approach.

Currie (1989) finds that in order to get board approval for investment in CAD, engineering managers often needed to play the system e.g. produce spurious predictions of increased productivity. She argues that to appreciate the strategic (intangible) benefits of a system e.g. the ability to support a greater product range, then 'a more strategic awareness needs to be developed at the apex of the organisation, which is not one solely based upon an understanding of simplistic cost-accounting techniques.' She adds that 'a change is required in the social definitions of what actually constitutes vital managerial skills for contemporary organisations.'

The issue of board members not understanding the strategic case for technology may be more pronounced in organizations where the finance director is responsible for IS investment.

Innovative methods of IS investment appraisal

Established practices are notoriously difficult to change, so a strong case would need to be made before new methods were considered by an organization. This section examines recent methods developed for the appraisal of IS investments. However, as there are many, the attributes of generic methods and an example of each are examined (Table 16.2). It should be noted that there is an overlap between the generic methods, but this does not affect their essential attributes.

Table 16. 2 *Bases of modern evaluation methods*

Basis of method	Example
Quantify intangible benefits	Silk's method
Assess people issues in addition to technical issues	Information economics
Examine in detail the costs of an operation	Return on management
Adapt another method of evaluation	Balanced scorecard
Produce a profile of intangible benefits	Prudential method

Silk's method

Silk (1990) suggests seven types of justification which sequentially 'harden up' the soft benefits and these are defined in Table 16.3. He identifies three generic benefits that suggest corresponding financial measures:

1 efficiency systems – judged by cost savings;
2 effectiveness systems – judged by ROA;
3 strategic/competitive edge systems – judged by growth (revenue or profit).

He claims that in the 1960s efficiency systems were common, and justifying savings in people by replacing them with mainframes was relatively straightforward. However, in the 1980s and 1990s it has become difficult to make sound financial estimates, and strategic systems have often been justified by acts of faith, because benefits are too soft or uncertain to be quantified in financial terms. This has led to polarization between the accountants and those who believe in strategic vision.

Table 16.3 *Silk's seven types of investment justification*

	Type	Definition
0	Must do	Special mandatory investments e.g. caused by legislation
1	Faith	Investment based on judgement or vision of senior management
2	Logic	Causal logic by which business improvement will arise is identified (size unspecified)
3	Direction	As Type 2, plus observable quantity is identified and measured after implementation to check whether business has moved in predicted direction
4	Size	As Type 3, plus size of change in observable quantity is measured
5	Value	As Type 4, plus the quantified changes are given a weighting so that disparate benefits can be compared with each other
6	Money	As Type 5, plus each of the benefits is given a financial value. They can be compared with each other, and the impact on the overall business financial and performance statements can be calculated

With reference to Table 16.3, the merit of following Types 3 to 6 is that managers must attempt to quantify benefits. Silk observes that 'faith' seems to be giving way to 'logic', and in the middle ground there is considerable scope for sharpening up business cases.

Silk's method is representative of an approach to quantifying intangible benefits. This would presumably appeal to proponents of traditional cost-benefit approaches, but the danger in quantification is that the subtleties of intangible benefits (and hence their possible importance) might be overlooked.

Information Economics

Information economics (IE) (Parker, Benson and Trainor, 1988) considers value and risks as opposed to costs and benefits, and assesses people issues in addition to technical ones.

Where 'saving in manpower' is an example of the potential benefit of a system, the risks and values of a system can be considered as different types of impacts. Values are positive impacts (e.g. whether the system is used by the workforce, whether training has been organized etc.), while risks are negative impacts (e.g. changing the roles of staff and possibly demotivating them).

IE is intended to present a common language for representatives from technology and business to agree upon attributes for a proposed IS, where those attributes encompass much more than costs and benefits e.g. competitive advantage or alignment with strategic IS architecture.

One strength of information economics is its use of the 7Cs as described by Wiseman (1994):

1 Comprehensiveness – address all relevant business, economic and technical issues;
2 Consistency – in decision making;
3 Clarity – of objectives, values and attitudes;
4 Communications – improved between functions;
5 Confidence – that projects have been thoroughly analysed and justified;
6 Consensus – between managers from different business units;
7 Culture – gap closing.

According to Willcocks and Lester (1994, p.72), critics of IE claim 'that it may be over-mechanistic if applied to all projects, it can be time consuming, and may lack credibility with senior management, particularly given the subjective basis of much of the scoring.' They also claim that there are statistical problems with the suggested scoring methods, and conclude that the method 'needs to be tailored, developed, and in some cases extended to meet evaluation needs in different organisations.'

Return on management

Strassman (1990) developed a concept of return on management (ROM) which measures performance based on the added value to an organization provided by management. He argues that the information costs of an organization are the cost of managing the enterprise. Hence, if ROM is calculated before and after IT is applied to an organization, the IT contribution to the business can be assessed. A drawback of ROM is that it relies upon meticulous measurement of costs in the business which are difficult to attribute to the correct sources, e.g. it is difficult to calculate the full costs of a PC when contributory costs come from hardware, software, support, user training and learning curve, etc.

Balanced scorecard approach

Kaplan and Norton (1992) formulate an approach to performance measurement for senior management which can be adapted to the needs of IT investment evaluation. They identify four views in a balanced scorecard as shown in Table 16.4.

A problem with this method is the difficulty of isolating the impacts of IT from other factors affecting business performance. It also tends to be an IS department's view of how it is judged.

Table 16.4 *The balanced scorecard views and measures*

View	Business measure	IT-related metric
Financial	View of shareholders?	Profitability per employee
Internal business	What to excel at?	Development efficiency
Customer/user	View of customers?	Level of service
Innovation/learning	How to improve continuously?	Time to adopt new systems

Prudential project appraisal method (PAM)

Coleman and Jamieson (1991) describe a methodology and a set of appraisal tools developed for Prudential Assurance. The tools are used to support the introduction of total benefit management and fall into the areas of financial appraisal, risk appraisal, and strategic or intangible benefit appraisal.

The tools for financial appraisal consist of spreadsheets for NPV calculation, etc., with macros to encourage the use of sensitivity analysis. Risk analysis tools are questionnaires on commercial and project risks, and a PC program which calculates the manageability of each risk based on assessments of its probability and potential impact.

The intangible benefits are supported in the appraisal system by a benefit profile and accompanying textual bullets. Together these provide a simple representation of the total contribution a project makes to the organization's objectives. The profile is constructed by managers completing a questionnaire which identifies project factors that could reflect on the organization's performance indicators or goals. Scores are taken along two dimensions:

1 the impact of the project on the benefit category;
2 the range or quantification of the impact, e.g. the number of customers that will be affected.

This provides an analysis of the total benefits of the project, and it can be used at any point in its life cycle.

A possible weakness of the method is that the benefits profile is constructed from the views of managers who make subjective judgements of the impact that their own project could have on the business. Thus the profile is liable to bias, as managers typically consider that their own function affects the performance of the organization more than any other.

Nature of IS infrastructure

Their appropriateness to any given organization depends upon a number of contingency factors identified by Farbey, Land and Targett (1992), such as the role of evaluation, the decision environment, the system, the organization, and cause and effect relationships.

A common factor between the methods is that a change in management approach to consideration of evaluation is required which is a considerable obstacle to overcome.

The choice of method is difficult, as in addition to the contingency factors all the methods have strengths and weaknesses. However, assuming an organization has decided to move away from cost-benefit methods to newer methods which take into account people issues and intangible benefits, then simply going through the process of considering contingency factors is likely to bring benefits. Employing a method will then bring broader issues into consideration and improve the choice of IS investments.

IS infrastructure, according to Earl (1989, p.20), 'comprises the processing power of computers, the highways of telecommunications, the foundations of data, and the fabric of basic business systems.'

Knowledge workers and IS infrastructure

Gunton (1989) identifies growth trends in IS which require the support of infrastructure and emphasise its importance. Traditionally, investment in IS was focused upon central data processing, but there is now growth in systems that support:

- staff who deal directly with customers;
- professional work groups engaged in research and development;
- management control and planning activities.

Additional trends include the integration of systems across functions, as in computer-integrated manufacturing, and the enhancement of systems to handle less structured information (graphics, images, knowledge), as well as data and text.

The requirements of knowledge workers can be summarized in three dimensions:

1 access to computer-held sources of information;
2 interworking (exchange of information with other people);
3 services (tools for handling information).

In addition, most knowledge workers also belong to work groups, where systems typically combine specific applications with utilities such as electronic messaging.

The legacy of partial solutions from the past (information frontiers) has delayed the adoption of these working practices, which, in turn, has delayed the realization of the benefits of adding value to information through its processing by knowledge workers. The requirement is for a knowledge work support architecture to be embodied in the infrastructure, and for this to happen organizations must appreciate the critical role of IS infrastructure. Organizations that do not establish a suitable infrastructure with the flexibility to support today's requirements and with a view to future developments will lose competitive edge to others that are more aware.

Types of infrastructure

Infrastructure naturally sub-divides into enabler and support categories.

Enabler infrastructure

Silk (1992) states that enabler infrastructure projects which allow the benefits of other IT investments to be realized are difficult to assess as they have no direct application and benefits accrue over a relatively long time period.

A similar view of enabler infrastructure is expressed by Way and Norris (1991), who considered it 'expenditure on enabling services which produce no direct returns, but are viewed as essential to the delivery of benefits from other, more applications-related investments'.

Hochstrasser (1994, p.153) states that 'infrastructure projects are hardware or software systems installed to enable the subsequent development of front-end systems'. Examples include the installation of networks, servers, extensive integrated programming environments, CASE tools, or multi-user operating systems. He feels that because enabler infrastructure projects enable the subsequent development of front-end systems, 'this makes a *standard* evaluation procedure for infrastructure projects impossible, particularly as the exact nature of the front-end systems subsequently to be developed is often still in the early planning stages'. He concludes that evaluation of enabler infrastructure projects is possible (presumably using a non-standard or general method in his terms) by taking the medium-term business strategy and matching it to the present infrastructure. A gap analysis can then be performed, and infrastructure requirements identified from the gap. However, this does not allow evaluation of investment in individual systems, and hence provides little opportunity for post-implementation review.

Support infrastructure

Support infrastructure provides services direct to the business without delivering benefits directly to customers. An example is given by Quinn (1992), who finds that advanced users of IT in service industries considered investment in infrastructure necessary for competitive service levels and/or survival.

In these cases standard financial evaluation is often inappropriate or useless. Quinn gave examples of support infrastructure projects as:

1 automate and integrate office activities across organizations;
2 interconnect knowledge workers through data networks so they can be better informed.

Support infrastructure can be evaluated as its benefits, although intangible, can be identified. This implies that an investment appraisal method which considers intangible benefits should be used to evaluate support infrastructure projects, and suggests that some newer methods of investment appraisal may be relevant.

Investment in IS infrastructure – an example

This section describes the background to an investment in IS support infrastructure – the development of an intranet system by Consult Ltd.

Intranet technology

An intranet is a system which employs characteristic features of the internet (in terms of tools, style and accessibility) to provide information on demand to a closed corporate user base, using a simple common interface. The intranet is defined by Pal (1997) as 'a private network of trusted Web servers used by a single organisation for intra-organisational applications'.

Consult Ltd

Consult Ltd is a major European systems house which has autonomous strategic business units (SBU) in each major country that it operates. Each SBU is set targets for turnover and profitability, and can determine its own strategy for achieving the targets. This is a corporate management style defined as financial control by Gould and Campbell (1987).

Consult Ltd operates in the IT industry where technology changes rapidly and the business opportunities do not fit any set pattern e.g. the changes required to systems by the year 2000. Burns and Stalker (1961) describe an organic structure for organizations that operate in a changeable environment. They say that the key attributes of a structure which can cope with this environment include information and decisions flowing vertically and horizontally throughout the organization. The continued survival of the organization depends upon excellent corporate communication supporting the continual development of ideas and innovations.

Identification of requirements for improved corporate communication

The majority of Consult Ltd's project work consists of undertaking consultancy on a time and materials, or fixed price, basis, where most work from new clients comes from competitive tendering. Here invitation to tender (ITT) documents are received and responses ('bids') are formulated to a tight deadline.

Excellent corporate communications can ensure that such information is available to the bid team on a timely basis, which is especially important when preparing bids in collaboration with other SBUs. Reduction in administration means that more time is available to enhance the content of the bid and improve the chance of winning the work.

This need accords with Hochstrasser's (1994) view that '70 per cent of companies suffer from a lack of accessible information'. He adds that information needs have often been neglected or have been analysed on a piecemeal basis, thereby losing any strategic coordination and control. This leads to two main problems; either:

1 divisions within a company suffer from a lack of shared data, or;
2 a company suffers from information overload, where the information is hidden in the data.

The SBUs are connected by e-mail but this does not identify the available information or give the opportunity to browse through it. As the company grows in line with its strategy, and larger pan-European projects are undertaken, the need will increase for a central repository of information about all the SBUs which can be readily accessed. There is also a threat of losing competitive edge to other companies in the market place that link their subsidiaries by high-bandwidth networks.

The intranet initiative

The inertia behind the call for improved corporate communications led to the formulation of the intranet initiative. The technical director agreed to back the submission of a proposal to the board for a company-wide communication system. Backing from a top manager is the key factor in achieving a successful implementation of office automation as identified in local authorities by Grimshaw and Kemp (1989).

The following key business requirements were identified:

- Support for:
  - international projects;
  - existing business;
  - interworking.
- Win more business;
- Promote efficiency;
- Promote innovation.

Other needs identified include: strengthen the corporate identity (espirit de corps); increase motivation by underpinning staff morale; and present a hi-tech image to build customer confidence.

The low level requirements for the intranet include:

- low cost;
- easy access;
- easy ability to find information;
- capture existing material;
- platform for future growth;
- reasonable level of security.

Promotion
A presentation of the proposed intranet investment was made to technical directors company wide (i.e. from all the national subsidiaries) to encourage them to buy into the concept. An intranet awareness programme was also undertaken to help build user buy-in, and a series of demonstrations of the system organized which stressed the positive features of the system:

- straight forward structure;
- existing documents already converted;
- good search facilities;
- good feedback mechanism.

Use
Technical directors have a brief to encourage staff to contribute to the intranet. Contributions are made by choosing a 'feedback' option on the intranet display. Selection of this option passes control to an e-mail system via which messages (with attachments as required) are sent to the intranet project manager. He has editorial authority and examines the quality of the material and its relevance before approving contributions.

The intranet is at an early stage of implementation, and this should be borne in mind when looking at current use of the system. For example, UK-based staff are the major users of the intranet, but this may be because the UK was the first country to implement the system, and certainly other SBUs are catching up as the roll-out proceeds.

Only the UK SBU has information on the intranet which is not exclusively technical, and the system is mainly used in the UK for preparation of contract tenders. Prior to the intranet it was necessary to use telephone and fax in order to prepare a proposal which included the CVs of staff from locations around the UK. The cooperation of colleagues from those locations was also required to elicit the necessary information. This work can now be undertaken by browsing the relevant material while based at one location.

Assessment of the intranet implementation

Ballantine et al. (1997) develop a model in an attempt to improve the understanding of IS success which can be applied to the intranet implementation. The model is based on an extension of work done by DeLone and McLean (1992), and separates success into three levels of IS effectiveness:

1 Development – technical;
2 Deployment – user;
3 Delivery – business benefits.

There are filters between each level which inhibit or encourage adoption of the system at the next highest level.

In addition to the filters between each level there are influencing factors of success which can act at one or more levels and between levels. Influencing factors are of two types:

1 endogenous factors (e.g. user skills/development methodology);
2 exogenous factors (e.g. political and economic).

Success measures based on the 3D model

The 3D model (Figure 16.1) gives a structure to evaluate the success of the intranet to date. However, it should be noted that the factors involved in the success of an information system are many and complex, and that the model represents a simplification of the real world in order to assist analysis.

Developers and users of the system were interviewed as to their experiences of the intranet and their proposals for its further development, and these views are categorized below.

Development level
The intranet is simple to use and runs on the standard (upgraded) desktop PC environment, and it has been developed by experienced IT staff who appreciate the attributes needed for a corporate system. In the UK there has been a

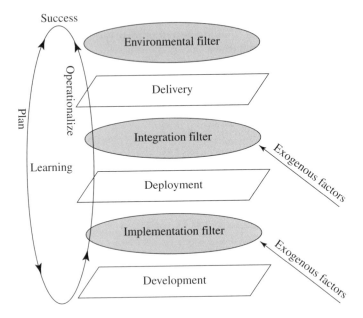

Figure 16.1 *3D model of information systems success*

reduction in the number of enquiries about write-ups of projects (project stories) than before for the same level of bid activity, so it may be assumed that UK staff are using the intranet to access information.

Implementation filter

The intranet project team are responsible for enhancement of the system, the distribution of the monthly updates, and have editorial control. Although this is an efficient and effective arrangement in terms of utilization of resources and concentration of skills, it means that the target users are not involved in the intranet's development, although it is being promoted as a corporate offering. The risk in this approach is that the users will have no feeling of ownership and hence might resist using the system.

Deployment level

The intranet project manager and support team are enthusiastic in their promotion of the intranet system, and partly due to their persuasiveness enough new information is acquired from contributors to allow the intranet to be updated monthly. However, the information on the intranet is not yet complete enough to put together a full response to an ITT (there are some project stories but no CVs or annual reports).

Users have contrasting views on the current monthly update of information on the intranet. One user said that the medium should be more dynamic with more topical updates at a greater frequency, while another user argued that the regular update meant that staff knew when to look for any new information, whereas random updates of information could be overlooked.

Integration filter

Across the SBUs in participating countries there is a predominance of technical rather than business information on the intranet, possibly because English is the business 'lingua franca'. Calori and De Woot (1994) state that the level of English spoken is extremely variable between the different European countries. They described how a CEO of a subsidiary of a French firm in Germany noted that where English was used as the working language, meetings consisted exclusively of presentations. Not one question was asked and there was very little interaction. In this case the choice of working language could sterilize inter-cultural exchanges and affect the strategic dimension of the relationships between the companies.

Delivery level

The true test of the success of project delivery is based upon summative evaluation and is whether the intranet has delivered solutions to the problems described in support of its adoption, and whether it has delivered its key business benefit – *improved corporate communications.* It is perhaps too early in its roll-out to come to a conclusion on whether the intranet is successful from this viewpoint, but an increase in cross-company work undertaken using the intranet would be required before it could be claimed to be successfully delivered.

Environmental filter

It is indeterminable whether the company's performance in the market place has improved due to the communications facilities offered by the intranet. However, having an intranet means that the company can use this as an example of in-house knowledge, skills, and implementation capability, and so could secure more work in this field than otherwise.

Organizational learning

There is a further concept in the 3D model – learning feedback – which loops around all levels and filters. It depends upon the organization having in place procedures and people who monitor the success or otherwise of any change process and who promote process improvement. In the intranet's example there is informal monitoring by the project team via verbal comments and contributions received via e-mail. However, no one is formally monitoring the change process, so presumably there is little learning feedback occurring.

Factors affecting success of the intranet project

Corporate management style

Consult Ltd's style of financial control of autonomous SBUs is highly conducive to profitability. However, according to Grant (1995, p.427) one of its weaknesses of this is 'its difficulty in exploiting synergies between each business, as each is treated as a single entity, and corporate headquarters lacks a mechanism for promoting coordination and cooperation between businesses'. An example of the difficulties the SBU structure brings is given by Feldman (1989). His illustration shows that where the autonomous behaviour of groups is given free rein, it results in destructive levels of autonomy in terms of the effective coordination of organizational activity as a whole. This indicates that control and autonomy are inseparable, and not alternatives.

Weill (1993) identifies that infrastructure projects have not been awarded the same priority as market-driven investments, and so development of infrastructure has not been coordinated across divisions as the divisions pursue their own initiatives. Hence it is difficult to reach agreement between divisions, especially where there is a multi-national flavour, and company-wide projects have been postponed to the detriment of the organization. In the case of the intranet, the project was not postponed, but success in terms of delivery in the 3D model has been limited.

Cultural differences

So far the intranet sites have been predominantly located within Europe where there are significant differences in culture and management style between countries. Johnson and Scholes (1993) quoting an article about the Anglo-French merger of Metal Box and Carnaud state: 'management styles are different throughout Europe and present a challenge to European corporate integration. Styles vary from the authoritarian Italian padrone to the German consensus approach.'

Calori and De Woot (1994) argue that the management philosophy in the UK is an exception in Europe, and that its philosophy, structures and practices are closer to the United States. They described UK management as having a short-term orientation towards shareholders, as opposed to management in mainland Europe which has a stakeholder orientation.

In the light of the above, and considering that the intranet has been designed exclusively by the UK team, one might imagine that the look and feel of the intranet would have a UK bias. However, this was not raised by the non-UK company interviewees, probably because the intranet uses standard internet features which are recognized by users from the other countries. Similarly, one might be tempted to argue that because the majority of the information on the intranet is in English and relates to the UK SBU, the UK regards the intranet as a local rather than a corporate system. This has less impact when it is realized that the Intranet was first rolled-out in the UK and that the UK has the best developed network, so it might have been expected to be the greatest contributor.

The one area where there does seem to be differences in the use of the intranet due to cultural variations is in the type of information stored. Only the UK has non-technical information on the intranet (e.g. project stories), while other (European) SBUs do not see the need for such information.

Organizational behaviour
The need to adapt business processes to achieve fully the benefits of the intranet was identified in a panel debate between end-users, analysts and suppliers from the Networks Expo show in Boston USA. Lauchlan (1997) reports that the panel concluded that 'the Intranet revolution must be matched by business process evolution if its full potential is to be realised.'

There needs to be significant and explicit attempts to change organizational behaviour if the intranet is to overcome resistance to cross-SBU communication. This accords with Keen (1981) who considers IS development an intensely political as well as technical process. He sees organizational change associated with a computer-based IS as requiring coalition building, which in turn requires IS managers with authority and resources for negotiation. Tactics include ensuring that the implementor has a contract for change, seeking out resistance as a signal to be responded to, relying on face-to-face contact, becoming an insider, and working hard to build personal credibility, and co-opting users early. None of these tactics appear to have been employed during the implementation of the intranet.

Improving the success of the intranet

It is self-evident that there is no simple remedy for the problems related to corporate management style, cultural differences, and organizational behaviour identified above. However, it is worthwhile investigating how investment appraisal methods might have helped.

Traditional appraisal methods
No formal business case was required to support the intranet investment, so the investment could be classified as an act of faith (Silk, 1990). In addition, a purely technical solution was proposed in answer to the problem of lack of corporate communications, which meant that discussion of its root causes was avoided, and resulted in corporate R&D driving what should have been a business-led initiative. However, the use of a formal appraisal method based upon cost-benefit principles would not have helped address the people issues, which leads to the consideration of more recent methods.

Newer appraisal methods

The use of newer appraisal methods would have highlighted the effect on the success of the intranet implementation of the people involved rather than purely technical aspects. This, in turn, would have focused more attention on the anticipated business benefits, which would have improved the buy-in of the SBUs and have given the intranet a better chance of fulfilling its corporate communication function.

The appraisal methods which would be best suited for the intranet investment are now discussed.

Choice of method

Given the premise that simply the process of utilizing a method of evaluation gives benefits, then the use of any of the methods would have been an improvement. The intranet is defined as infrastructure as it is predominantly a means of communication for the organization rather than supporting a business process. However, it does more than simply enable the use of other applications, so can be regarded as support infrastructure as opposed to enabler infrastructure. Therefore, the key element from an evaluation standpoint of the intranet is to use a method which copes well with intangible benefits.

Some recent methods tend towards conversion of intangible benefits into equivalent financial measures e.g. Silk's method and Strassman's ROM method, while the balanced scorecard approach of Kaplan and Norton also seems to suggest quantification of benefits. However, the key issue here is to maintain the visibility of the people issues and the benefits to be gained from changes in working practices.

A classification of projects for the purpose of identifying suitable methods of investment appraisal is proposed by Farbey, Land and Targett (1992). They identify a number of contingency factors which are used to examine the intranet project (Table 16.5).

The classification indicates that information economics would be an appropriate choice for intranet evaluation. Willcocks and Lester (1994, p. 63) also suggested that 'where benefits and inputs are becoming increasingly intangible but sizeable, as is usual with innovation and competitiveness objectives, then the Information Economics approach of Parker, Benson and Trainor (1988) becomes more appropriate'.

The key strength of information economics would have been the facilitation of:

- improved communications between functions;
- arrival at consensus between managers from different business units;
- closing the culture gap.

However, the time consuming nature of IE and its problems with gaining

Table 16.5 *Classification of the intranet by Farbey, Land and Targett's contingency factors*

Contingency factor	Intranet characteristic
Role of evaluation	No formal evaluation was undertaken, but it could be assumed that evaluation should occur at the requirements stage and at the strategic level
Decision environment	Decision processes are ad hoc and benefits are qualitative
The system	Provides infrastructure
The organization	The industry is turbulent and Consult Ltd are a leader
Cause and effect relationships	The system will have an indirect impact on the business and the impact is unpredictable

credibility with senior management (Willcocks and Lester, 1994) do not suggest that it would be suitable for an organization like Consult Ltd, as this would be a significant change from its current informal approach to project evaluation.

Indeed, the apparent simplicity of the benefits profile produced as part of the Prudential project assessment method of Coleman and Jamieson (1991) seems to offer both the maintenance of visibility of intangible benefits, and a low key approach to implementation. This method would therefore seem to be the most appropriate in this case.

Benefit tracking
There is no mechanism in place for tracking the success of the intranet initiative because the benefits (or values from an IE perspective) of the system have not been formally recorded. Therefore, the formal feedback loop in the organizational learning process is missing.

Benefit tracking (and value tracking) would have been invaluable in this situation, as difficulties (for instance, cultural) could have been more readily identified and justifiably escalated. For example, as suggested by a user, the number of project stories put on to the intranet by each SBU could be reviewed at board meetings. It would then be obvious which SBUs were falling short in involvement, and would hopefully promote discussion of the root causes.

Conclusions

There are many reasons for evaluating IS projects, ranging from assessing whether or not to invest, to eliciting information to guide incremental improvements. Traditional methods of investment appraisal rely on assessments of the financial benefits of a project versus the costs of implementing it. More sophisticated methods also take into account the time value of money. As the shift from manufacturing towards the service sector grows, so benefits from projects become less tangible and, hence, less amenable to cost-benefit analysis.

The success of IS projects in particular (and hence their potential for delivering benefits) is closely linked to the participation and involvement of people. In essence, modern IS projects are people projects with a technical element, rather than technical projects with a people element. There is a need to consider the users of the system when identifying the potential benefits of the proposed system, and to track the delivery of these benefits during implementation, and to assess and learn from the success of their delivery in the post-implementation phase.

The need to take people issues and intangible benefits into account has led to the development of new methods of evaluation, and each of which attacks the problems from a different angle. However, there is little guidance in the literature as to which methods are most appropriate to evaluating investments in IS infrastructure.

When considering the purposes of evaluation, the use of newer methods to evaluate investment in support infrastructure is more likely to improve the success of implementation rather than indicate whether or not to proceed with the investment. This is because, although some methods recommend quantification of intangible benefits (e.g. Silk, 1990), the actual benefits realized depend to a great extent upon actions undertaken to promote participation and involvement in the use of the system e.g. through associated change initiatives and promotion of the system.

Where the investment in IS infrastructure involves new technology there can be a tendency for the technical department to encourage its adoption while bypassing a thorough evaluation, a form of technology push. In Consult Ltd the technical department in each SBUs did successfully implement an environment which enabled the intranet to function. However, the initiative was propagated through the technical directors of the SBUs, which meant that the business users had limited involvement. This resulted in most of the information on the intranet being of a technical rather than business nature.

Cultural differences between the countries involved in the pan-European roll-out and the problems inherent in certain management styles appear to have prevented the full realization of the business benefits that were foreseen at the initiation stage. The use of recent evaluation methods might have enabled such problems to have been identified at the evaluation stage and actions to address them could have been put in place. Such methods might also have led to the identification of benefits and values that could have assisted in organizational learning, which might have increased the chance of success of similar developments in the future.

The use of any recent method would probably have been beneficial, as simply the process of using a method can reveal factors that would otherwise remain hidden. Both information economics and the Prudential method appear to be suitable for evaluation of support infrastructure, and the Prudential method seems the simpler to implement. Use of these methods could have facilitated improved communications between functions, and assisted managers from different business units arriving at a consensus on use of the intranet. It could also have helped to close the culture gap between staff from the various countries.

When considering results of the investigation into the intranet implementation, it must be remembered that Consult Ltd's implementation is not yet complete, which means that conclusions have to be drawn from a snapshot of the project. Angell and Smithson (1991) argue that the judgement of when to carry out an evaluation can make a considerable difference to the result. For example, immediately after installation users find the system awkward, further along the learning curve they will find the system is working well, and, further still, fresh problems and opportunities start to emerge. In the case of the intranet, the UK is much more advanced in its roll-out than its counterparts in the other SBUs, which might have influenced the contrasting views of interviewees from different countries.

References

Angell, I. O. and Smithson, S. (1991). *Information Systems Management – Opportunities and Risks.* Macmillan Education Ltd, Basingstoke.

Avison, D. E., Horton, J., Powell, P., and Nandhakumar, J. (1995). Evaluation incorporation in the information systems development process. *Proceedings of the Evaluation of Information Technology Conference,* Henley, July.

Ballantine, J., Bonner, M., Levy, M., Martin, A., Munro, I. and Powell, P.L. (1997). Developing a 3D model of information systems success. *Information Resource Management Journal,* September.

Blackler, F. and Brown, C. (1988). Theory and Practice in Evaluation: The Case of the New Information Technologies. In *Information Systems Assessment: Issues and Challenges* (N. Bjorn-Andersen and G. B. Davis, eds) North Holland.

Burns, T. and Stalker, G. M. (1961). *The Management of Innovation.* Tavistock.

Butler Cox Foundation (1990). Getting value from information technology. *Research Report 75,* June, Butler Cox Foundation, London.

Calori, R. and De Woot, P. (1994). *A European Management Model.* Prentice-Hall.

Coleman, T. and Jamieson, M. (1991). Beyond return on investment. In *Information Management* (Leslie Willcocks, ed.), Chapman & Hall.

Currie, W. L. (1989). The art of justifying new technology to top management, *Omega*, **17**(5), pp. 409–418.

DeLone, W. H. and McLean, E. R. (1992). Information systems success: the quest for the development variable. *Information Systems Research*, **3**(1), pp. 60–95.

Drury, C. (1992). *Management and Cost Accounting*. Chapman and Hall, pp. 372–374.

Earl, M. (1989). *Management Strategies for IT*. Prentice-Hall International.

Farbey, B., Land, F. and Targett, D. (1992). Evaluating investments in information technology. *Journal of Information Technology*, **7**(2), 100–112.

Feldman, S. P. (1989). The broken wheel: the inseparability of autonomy and control in innovation within organisations. *Journal of Management Studies*, **26**(2), 83–102.

Gould, M. and Campbell, A. (1987). *Strategies and Styles*. Blackwell.

Grant, R. M. (1995). *Contemporary Strategy Analysis*. Blackwell.

Grimshaw, D. J. and Kemp, B. (1989). Office automation in local government. *Local Government Studies*, March/April, 7–15.

Gunton, T. (1989). *Infrastructure – Building a Framework for Corporate Information Handling*. Prentice-Hall.

Hamilton, S. and Chervany, N. L. (1981). Evaluating information system effectiveness – Part I: Comparing evaluation approaches. *MIS Quarterly*, **5**(3).

Hochstrasser, B. (1994). Justifying IT investments. In *Information Management: The Evaluation of Information Systems Investments* (Leslie Willcocks, ed.), Chapman & Hall, p. 153.

Johnson, G. and Scholes, K. (1993). *Exploring Corporate Strategy*. Prentice-Hall.

Kaplan, R. and Norton, D. (1992). The balanced scorecard – measures that drive performance. *Harvard Business Review*, January–February, 71–9.

Keen, P. G. W. (1981). Information systems and organisational change. *Communications of the ACM*, **27**(12), pp. 1218–1226.

Lauchlan, S. (1997). Report on the Networks Expo show in Boston USA. *Computing*, 27 February, p. 24.

Legge, K. (1984). *Evaluating planned organisational change*. Academic Press.

Pal, A. (1997). Intranets for Business Applications. *Ovum Report*, London

Parker, M., Benson, R. and Trainor, E. H. (1988). *Information Economics: Linking Business Performance to IT*. Prentice-Hall.

Quinn, J. (1992). *Intelligent Enterprise: A Knowledge and Service Based Paradigm for Industry*. Free Press, New York.

Silk, D. (1990). Managing IS benefits for the 1990s. *Journal of Information Technology,* **5**(4), pp. 185–93.

Silk, D. (1992). *Planning IT.* Pitman.

Strassman, P.A. (1990). *The Business Value of Computers.* The Information Economics Press, New Canaan, Connecticut.

Walsham, G. (1993). *Interpreting Information Systems in Organisations.* John Wiley & Son.

Way, R. and Norris, G. (1991). *Value from Investment in Information Technology: A Framework for Assessments.* Electricity Audit Company, South Wales.

Weill, P. (1993). The role and value of IT infrastructure. In *Strategic IT Management: Perspectives on Organisational Growth and Competitive Advantage* (R. Banker, R. Kauffman and M. Mahmood, eds), Idea Company Publishing, Harrisburg.

Willcocks, L. and Lester, S. (1994). Evaluating the feasibility of IS investments: recent UK evidence and new approaches. In *Information Management: The Evaluation of Information Systems Investments* (Leslie Willcocks, ed.), Chapman & Hall, pp 49–77.

Willcocks, L. (1994). *Information Management.* Chapman & Hall, London, p. 5.

Wiseman, D. (1994). Information economics: a practical approach to valuing information systems. In *Information Management: The Evaluation of Information Systems Investments*

17 The development of an EIS within a hospital trust – pitfalls and lessons

Joan Ballantine
Warwick Business School, University of Warwick

Introduction

The UK National Health Service (NHS) has seen enormous change in the last decade, not only in the provision of health care, but also in terms of how the service is managed. The implementation in 1991 of the 1989 White Paper ('Working for Patients') resulted in the separation of purchasers of health care services from providers of such services, the separation requiring purchasers and hospital providers to contract for the provision of services. The reforms have implied a need to reform management information systems (MIS) within healthcare organizations. Increasingly, the production of accurate, relevant and timely information within such organizations have become key features relevant to their success. However, the difficulties inherent in producing such information have been exacerbated by the inability of healthcare organizations to extract meaningful information from existing operational systems (for example, patient administrative systems). This problem has to some extent been addressed in the NHS Management Executive information management and technology strategy, developed to support the 1989 reforms. A key element of the strategy relating to the needs of large acute hospital trusts was the development of a full range of integrated, patient-based, operational systems which were to be linked to appropriate managerial systems, thereby creating a hospital information support system (HISS) (see Figure 17.1).

A HISS is an integrated patient-based IT environment which has applications of both a hospital-wide (e.g. patient administrative system) and departmental (e.g. pathology) nature, together with a data communications network

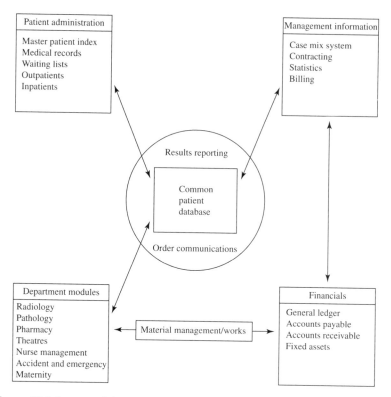

Figure 17.1 *Integrated hospital information support system (HISS). Source: Keen, 1994*

and an order communications system. Applications in a HISS environment are designed to operate in an integrated manner to ensure that data is entered once and only once, and is then made available to a variety of users as and when required. The target date for all large UK acute hospitals to acquire such systems is the year 2000 (Millar, 1994). However, the cost of HISS systems have largely been prohibitive to their widespread introduction. In addition the so called 'big-bang' approach to systems development and integration, clearly visible in HISS development, is currently being questioned in terms of its efficacy, largely as a result of the difficulties associated with installing complex, corporate-wide integrated systems in a relatively naive information technology culture (Willcox, 1994). The more favoured approach to the development of corporate-wide integrated systems within the National Health Service is the incremental approach, whereby changes are gradually made to existing operational systems, and flexible and user-friendly software tools are used as the 'glue' to connect disparate operational information.

In common with a number of acute providers, the hospital trust discussed here was unable to commit the funds required to develop a fully integrated HISS. As an interim solution, the trust identified the possibility of extracting data from existing core operational systems and manipulating that data through an executive information system (EIS), thereby providing relevant information in a form suitable for both clinical (e.g. consultants and clinical managers) and managerial staff (e.g. contracts manager, finance director and the chief executive officer) within the organization. This chapter reports on the development and implementation of the EIS within the hospital trust. The remainder of the chapter is structured as follows: first the background to the case site is discussed as is the systems environment within which the EIS evolved; the stages of EIS development are then considered before discussing the experiences and problems of using the EIS to date. Finally, some tentative conclusions regarding the success of the EIS to date are drawn.

The case site and systems environment

The hospital trust is situated in the southern part of Northern Ireland and operates from one major general hospital site which has been operating as a provider of acute services since it opened in the early 1970s. The main site offers a full range of inpatient, outpatient and day care services. Two subsidiary hospitals also exist, one of which provides services for the elderly, including day hospital procedures, assessment, rehabilitation, respite and continuing inpatient care. The third site provides key support to the main hospital site, and offers services including outpatient, day and inpatient services for medical, surgical and geriatric patients [although this site closed at the end of 1997]. The Trust has a bed complement of approximately six hundred, an annual estimated contract income of £42 million, and currently serves a population of approximately 250,000, with an average of 20,000 inpatients and 80,000 outpatients treated each year.

Prior to the reforms of 1989, the hospital trust operated an operational patient administrative system (PAS) which was purchased in the early 1980s. The PAS was (and is currently) primarily used to record information regarding the admission, transfer and discharge of patients to the hospital. Written in a third generation language (MUMPS), the system has limited capabilities in terms of producing management reports for decision making and control activities. Despite this inflexibility, the system met many of the management and operational information requirements prior to 1989. For example, the PAS facilitated reporting of impatient and outpatient statistics, and details of waiting lists. However, these reports were difficult to interpret. In addition the PAS did not facilitate the production of ad hoc reports. This inevitably led to a feeling of alienation among the users of the system, and in particular clinical staff who were unable to access information which might help them understand why patient activity had altered from one period to the next.

The reforms of 1989, however, resulted in significant changes in the information requirements within the trust. Managers and clinical staff alike now required information which enabled them to negotiate contracts with purchasers, monitor and control service levels and monitor performance against other similar provider units in the region. For example, in order to negotiate contracts an accurate picture of patient activity by speciality was required, as was the need to monitor actual versus planned activity. The inflexibility of the PAS to provide such information was partially addressed during the early 1990s by the development of a decision support system (DSS) which captured data from the PAS and held it within relational database tables. A structured query language was used to facilitate the production of more relevant and timely information used for planning and control purposes. Despite this development, however, the DSS could not be directly used by the decision makers within the organization since a relatively high degree of computing skills were required to extract and manipulate the required information. As a result the operation of the DSS relied heavily on the skills of an in-house information technology (IT) unit who spent a considerable amount of time producing the required paper based reports. This situation inevitably led to time delays in reporting relevant information to key decision makers. In addition, feedback to the IT unit suggested that the recipients of the paper based output were not using all of the information requested from the IT unit. As a result, the DSS, whilst providing more relevant information than previous, did little to address the real need of the reforms to provide more relevant and timely performance information to enable managers and clinical staff to adequately plan, monitor and control activity. Additionally, the need for managers and clinical staff to directly explore the reasons for trends in activity levels (i.e. increases in patient activity within specialities) and how these affected the cost base of the organization was not facilitated by the DSS.

In order to overcome the limitations of the DSS and the ever increasing demands made of the in-house IT unit, the trust made a decision to acquire and implement an EIS. They believed this would enable clinical and managerial staff at various levels of the organization to access relevant decision making information. Whilst earlier discussions within the trust regarding the possibility of introducing an EIS had been previously discounted as a result of the prohibitive cost involved, and the perceived high risk of such a strategy, both these concerns were challenged when a commercially available EIS was offered to the trust at a substantially reduced price. The supplier hoping that a successful project would result in additional orders throughout the region.

As a result of discussions with the software supplier, it was agreed that a consultant would work with the in-house IT unit for a limited period during which time a prototype EIS would be developed to incorporate data from the trust's PAS and DSS. The development of the prototype was subsequently followed by presentations to senior management and clinical staff to assess their reactions and views concerning the systems. Feedback from these sessions was considered before a final decision was made to purchase and implement the fully-blown EIS.

According to Butler (1992), an EIS is used by executives to extract, filter, compress and track critical data. Rinaldi and Jastrzembski (1986) argue that EISs have become the favoured tool for providing top management with information on the organization's key performance indicators (see also Harvey and Meiklejohn, 1989; Fireworker and Zirkel, 1990; Watson, Rainder and Koh, 1991). O'Brien (1993) identifies the key purposes of an EIS as follows:

- to provide on-line access, trend analysis, exception reporting and drilldown capabilities;
- to present information in a variety of forms;
- to enable executives to monitor organizational performance;
- to enhance communications between different groups of an organization (see also Friend, 1986; Kogan, 1986; Zmud, 1986).

An EIS provides sophisticated software tools which enables data to be integrated, processed and presented to executives in an easy-to-learn and highly user-friendly format (Minear, 1991). Thus EISs integrate and present data already held in existing information systems. Generally they do not create data. O'Brien (1993) identifies the key features of an EIS as comprising: executive workstations typically networked to a mainframe, microcomputer or local area network file server through which access to the EIS is enabled. The EIS works with database management systems (DBMS) and communications software which enable executives to gain access to external, internal and special database information. For example, external databases are likely to provide access to information on, for example, competitors (benchmarking data), customer preferences for services, regulatory information and regional economic indicators. Internal databases, on the other hand, might provide information on relevant internal performance dimensions, including for example, financial performance, quality and resource utilization. Special management databases are likely to provide specialist internal information, for example, relevant cost analysis, information relevant to make or buy, special pricing or capital investment decisions.

Mohan, Holstein and Adams (1990) argue that whilst much progress has been made in terms of the development of EISs within the private sector, far less progress has taken place within the public sector. One of the reasons for this they argue is the cost of an EIS which is far less an issue for private sector organizations. However, cost is frequently a factor which is prohibitive to the introduction of EISs within public sector organizations. As discussed earlier cost was a major factor in terms of making the decision to introduce an EIS within the hospital trust described here.

EIS Development

The development and implementation of the EIS within the trust was planned to take place in an evolutionary manner, consisting of three phases. The first phase [completed towards the end of 1996]) sought to provide senior clinical and managerial staff access to the information that was previously available through the paper-based output of the DSS. However, those requiring information from the EIS could now use the system in an interactive manner without the intervention of the in-house IT unit. The provision of an interactive system was hoped would help focus the information needs of clinical staff in particular. The objective of the EIS was to provide flexible reporting facilities and graphics capabilities, which would allow the users to explore underlying trends. The EIS would enable clinical and managerial staff to query cumulative and monthly patient activity information, broken down by speciality, and consultant within speciality. Activity levels could be further categorized into inpatient, outpatient and day care activity. In addition, the EIS tracked information related to bed statistics, bed performance and method of admission (e.g., referred from local general practitioner, split between fund and non-fund holders, elective and emergency data).

The second phase of development [completed towards the end of 1997] sought to integrate financial and patient activity data related to one of the trust's key resource areas, its laboratories. The rationale for the second stage of development stemmed from concerns regarding over-spending of laboratory resources which were considered to be a substantial cost element of the trust. In addition, since financial and patient activity data related to laboratories were not in any way linked before the second stage of EIS development, it was difficult to see the extent to which individual specialities, or consultants within specialities, were consuming laboratory resources and hence driving the costs of such resources within the Trust. The second stage of EIS development greatly added to existing information needs. For example, the following sources of information were made available to decision makers: number of tests by speciality; number of tests by consultant within specialities; number of out of hours requests for tests (which has a knock-on effect on overtime payments); and cost of requests for individual laboratory services (e.g., haematology, microbiology).

The final phase of EIS development [still ongoing from 1998] aims to integrate patient activity and financial data across all specialities and support services. In order to collect the data required for stage three development, the trust is currently running a number of pilot studies which are investigating the extent to which costs vary as patient numbers increase/decrease at speciality level. In addition, the final stage of EIS development is being aided by the parallel development of a speciality costing system (which is largely under the control of the finance function) which will enable costs to be integrated with patient activity data. Whilst the final stage of EIS development will provide more relevant performance related information, the trust recognizes that integration will only be possible at an aggregate level (i.e. at speciality level), due to the nature of data currently captured by the trust's operational systems. Thus, whilst the long-term aims of the trust are to integrate activity, cost and quality (i.e. outcomes) data at a patient level, the EIS, in either its current or completed form, will not make such integration possible. Thus, the trust recognizes that the development of an integrated HISS is an issue which will need to be addressed in the future if integrated activity and cost data at the individual patient level are to be made available to key decision makers.

Experiences and problems

To date the experiences of the users of the EIS indicate a somewhat mixed response. Whilst there is general agreement among both clinical and managerial users that the system has improved access to relevant information, there are also concerns that the EIS has led to information overload problems within the organization, particularly among clinical staff. The following section discusses in more detail the experiences of EIS use within the trust.

Prior to the first phase of EIS development, a process of consultation with the intended users (both clinical and managerial) of the system took place, during which the rationale for the system's introduction was discussed. This process also enabled the objectives of the EIS to be defined (see Table 17. 1), although it has since been recognized that the objectives were largely defined by the management of the trust, with less input from clinical staff. The initial consultation process also provided a means of sharing concerns regarding the introduction of the system. Subsequent to this, a programme of training was carried out which gave the users the opportunity to explore the detailed workings of the EIS. Problems identified during the consultation and training process were subsequently addressed by the development team before implementing the full-blown EIS. During both consultation and training, however, resistance to the introduction of the EIS had not become apparent.

Since its initial development and implementation, the EIS has been widely used by two user groups in particular: the executive management (the CEO and the director of business and planning, who is responsible for negotiating contracts) and clinical nursing managers (within surgery, medicine, outpatients, obstetrics and gynaecology). However, the system is less widely used by senior clinical consultants. Despite the lack of use by senior clinical staff,

Table 17.1

Objectives of the EIS System	Degree to which met?
1 Improve access to PAS activity and performance information	Achieved
2 Allow graphical analysis and presentation of information to decision makers	Achieved to some extent
3 Provide a means of improving data quality in the organization through feedback via the EIS	Questionable
4 Devolve the analysis and use of management information into the specialties through deployment of the EIS	Questionable
5 Allow Clinicians to become involved in managing their specialties and themselves through providing regular patient activity against contracted volumes	Achieved

feedback from the users of the EIS suggest that the first two objectives outlined in Table 17.1 have been achieved. The EIS has improved access to PAS data not least because of the flexible nature of the system. Additionally, the EIS also makes extensive use of graphics, which has not only aided understanding of the underlying data reported, but has positively improved its acceptance as a planning, monitoring and control tool by both managerial and clinical staff. The second stage of EIS development has clearly facilitated the integration of patient and activity data for laboratory services, thereby partly achieving the third objective of Table 17.1 to some degree. However, it will be some time before the trust is able to fully integrate financial and activity data, even at an aggregated speciality level.

Despite relative success in addressing the first three objectives outlined in Table 17.1, it is debatable whether the remaining objectives of the EIS have been met. For example, whilst the EIS has to some extent improved the quality of performance information within the organization in terms of more timely and relevant information, it has done little to address the need for more diagnostic information. For example, whilst the EIS gives managers a clear picture of how patient activity has altered over a period of time, thus aiding monitoring and control activities, it does little to help the users understand why activity has altered. The emphasis on measures which indicate what has happened (i.e. resource utilisation measures in particular), as opposed to why they have occurred, can be partly explained in that such measures are part of the information set that must be reported to government on a regular basis. Thus, one would expect there to be a greater emphasis on such measures. However, increasingly the users of the EIS are becoming more aware that the existing information set provided by the EIS is insufficient to enable them to plan and control operations because there is a lack of information which helps explain why activity has altered.

Finally, while the EIS has facilitated increased devolvement of decision making down to speciality level, in particular to clinical nursing managers, it has been less successful in terms of devolving responsibility for managerial tasks to senior clinicians.

More recently, recognizing some of these limitations, the Trust have subscribed to an external database facility which enables external comparisons of performance with other UK Trusts using data from nationwide PASs. Whilst the database was initially used by senior management staff for monitoring activity data such as length of stay and throughput statistics, it is becoming more widely used by nursing and clinical staff. However, the limited information on comparative case mixes, and the fact that it only reports on inpatient data still constrains the systems' utility to provide diagnostic information.

Early experience also indicates that considerable disparity exists between the levels of EIS use by senior clinical and management staff. In addition the senior management group appear to use substantially more of the features and functionality of the EIS system than the senior clinical group (this, however, is not the case with clinical nursing managers), with the former group using the system not only for control purposes, but also to address long- and medium-term planning issues. A number of reasons might explain this anomaly including inadequate training, lack of time to devote to managerial tasks, technological phobia, poor analytical skills and a lack of understanding of the underlying data held. An additional possible explanation is the change in consultant–nurse professional relationships which has taken place. Historically, the relationship between consultants and clinical nursing managers has been one where consultants have been viewed as the key decision makers within specialities, in addition to ranking higher in the organizational hierarchy than nursing managers. The clinical directorate model (Disken et al., 1993) of management adopted by the Trust, in which consultants and clinical nursing managers now work more closely together to manage patient activity and spending levels within specialities, has changed this relationship to one of almost equal partners from a managerial point of view. The introduction of the EIS has only further exasperated this situation by raising questions regarding the management of specialities, from both a clinical and business perspective.

Implications and conclusions

The experiences outlined in this paper are likely to have implications for other healthcare providers who are considering the introduction of an EIS. The introduction of the EIS within the clinical directorate model of management adopted by the Trust (that is, one of using senior nursing, as opposed to business managers) has highlighted a number of problems. Whether or not an alternative model of management in which business managers manage directorates would have been better suited to the implementation of an EIS is questionable given that little evidence exists to either support or refute this. Even if business managers had been in place within the trust it is highly questionable whether the EIS would have been developed to provide access to diagnostic information and that information overload problems would not also have resulted.

Mohan, Holstein and Adams (1990) argue that the implementation of an EIS within the public sector is contingent on the following factors:

- the role and commitment of top management;
- modularity in systems development;
- prototyping with live data;
- push-button ease of use;
- low cost;
- the need for detailed data in the system;
- the ability to access data at any level, detailed or aggregated;
- an iterative approach in developing new data where none existed.

Whilst the EIS developed within the trust meets the majority of the factors identified by Mohan, Holstein and Adams (1990) (for example, low cost, prototyping, the need for detailed data and push-button ease of use), problems still exist with the system, particularly in terms of information overload and the need to provide more diagnostic information to the users of the system.

An additional, and related, implication of the experiences reported here concerns the appropriateness of decentralizing information systems within the healthcare sector. While there has been a general trend, particularly within private sector organizations, to decentralize information systems use, the experiences outlined here shed some doubt on the appropriateness of this policy. Whilst there are clearly benefits of decentralization, it is questionable whether the necessary computing and information management skills and competencies exist within, for example, individual specialities within a hospital setting, to fully exploit the move from centralized to decentralized systems.

Clearly further development of the EIS will require that some of the above problems be explored. However, the project has provided the trust with some insights into the potential pitfalls and problems inherent in the introduction of an EIS within the healthcare sector.

References

Butler, J. (1992). Executive essay. Mortgage Banking, March, pp. 72–4.
Department of Health. (1989). *Working for Patients*, London, HMSO.

Disken, S., Dixon, M., Halpern, S. and Schocker, C. (1993). *Models of Clinical Management.* IHSM The Evaluation of the Clwyd Resource Management Project, Final Report 1990, Welsh Office Publisher.

Fireworker, R. and Zirkel, W. (1990). Designing an EIS in a multidivisional environment. *Journal of Systems Management.* **41**(2), pp. 25–31.

Fitzgerald, B. and Murphy, C. (1994). Introducing executive information systems into organizations: separating fact from fallacy. *Journal of Information Technology.* **9**, pp. 288–296.

Friend, D. (1986). Executive information systems: successes, failures, insights and misconceptions. *DSS 86 Transactions*, The Institute of Management Sciences, Providence, RI, pp. 35–40.

Harvey, D. and Meiklejohn, I. (1989). *The Executive Information Systems Report.* Business Intelligence, London.

Kogan, J. (1986). Information for motivation: a key to executive information systems that translate strategy into results for management. *DSS 86 Transactions*, The Institute of Management Sciences, Providence, RI, pp. 6–13.

Millar, J. (1994). Has HISS run out of Steam. *Health Services Journal*, July, 24–26.

Minear, M. N. (1991). Implementing an executive information system. *Computers in Healthcare*, July, pp. 34–40.

Mohan, L., Holstein, W. K. and Adams, R. B. (1990). EIS: It can work in the public sector. *MIS Quarterly*, pp. 435–448.

O'Brien R. C. (1993). *Management Information Systems: A Managerial End User Perspective*, Irwin.

Rinaldi, D. and Jastrzembski, T. (1986). EIS: the golden opportunity. *Computerworld.* **20**(27), pp. 28–34.

Watson, H. J., Rainder Jr, R. K. and Koh, C. E. (1991). Executive information systems: A framework for development and a survey of current practices. *MIS Quarterly*, pp. 13–30.

Willcox, D. (1994). NHS still cheers on Hiss projects. *Computing*, September, p. 6.

Zmud, R. W. (1986). Supporting senior executives through decision support technologies: a review and directions for future research. In *Decision Support Systems: A Decade in Perspective* (E. R. McLean and H. G. Sol, eds), pp. 87–101, Elsevier, North-Holland, Amsterdam.

18 The 'Know How Fund' project database

Sam Smith, Lawrence Zentner, James Robson, David Welch, Nick Woellwarth
Cranfield School of Management, Cranfield University

Preamble

An existing database within the UK Overseas Development Administration is under used. The reasons for this are examined in terms of people, processes and technology. The system is examined within the context of the overall information systems portfolio. Key staff are interviewed and recommendations are made for gaining benefits from revisions to the current database.

Introduction to the Know How Fund

Fund objectives

The Know How Fund (KHF) is Britain's programme of bilateral technical assistance to the countries of Central and Eastern Europe. First established in 1989, its aims in 1996 were to support their transition to pluralistic democracies and market economies by funding the provision of British skills (or 'know-how') in a range of key sectors:

- financial services;
- privatization;
- public administration;
- management;
- good government;
- EU integration.

Projects aim to transfer best practice and experience through training (e.g. for bankers, managers, judges, media) and advice on how to operate new institutions (e.g. stock exchanges, privatized businesses, courts). A typical project might involve a UK contractor training a local to train others.

The UK also contributes to EU projects in these regions. Other European countries also have their own bilateral aid programmes. So the KHF is not the only organization operating in the region.

Administration by the Joint Assistance Departments (JADs)

The KHF was funded by Britain's Overseas Development Administration (ODA). Since the chapter was written in 1997, the KHF has transferred to become part of the Department for International Development. Spending in 1995/96 was £86.5 million.

It was administered by two (JADs) – one covering the former Soviet Union (FSU) and one for Central and Eastern Europe – which were jointly run and staffed by the ODA and the diplomatic wing of the Foreign Office. There are sixty staff, organized in sections by geographic area. Most are in London, but a handful are based in embassies (e.g. three in Russia). Many staff were on short-term, two-year secondments.

Advisers

Back up is provided by a team of professional advisers – both on contract and from within the ODA – who add coherence through their technical expertise and knowledge of the region. (The Foreign and Commonwealth Office (FCO) Minister of State also chairs a three monthly Advisory Committee of luminaries from business, academe, etc.).

Project appraisal and funding

New proposals for KHF support come from outside bodies – whether in the recipient country or the UK. JAD staff in the appropriate country section conduct appraisals against detailed country plans and other criteria, aided by comments from the adviser and 'posts' (local embassies). About 70 per cent of proposals are accepted.

There are two funding options:

1 100 per cent support – in which case the contract to deliver the project is competitively tendered;

2 50/50 co-funding with the UK private sector.

Support is delivered by UK contractors, who handle the project in the field for the KHF, in liaison with the local 'partner' body and with the support of the embassy-based staff. The ODA Contract Branch (ODAC), based in East Kilbride, handles tendering and the issuing of contracts.

Stage payments must be approved by KHF staff, who monitor projects, for example, via the progress reports delivered at agreed milestones and visits to the country.

Background on the database

Inception of the database

The project database was set up in 1993, as a four-week project led by the then IT officer. The available information on its inception is limited, but a 1993 document shows that the intended benefits were easier and faster storage and retrieval of growing amounts of project information held on paper files. It was expected that this would in turn

'… allow reports to be produced that until now have been compiled manually from paper file records or spreadsheet records.'

The database holds information in ten types of record, which together show:

- the project description, country and sector;
- the names and addresses of all the parties involved;
- the status of the project and the funds committed/spent/outstanding;
- details of monitoring arrangement;
- a summary of the post-project appraisal.

(Annex A gives a fuller list.)

Information technology in the JADs

The JADs get advice and support from the ODA's IT section and uses the ODA's funding databases (e.g. MIS – an ODA-wide financial system primarily intended to tract expenditure commitments and payments). Until recently the IT systems were keyboard command based. Last year the JADs converted to Windows '95 with e-mail. Most staff were unfamiliar with the new systems, so training was provided (and is given to new staff arriving from the FCO without Windows experience).

The new systems provide potentially easier ways of sending messages. But in the case of producing reports, they have not replaced traditional paperflows which continue in parallel. The 'old world' databases (MIS and the project database) also continue in use unaffected by Windows.

A draft ODA report dated December 1996 suggests that the ODA should develop an integrated project database, which would improve the organization's ability to monitor and appraise projects after the approval and funding stages. However, we understand that this is currently only a proposal, and would take eighteen months to two years to implement.

Current information flows in the JADs

Several parallel systems exist

Project information is stored in several places at once:

- the official paper files for each project;
- working papers, diary entries and ad hoc computer files held by individual officers/sections;
- the management information system ('MIS') database;
- the office forecasting spreadsheet ('OFS') – for forecasting expenditure;
- the JAD project database.

Figure 18.1 plots these systems on a applications portfolio. The KHF's key operational processes are the approval and subsequent funding, and monitoring of individual new projects. While monitoring and post-project appraisal are taken seriously, finding and appraising good new projects to support is the key task. The separate information flows when a new project is proposed are shown in Figure 18.2. This shows that:

- the key decision making information flows for new proposals are handled on paper;
- the key financial information flows are handled on paper and/or via the MIS.

The database is not therefore a key operational system for new project approvals.

Producing aggregate reports

As well as approving individual projects, the JADs need to be able to aggregate information on projects to see the overall position. This is important for

STRATEGIC SYSTEMS	HIGH POTENTIAL SYSTEMS
Potential use of projects database for: ● Contractor selection ● Post-appraisal of projects	
KEY OPERATIONAL SYSTEMS	SUPPORT SYSTEM
Paperflows Filing systems Conventional fax/post links with embassies ODACO etc. MIS (financial system) Finstat OFS (spreadsheet system)	Windows E-mail **Project database** at present (but ineffective)

Figure 18.1 *Know How Fund information systems applications portfolio*

management who need to be able to look across sectors/countries. It is also particularly important for financial reporting, since the JADs are responsible to Parliament and the National Audit Office (NAO) for spending taxpayers' money. The MIS and OFS fulfil this function (as well as providing good management tools).

Non-financial aggregated reports are also helpful, to give an overview for a wide range of management and reporting purposes. For example, it may help users to answer parliamentary questions or brief for ministerial visits if they can find out:

● how many live or old projects there are in a particular country or sector (or both);
● the status of one project officer's projects;
● all the projects in a country involving a specific contractor or partner.

One intended benefit of the database was to make producing such reports

PAPERFLOWS	MIS	OFS	PROJECT DATABASE
Outside bodies ↳			
Proposal ↳			should be entered as proposal
New project file ↳			
Appraisal: papers copied to — project officer — advisers — section head — posts ↳			
Approved/rejected ↳			should be entered as approved/rejected and details updated
ODACO form sent to ODAC who tender and issue contract ↳	MIS code must be updated enter project on MIS database		
monitoring progress reports ↳		enter on spreadsheet system	updated
payments authorized ↳	ODACO section (?) update MIS	? update payments progress ?	updated
completion post appraisal			updated

Figure 18.2 *Information flows on a project*

easier. The database's report function does allow forty-five different types of aggregate report to be printed. Several of these report options were added to meet specific requests from project officers.

The reports produce a simple printout. There is no facility to print the information graphically (charts, graphs, etc.). Further analysis and synthesis of the raw data produced may be required to put it in a useable format.

Nevertheless, we were surprised by the gap between the common perception of the system and the wide range of reports it could actually produce. The system's full capabilities are not widely known. This report facility clearly has strategic potential, which is not being realized because of a lack of inputting and use, and because people do not understand the potential.

Use of the database in practice

Inputting and updating the computer records are usually delegated to administrative personnel. There is no common procedure or timetable set down for when new computer files are supposed to be completed, for example there is no requirement to create a computer record before the section head approves expenditure.

Database information is used occasionally by most staff at section head and below – whether to answer simple queries, check status, or gain an overview on a topic. Attitudes towards the database's usefulness – and hence towards updating it – vary between sections. For example, of those we interviewed:

- in one section the database is seen as of some use and effort is directed to update it, subject to other priorities;
- in another the database had not been used by anyone for over a month, and a staff member who arrived three months ago was unaware of its existence.

Nevertheless, the general consensus is that the database is of little use because it is not up to date. Staff at all levels say they often, or always, look elsewhere for information on a project or projects – e.g. by asking/phoning a colleague, looking on the file, or using the MIS financial system. MIS is more reliable since it must be updated, but its contents stress the financial aspects and some people find it as difficult to use as the database.

On the other hand, people acknowledged that the absence of good aggregate data, available quickly, does cause problems, eg:

- Database information is regularly sent to KHF staff in embassies and to the G7 Organisation as an update. There are sometimes complaints that it is not accurate.
- It is difficult and time consuming to compile reliable briefing for high-profile ministerial visits.
- Answering straightforward queries from Parliament, the public, etc, can be difficult; for example, the answer to one straightforward parliamentary question, seeking historic data on support to a region of the FSU, had to be laboriously hand-compiled from the paper files, taking several days.
- On one occasion two businessmen on a plane had discovered in conversation that they were working as KHF contractors on separate projects in the same town – different project officers were responsible for each and had not realized the connection: there could have been synergies here in terms of briefing, contacts, etc. This sort of incident is not uncommon.
- A problem unique to the Russian section is that the database does not distinguish between regions of Russia, which is often the level at which aggregated data is needed.

Analysis of database as an information system

A successful 'information system' is about more than just computer hardware and software. The system has four components: data, processes and people, as well as technology. Examining these four areas we can see why the project database has not fulfilled its intended potential:

Processes

The database is not integrated into workflows, instead it forms a separate task. There are no set procedures telling people how they should interrelate these tasks (e.g. using the database to aid the monitoring process).

There are many duplicate work processes (i.e. paperflows, MIS, OFS project database, contract paperwork and forms, reports for PIMS – ODA's database which breaks down aid by purpose).

The database ranks as a low priority amongst all these processes, as it is essentially regarded as 'nice to have' rather then key operational. Staff regard the real work, as going on elsewhere, for example MIS *must* be updated if funds are to be paid out.

The fact that the database is out of date creates a vicious circle. Staff do not trust the database to give accurate information, so they do not use it and tend to see updating as low priority. The database therefore becomes more out of date.

Data

Project data is often not up to date. People dealing regularly with a live project know its status, or can check quickly on paper files or the MIS. However, problems occur dealing with historic or aggregated data; or with live projects when the individuals who know about them are unavailable or have left the department.

People

Staff turnover is rapid, with two year secondments the norm. This limits the amount of user knowledge, which can develop in terms of system use and benefits. (The JADs also rely on the longer-serving advisers and senior personnel to act as the organization's memory in a more general sense.)

Although training/assistance is available, the take up is often low because of perceptions of the system's low importance.

Lack of use in turn means that many users are unaware of the potential benefits.

A few staff changes can remove a section's 'IT experts'. Sections tend to be inward looking, and old-fashioned 'closed' accommodation may further hamper support and skill sharing between sections.

We were told that FCO secondees generally came from a less computer-oriented 'culture' than ODA secondees (who might already have used similar systems) and so were less likely to utilize the database regularly.

Technology

The command-based computer system is not user friendly. It is complex to use relative to the information it provides – effectively it is an electronic card box of project records. The instructions are hard to follow for the non-computer literate. The system is less user-friendly than Windows, with no help function if people get stuck. Staff regard it as hard to access, use and print from. These problems are compounded by lack of use.

This is exacerbated by the introduction of Windows for everyday needs, as the contrast is stark. Users must also take a conscious decision to return to the 'old world' by clicking on an icon, and then key the command for the database.

Potential benefits

Need for the database

There is a clear need for a simple, up-to-date computer index of all projects, that is accessible to, and shared by, all staff. This is shown by the fact that most staff create their own ad hoc computer indexes or paper records to cover the projects or the contractors they deal with. Several people told us that that a good, up-to-date database would be very useful:

- Project officers, assistant project officers and section clerks need to know the status of specific projects for which they are responsible.
- Section heads need an overview across their countries/regions.
- More senior staff need a clear overview picture of the KHF's work if they are to steer strategy. MIS gives them this as a quantitative overview in terms of spending. But they also need qualitative information.

Good aggregate historic data is becoming increasingly important as the KHF grows older and develops a long tail of past projects. There needs to be continuity and a good 'memory' about past projects, partners and contractors. This is made more important by the staff turnover.

Operational benefits

If the current system was kept up to date potential benefits could be as follows:

- Answering important briefing requests (e.g. parliamentary questions) would be quicker and easier.
- Time would be saved answering everyday queries (e.g. from the general public).
- Knowledge gaps and mistakes (which reflect badly on the image the KHF is trying to project for HMG to partners, contractors, etc.) would be avoided.
- Monitoring projects would be easier – with database entries used as reminders.
- Senior staff could better judge the balance of work between sections at any given time (e.g. where on the approval cycle most projects were).
- Other communication/reporting flows could be reduced, as all staff (not just project officers) could quickly ascertain the status of any project.
- The number of paper records could be reduced.
- Ad hoc duplicate/parallel systems which individuals have been forced to develop would no longer be needed, saving time and resources.
- Embassies and the G7 Organization would have good quality information.

Strategic benefits

Good, accessible appraisal records for past projects could help project officers assess the proposed contractors and partners for new proposals.

Completed appraisal fields would allow more rigorous assessment of how well projects overall were delivering their expected benefits.

Senior officers would get a clearer strategic picture of the JADs work by country/sector, eg:

- plotting trends over time;
- throughput and caseloads across the organization;
- the pattern of post-project appraisal results.

An up-to-date system would act as the KHF's 'collective memory', reducing problems caused by the lack of staff continuity and the resulting reliance on the advisers.

Against these factors, there are underlying problems with the format and user friendliness of the current database. There can be no guarantee that people will use it even it if it up to date; but steps can be taken to make this more likely.

Recommendations

We recommend the following steps to achieve the benefits which the project database is capable of delivering:

People

Clarify the potential benefits

People need to understand why the database is important to the KHF and also how keeping it up to date can help them:

- Clarify and quantify what an up-to-date system would deliver, for example ask staff to systematically quantify over a period the amount of time they spend on data collection, parallel personal records, or asking other staff for updates which a current database would obviate. Then put a value on the cost of this time (staff salaries plus overtime plus overheads).
- Initiate and encourage discussion among all the staff on the potential benefits, e.g. via informal workshop sessions. We were impressed by the level of thought and interest which the people we interviewed at all levels showed about the way the work is organized. This source of ideas needs to be tapped into more effectively, helping to build a vision of what needs to be done that is shared across the KHF.
- Seek feedback from embassies and the G7 Organisation on the database's importance to them (NB they may be unaware the data they have is not as current as it could be).

Management lead

Top level managers collectively need to decide that an updated database is sufficiently valuable to make the work required worthwhile.

They then need to give a clear, consistent message to their staff that the database is a priority. Inconsistencies in the delivery of this message will undermine the goal.

Appoint a 'project champion', probably at the section head level, to support a relaunch of use of the database across the organization. This practical role, which would be supported by the IT Committee, would involve:

- coordinating the work required (e.g. user guidance, the proposed monthly report);
- acting as a focal point across the organization for feedback, ideas, problems, etc.

Demonstrate the benefits/gains acceptance

Use a pilot stage, where the database in one section would be brought and kept up to date, as a demonstration. The benefits expected from doing this would be spelt out beforehand, and the benefits actually achieved (time saved, problems avoided) monitored. This would allow management to judge whether to go ahead across the organization.

Introduce a monthly bulletin using the database information to update staff at all levels on KHF activities. This would have several benefits:

- Providing useful information, demonstrating the database has use and fostering wider awareness of the KHF's activities amongst staff.
- Helping to ensure staff were aware of other projects in their area, avoiding embarrassing knowledge gaps.
- Sharing useful tips, problems, etc.
- Encouraging people in a positive way to ensure their entries showed the current position.

Processes

Establish ownership
Guidance/procedures should leave no doubt about who is responsible at each stage – for example on receipt of the contractor's progress report, the project officer should notify the section clerk, so they can complete the relevant fields on the database.

Make up-to-date project database records one of the specific reporting goals on which all staff are measured each year (with phase-in targets, if necessary). This would not, of course, be the primary criterion, but it would be one of them, signalling the issue's importance.

Monitor performance – for example, monthly returns.

Improve procedures
Clear instructions and procedural manuals for both new and existing staff. People need clear 'desk instructions' for each type of officer involved, for example:

- flow charts/checklists showing people mechanically the steps needed;
- a 'how to' guide which uses visual aids, e.g. pages showing how the database appears on screen with arrows/text boxes explaining what it means and where to move/what commands to give at each point.

Issue everyone with a plastic card, showing/reminding them of the key operating instructions in a handy format.

Identify stages at which the database would be updated, what the triggers are for action, who is responsible, and how this would be monitored.

Involve users with a good knowledge of the system in designing and providing training and guidance in cooperation with the IT officer.

Technology

Improve the system
Working within the resource constraints, improve the system's capabilities, for example:

- Solicit additional report functions that staff would find useful, e.g. adding a facility to identify the region of Russia concerned and print reports on this basis.
- Develop an icon, which allows direct access to the database from Windows (i.e. without going through the 'old world' icon).

Data

Update the system
Get the system up to date. It would be tempting to suggest using agency data processing personnel. But we understand this has been done in the past, only for entries to fall behind again. There is a danger that there is no 'ownership' or commitment unless people get the system up to date themselves. But over-time could be an appropriate incentive and signal the task's importance.

The pilot approach would mitigate the resource implications of this.

Updating all past records would be a massive task. Live projects are also more important day to day than completed ones. So the initial focus should be to update all current and future projects.

This does not deal with the poor historic data problems. A second phase dealing with historic projects could be rolled out gradually once current projects are up to date.

Consider more integration with workflows, eg:

- require staff to use the monitoring and appraisal tools;
- section heads to only authorize spending on a new project if its database entry is up to date.

Summary

The project database was intended to ease storage and retrieval of data previously held on paper, and make it easier to produce aggregated reports. This aim has not been realized.

Current information flows

An 'information system' (IS) consists of people, processes and data, as well as technology. The JADs project database is not integrated into everyday project approval and funding processes – as a result it is regarded as low priority.

Use of database in practice

This in turn has led to the data on it becoming out of date, creating a vicious circle – because the database is out-of-date people do not value it, and therefore do not see any benefit in using it or updating it.

This problem is compounded because people do not find the computer system user friendly. Although training and guidance are available, there is a psychological barrier to using the 'old world' system. Staff also place a higher priority on mastering recently introduced Windows systems, which they need for everyday tasks.

It would be tempting to suggest a new user-friendlier Windows-based database to overcome these problems – suitable off-the-shelf commercial products are available. This is an option many of those we interviewed favoured, though they recognized resource constraints made it unlikely. However, we believe that the use of the database is *primarily* about people and processes, not about technology. The MIS system – which is noticeably user friendly – is kept up to date because it is seen as essential.

Potential benefits

We have identified potential benefits from an up-to-date database. These go beyond aggregating historic data, to using the database as an operational and strategic tool to improve communication and project monitoring and appraisal.

Recommendations – how to achieve the benefits

To break the vicious circle, the JADs need clarity about how an up-to-date database would benefit the KHF's key activities, and a clear management decision that achieving these benefits is a priority.

We have made some detailed recommendations on how to achieve this, including:

- A pilot phase where the system is brought and kept up to date in one section as a demonstration. The benefits expected from doing this would be spelt out beforehand and the benefits actually achieved monitored and appraised.
- Establish clear procedures spelling out where the database needs updating

in the project appraisal cycle and who is responsible (e.g. project officer must notify section clerk).

- Monitor results monthly; make the results one criterion in people's reports.
- Improve the guidance material on how to use the database and communication of the facilities which the system has available, for example:
  - a user guide with visual aids showing how the database appears on screen, annotated with instructions;
  - a plastic card issued to everyone showing the key instructions.
- Integrate the database with workflows, for example:
  - require people to use the monitoring and appraisal fields;
  - section head not to authorize expenditure unless database updated.
- Introduce a monthly bulletin which uses the database information to update staff at all levels on KHF activities, trends, etc.
- Improve the existing system to better user requirements – e.g. examine feasibility of user requests for new report fields, a facility to search by region in Russia.

Longer-term plans

The ODA are considering whether to introduce an integrated project database across the organization. This could take two years. Better use of the existing project database is a cost-effective way for the KHF to achieve benefits in the medium term, given that major IS expenditure is unlikely while the ODA-wide system is under development. The KHF must ensure that any ODA-wide system meets its needs.

However, in the longer term there is potential to integrate paper and computer information flows, with all the working records and updated project information held on easily accessible team systems (which are also open to ODAC and the embassies.) This would require a new software system, which we understand is not currently a realistic objective. Even if resources were available, it would be a mistake to deal with the issue solely by looking to new technology to provide the answer, without first tackling the people and process issues – otherwise any expenditure could be wasted.

Conclusion

We believe the project database can deliver operational and strategic benefits to the KHF. This will provide a cost-effective way of using the existing IT resources in the medium term, while the KHF is awaiting the outcome of longer-term ODA plans for an integrated database.

In order to achieve this, the data on the system has to be brought up to date, and the people and process issues have to be addressed. Technology is not the over-riding issue.

Buy-in at all levels of the organization is crucial.

Annex A Project database fields

The ten fields on the project database provide the following information:

Project	The project number; officer; description and country; the contractor and partner; current status and approved costs.
Country	The country and sector.
Staff	The project officer's details (name, address, phone).
Contractor	Contractor's details (name, address, phone, contact person).
Partner	Partner's details (as above).
Appraisal	Recording when a proposal is sent for appraisal; the advisers it was copied to; and when their comments and the embassy's comments were received.
Approval	The financial details and planned timing of an approved project. These details are automatically transferred onto the JAD from the MIS once the MIS code assigned to the project is typed into this field.
Contractual and monitoring	This shows whether there was a competitive tender; the contract issue date and number; any sub-contractors; the dates when contractor reports are due; and agreed monitoring arrangements (who is to visit and when).
Completion	This measures performance of the completed project with an 'output achievement rating' (rated 1–9); ratings for how far inputs were appropriate, timely, well coordinated and efficiently procured; and the likelihood that the project will meet its objectives and be sustainable. This field parallels information in the paper-based project completion records.

Index